THE EUCHARIST

ESSENCE, FORM, CELEBRATION

Johannes H. Emminghaus

Translation by
Linda M. Maloney
from the 1992 edition
revised and edited by Theodor Maas-Ewerd

A Liturgical Press Book

THE LITURGICAL PRESS
Collegeville, Minnesota

1	2	3	4	5	6	7	8

Library of Congress Cataloging-in-Publication Data

Emminghaus, Johannes H.
    [Messe. English]
    The Eucharist : essence, form, celebration / Johannes H. Emminghaus ; translated by Linda M. Maloney from the 1992 edition ; revised and edited by Theodor Maas-Ewerd.
        p.   cm.
    Includes bibliographical references and index.
    ISBN 0-8146-1036-6
    1. Mass.   I. Maas-Ewerd, Theodor, 1935–   II. Title.
BX2230.2.E4513   1997
264'.0203—dc21   97-496
                                                      CIP

To

Pius Parsch

Augustinian Canon of Klosterneuburg
(18 May 1884–11 March 1954)
in grateful remembrance

Contents

Translator's Note

In order not to diminish the readability of the work, I have avoided the use of the highly abbreviated symbols that are commonly used in scholarly works, since they demand that the reader refer frequently to the list of abbreviations. The abbreviations that are used here are easy to decipher by themselves.

Biblical texts are taken from the New Revised Standard Version, and when possible they are not given as mere verse references, but are quoted or summarized. However, it is often advisable to take note of the context, and for that reason the reader should keep the Bible at hand while reading this book. The abbreviations of the biblical books and the spellings of names follow the *JBL* guidelines.

The constitutions and decrees of Vatican Council II are cited according to their official titles (with abbreviations based on the first two initials) and from the translations in Walter M. Abbott, S.J., ed., *The Documents of Vatican II* (New York: Guild Press, 1966).

Liturgical and patristic texts were given new translations by the author; for the translation, the newest English versions have been consulted. Historical conciliar texts are cited according to the Denzinger-Schönmetzer edition (*Enchiridion symbolorum. The sources of Catholic dogma.* Translated by Roy J. Deferrari from the 30th ed. [St. Louis: Herder, 1957]).

Texts of the rubrics for the celebration of Mass *(Ordo Missae)* are taken from Ralph A. Keifer, *To Give Thanks and Praise. General Instruction of the Roman Missal* (Washington, D.C.: Pastoral Press/NAPM, 1980).

Texts of the *General Instruction of the Roman Missal* are from *The Sacramentary* (Collegeville: The Liturgical Press, 1974, 1985).

Foreword to the First Edition

For nearly fifty years, I have felt a great gratitude to Pius Parsch. When I was a boy, wise pastors in the parish of St. Meinolf in Bochum not only taught me how to be an altar boy, but at the same time instructed me in the liturgy. Even before I received my first "Schott"* as a Christmas present from my parents in 1928, I was collecting the "Sunday leaflets" by Pius Parsch (entitled "Live with the Church") that were used in the congregation. Later came his "explanation of the Mass" and "liturgical calendar," which were combined in three handy volumes under the title *The Church's Year of Grace*, and furnished the spiritual accompaniment to my theological studies. When good guidance brought me to the University of Vienna in 1967, and I chose Klosterneuburg, nestled between the Vienna Woods and the Danube, as my home, in my gratitude I formed a plan to prepare a new edition of Parsch's "explanation of the Mass" (the third edition of which had appeared in 1950) for our own time.

Now, after the Council, it is impossible simply to re-edit or revise it; neither the content nor the language is suitable any longer. But Parsch's fundamental principle was correct, and it remains so today: the *essence* or *nature* of the liturgy can only be explained on the basis of Christ's institution, as witnessed in scripture, and the traditional teaching of the Church; its *form*, in turn, with its many changes, its high and low points, is explicable also from scripture and history; but *the manner of its celebration* can only be explained from the form as we know it and especially from the concrete faith of people at any given time. Thus the dedication of this little volume to Parsch is more than a symbol of devotion and gratitude; it indicates the program and purpose of the book.

The book's intention is utterly practical: It is meant as an aid to an appropriate and responsible celebration of the congregational Eucharist.

By "practical," however, I do not mean something that is quick and easy to use, like many handouts and texts that are widely available. I do not desire to spare the reader the task of study and reflection. The intended result is not only an *active* participation, but also one that bears fruit because it stems from faith. That is what appears to me especially crucial at the present time. Our task now is to live with the renewed liturgy, to integrate it more and more fully into our lives, and at the same time to understand and celebrate it as a sign of salvation and as the Church's self-expression. That constitutes the "practical" purpose of this book.

As I am writing, I think especially of my companions in priestly ministry as the readers and "consumers" of this book, but also of teachers, catechists, and members of parish liturgical committees and study groups, and by no means least my own audience in Vienna, to whom I feel especially close. Therefore I have made an effort to make the book readable. I have dispensed with footnotes, but I hope, in spite of that, that I have never betrayed the degree of confidence that the reader of a piece of professional literature bestows on the author. I want in our own time to further Pius Parsch's desire that living liturgy be celebrated in living communities.

Johannes H. Emminghaus
Klosterneuburg, April 1976

———————

*The most common German form of the "daily missal," known by the surname of its author/editor.

Foreword to the 1992 Edition

It has been fifteen years since Dr. Johannes H. Emminghaus, professor of liturgiology and sacramental theology at the University of Vienna, submitted his manuscript *The Mass: Nature, Form, and Celebration* to the Austrian Catholic Biblical Publishers (Österreichisches Katholisches Bibelwerk). It would represent false modesty were I not to admit that the fact that I had given him the suggestion for this book fills me with joy and some pride as well. In any case, Professor Emminghaus and I, in our first discussions, were planning a revision of Pius Parsch's "explanation of the Mass," but it soon became apparent that such a project was impossible; there had been too much intervening development in theology and in the Church.

Thus what emerged was a new book that quickly became a standard work on the eucharistic celebration, and was particularly successful as a textbook for those studying theology. The publisher, in consultation with Professor Emminghaus, deliberately chose to use the word "Mass" in the title, rather than "eucharistic celebration," which would have seemed natural in the wake of the Council. On the one hand, we wanted to indicate continuity, and on the other hand we wanted to appeal also to people who do not consider themselves ecclesiastical "insiders," but whose overall education has made them open to an interest in Church history and its developments.

The unexpected death of Johannes H. Emminghaus in 1989 prevented him from undertaking the revisions of the book that by then were necessary. Hence I am very grateful to Monsignor Theodor Maas-Ewerd, professor of liturgiology in the theology faculty of the Catholic University of Eichstätt in Bavaria, for having agreed to look over the work. He has incorporated the insights of recent research, brought the bibliography up to date, and in addition has given a new formulation to many passages, because there have been some important changes in thought and language since the first edition. Thus this standard work is again available as an up-to-date and readable book. At the conclusion of this book, Professor Maas-Ewerd offers an affectionate memorial to his fellow countryman and colleague; it conveys the personality of Johannes H. Emminghaus to the readers in impressive fashion.

Professor Emminghaus, who was both a historian of the arts and a person deeply interested in "eastern Europe," would certainly have rejoiced in the new cover illustration for his work, the Last Supper panel from a work by the Master of Raigern. At a time when the Benedictine monastery at Raigern (Rajhrad), in southern Moravia near Brno is again open to "western" visitors, the round table can symbolize the unity and community of all who celebrate the Eucharist.

Norbert W. Höslinger
Altmünster, July 1991

Introduction

Nature and Celebration of the Mass

This book is intended as an aid to understanding and to a formally correct celebration of the eucharistic liturgy as it was renewed after Vatican Council II; it is therefore an "explanation of the Mass," as Pius Parsch, to whom this work is dedicated, understood it. It is, in fact, an explanation—entirely within the programmatic intention of Parsch—both of the biblical foundations and the historical development of that liturgy within a tradition extending over almost two thousand years, with its high and low points, promising moments for future development as well as obvious dead ends, repeatedly calling for improvement and reform. We must therefore inquire into both aspects—Jesus' foundational intention and the Church's long tradition of celebrating the Lord's legacy—in order to obtain a clear picture of the enduringly valid form of the Mass at all times, including its present realization. Neither of the two criteria can, by itself, constitute the necessary foundation: A naive reliance on the biblical evidence alone would deny the historical dimension—the ecclesial character of the liturgy—while concentration on its purely historical development, or its temporary adaptation to the demands of any given time, without a continual reference to its institution by Jesus, could easily eliminate the sacramentality and thus the salvific efficacy of the celebration of the Mass. After all, the Church, in celebrating the Mass, is not merely in a position to do something edifying; it is fulfilling the command of Christ.

However, at the present time, in the wake of the successful reform of the liturgy, this book requires a certain amount of justification. Is it at all possible or desirable to "explain the Mass"? Instead, should not the Mass itself, if it is correctly celebrated, be immediately transparent and self-explanatory? And whatever is not immediately obvious—is that not simply the "mystery of faith," as it is called in the acclamation after the consecration?

Liturgy as Sign of Faith

The liturgy of the Mass, like all sacramental signs, is a "sign of faith." But neither signs nor faith are static: they are very dynamic realities. Life is immediately involved with "history," the sequence of events. Thus in the first place faith is, surely, a grace given to human beings by God, but at the same time, from the human perspective, it is also something like a "learning process" derived from proclamation, considered experience, stimuli, and "mystagogy." It is not something that exists as a finished reality in itself. Consequently, faith must always be nourished from Scripture and the Church's teaching; in the present case, we refer particularly to the doctrines of the faith regarding the Mass. The history of the celebration of the Mass reveals the development of this faith, but also the "creeping in" of foreign traits "less harmonious with the intimate nature of the liturgy" (Constitution on the Sacred Liturgy[1] 21), as indicated by the need for reform after the last Council. Therefore it will be a good thing if we first present and explain the sound teaching of the Church in its biblical context.

At the same time, however, the sacramental sign of faith certainly requires explanation. It is true that it was instituted by Christ as something that is coherent and comprehensible. But not even natural signs have meaning in themselves; they continually derive their vital power in large part from the experiences and conventions of a particular group. In the case of the sign of faith, that means the Church. Liturgy, by its very nature, is "organic liturgy." Therefore the second goal of the present reflections is to make the meaning of the signs "more transparent," more available to experience. That was the pastoral purpose of the whole conciliar constitution on the liturgy, and many people have been working toward that end for years, certainly with a great deal of success. Nevertheless, this work also requires ongoing explanation and reflection: for example, so that the overcoming of the language barrier will not lead us to convert the whole liturgy into words; so that the mystery may retain its place in balance with comprehensibility and rationality; so that the signs are not perfected purely for their own sake, but may be and remain in future the signs of faith. Thus the second purpose of this explanation of the Mass will be to explain the signs and, through interpretation, to make them more accessible to experience, in order that faith may be realized in these signs. In the future, that will have to be the task of a "second reform of the liturgy," now that the first has revised the rituals and the books for the various rites. Faith must be supported and nourished by signs that are more vital and easier to understand.

The Mass as Center and High Point of Sacramental Life

The present missal, in the first articles of its *General Instruction*, briskly summarizes the Church's teaching about the celebration of the Mass: it is, in fact, intended to be a short explanation of the Mass. The initial article begins by giving a taut and concise description of the nature of the Mass:

> The celebration of Mass, the action of Christ and the people of God arrayed hierarchically, is for the universal and the local Church as well as for each person the center of the whole Christian life. In the Mass we have the high point of the work that in Christ God accomplishes to sanctify us and the high point of the worship that in adoring God through Christ, his Son, we offer to the Father. During the cycle of the year, moreover, the mysteries of redemption are recalled in the Mass in such a way that they are somehow made present. All other liturgical rites and the works of the Christian life are linked with the eucharistic celebration, flow from it, and have it as their end. (*General Instruction*,[2] 1).

Accordingly, the Mass is both the center and the high point of Christian life. Through baptism in water and Holy Spirit human beings are reborn in faith from the condition of sin and alienation from God into which they were born and enter into a new state of being as children of God; they receive forgiveness of all sin and are received into communion with Christ and membership in the People of God. Through the gift of the Spirit in confirmation they are conformed still more to the Lord and enabled to witness to Christ before the world through their lives of faith. In the eucharistic meal, under the forms of bread and wine, they partake of the body and blood of Christ and make visible and tangible the unity of the People of God in fraternal and sororal love and community. In the Church's eucharistic sacrifice they are drawn into the real memorial of the one, universal sacrifice of Christ. While baptism and confirmation incorporate Christians once for all into the People of God, the celebration of the Mass is the ongoing sign of the closest communion with Christ, and at the same time of the Christian's own surrender of his or her life to God. Thus the Eucharist is the enduring proclamation and real application of the redemption given once for all through Christ's death and resurrection, until he comes in glory. In its common celebration of the holy Eucharist, the Church grows, and the individual Christian also grows to full maturity in Christ. To this extent the Mass is the center and high point of Christian life, a life based on faith.

The Mass is more than simply an act of worship: It is primarily a sacramental application of redemption. In every sacrament God anticipates all human action; God begins the work of our salvation, and without God we can do nothing (John 15:5). In a faith that calls upon the sacraments, human beings accept God's offer of salvation, and only through and by means of that offer are they able, through Christ and in the Holy Spirit, to worship God and incorporate their lives in God. The Mass is the primary locus of this saving action of God for the baptized, and at the same time of the worship of God "in spirit and truth" (John 4:24) by the faithful People of God. The celebration of the Mass brings human beings into a dialogue with God. This twofold movement from God to human beings and then from them to God, simultaneously "the action of Christ and of the people of God" is characteristic of the celebration of Mass. Salvation is never simply imposed on people; each person, in his or her dignity, is taken seriously by God, and each person cooperates in her or his own salvation. Therefore, not only in life, but also in the Mass, each person is not merely a recipient, but also a conscious, active, devout, and community-conscious participant and actor.

In the Mass salvation is applied to us not merely in abstract validity and as something complete and already accomplished, and not simply as the effect of a previous saving action of Christ (in his incarnation, death, resurrection, and ascension); instead, the event of salvation itself, which happened once in historical time, becomes present, "sacramentally" present, in sensible signs. We are thus drawn, as living beings, into Christ's saving action "for us," because the historical, once-for-all Christ event is given to all times, both objectively and as a real presence in every moment. Time is, after all, only relative; that is, it is simply a quality of our created order (according to place and time) existing in the succession of events. God's action transcends and surpasses time. In the ritual symbol, therefore, Christ's action is really and continually "present." The agent of this ritually symbolic celebration is the Church, that is, the Lord himself who continues to live and work in it. That is why *GI* 1, cited above, also says that the mysteries of redemption are "in some way made present," that is, in the order of space and time.

The whole complex of mysteries of our redemption unfolds in sequence in the course of the liturgical year. This represents more than simply a didactic concern for the limited ability of human beings to grasp things at a given time. It is not only the proclamation in the liturgy of the word throughout the year that manifests this unfolding, although it appears most clearly there; the celebration of the Mass as a whole is sustained by the mystery of each individual feast. SC 102 therefore says: "Holy Mother Church is conscious that she must celebrate the saving work of her divine Spouse by devoutly recalling it [in real symbols] on certain days throughout the course of the year. Every week, on the day which she has called the Lord's day, she keeps the memory of His resurrection. In the supreme solemnity of Easter she also makes an annual commemoration of the resurrection, along with the Lord's blessed passion. Within the cycle of a year, moreover, she unfolds the whole mystery of Christ, not only from His incarnation and birth until His ascension, but also as reflected in the day of Pentecost, and the expectation of a blessed, hoped-for return of the Lord. Recalling thus the mysteries of redemption, the Church opens to the faithful the riches of her Lord's powers and merits, so that these are in some way made present at all times, and the faithful are enabled to lay hold of them and become filled with saving grace."

The Mass as Center of the Church's Self-Realization

The Mass is also the center of the Church's life, that is, it is embedded in a larger whole, but not identical with that whole. The second Vatican council's Constitution on the Church (Lumen gentium) clearly states that the nature and activity of the Church are manifested in three ways: In its proclamation, which awakens and gives life to faith, in service to the world (so-called diakonia or caritas), and in the liturgy (cf. SC 9 and 10). "Liturgy" here is only another name for "sanctification through the sacraments." These three elements: proclamation, caritative service, and liturgy, together constitute an indissoluble unity. One element cannot exist without the other two. Therefore the Church very early combined its proclamation (service of the word) and its charitable efforts (community meal, later a collection for the special needs of the poor) with the eucharistic celebration, at least symbolically. But preaching and missionary efforts on behalf of the good news and the Church's service to the world necessarily extend beyond the celebration of the Mass and are not fulfilled within it. Still, the Eucharist is the center and summit of the whole. Other worship services as well (separate liturgies of the word, catechesis for adults and children, participation in the liturgy of the hours, etc.), and all occasions when Christians assemble or live together in the name of Jesus Christ, and the

Lord is present among them (Matt 18:20)—all these take their life from the mystery of the Eucharist, "leading up to it and flowing from it." Moreover, such things as meditation, private reading of Scripture, personal prayer, adoration of the eucharistic species outside Mass, etc., are necessary to support the liturgical event and fill it with personal life. The isolated celebration of the Mass by itself cannot fulfill these necessary purposes, especially since the worship service is often subject to time constraints. Only in this larger context is the Mass really the center of all devotion and a dedication of one's life to God.

The Hierarchically Organized People of God as Agent of the Liturgy

The People of God does not gather to celebrate the Mass as an amorphous, indifferent assembly of people; it is "hierarchically assembled." It is true that as a whole, since their baptism and confirmation, the people have the dignity of a chosen race, a royal priesthood, a holy nation and a people of God's own choosing (1 Pet 2:9). It is a holy priesthood that offers spiritual sacrifices to God (1 Pet 2:5). But there exists also within the Church the special office of servants of Christ and stewards of God's mysteries (1 Cor 4:1). Just as Christ was sent by the Father as shepherd, teacher, and priest, so he sent the apostles in the same way (John 20:21), and they, through the laying on of hands, sent their successors in the same office of proclamation, leadership, and administration of the sacraments, reflected in the orders of bishops, priests, and deacons in the Church. It is true that, ultimately, it is always Christ himself who teaches, unites and sanctifies; but those in office represent him—that is, they stand for him and act in his name. That is why they are entitled to leadership in proclamation during the liturgy of the word and in the Eucharist; moreover, the collegiality of all bishops and their priests, beyond the limits of the local diocese, guarantees the unity of the Church of Christ, whose highest office of service is the Petrine office of the bishop of Rome. Nonetheless, all offices and special callings and abilities (charisms) are together responsible for the building up of the body of Christ: "to equip the saints for the work of ministry, for building up the body of Christ, until all of us come to the unity of the faith and of the knowledge of the Son of God, to maturity, to the measure of the full stature of Christ" (Eph 4:12-13). Ultimately, it is Christ himself who gathers together the whole body of the Church and holds it in unity (Eph 4:16), and he himself is always present and active in the sacrifice of the Mass, represented in the person of the priestly minister, and especially, but not solely, under the eucharistic species (and in all the sacraments). He is also present in his word, which he himself utters in the person of the proclaimer when sacred scripture is read in the Church; finally, he is present in the prayer and singing of the priestly people of God, the community—for he is always present where two or three are gathered in his name (Matt 18:20; for the whole, cf. *SC* 7a).

The organic structure of the Church and also of the worshiping community requires a unified, but not necessarily a uniform organization. "For as in one body we have many members, and not all the members have the same function, so we, who are many, are one body in Christ, and individually we are members one of another. We have gifts that differ according to the grace given to us" (Rom 12:4-6). Equality in the Church, as in every society, does not consist in uniformity and levelling, but in equal dignity and calling. Of course, any kind of privilege that was not coupled with a readiness to serve on behalf of all would be the opposite of what is right. Office exists in the Church only for the sake of the community of Christ, as an office of service for and within it.

Those exercising office are not to "lord it over" the faith of the community (2 Cor 1:24); in the same way, they are not lords of the liturgy. Growing out of the fundamental structure of the sacramental signs, but also developing over the nearly two thousand years of the liturgy's history, there have come to be liturgical laws that are above all subjective caprice and signify in themselves the unity of the whole Church. The unity must be as great as possible, but also only as great as necessary. Common worship requires a balance of order and spontaneity. Whims of the person presiding over the service, going beyond the variable norms of the liturgical books, represent bad forms of clericalism: the result is that the community is subjected to the favorite ideas and private notions of the presider. Law in the Church does not contradict its character as a Church of love, because in the Church the order of law cannot and should not be the instrument of the exercise of power, but should benefit and guarantee a realm of freedom for every Christian. Among the fundamental rules of social life at the present time is that those who are affected must be heard. Only then can the participation of the whole Church be active, mutual, and spontaneous. Hence *GI* 1, §2 reads: "It is of the greatest importance that the celebration of the Mass, the Lord's Supper, be so arranged that the ministers and the faithful who take their own proper part in it may more fully receive its good effects. This is the reason why Christ the Lord instituted the eucharistic sacrifice of his body and blood and entrusted it to the Church, his beloved bride, as the memorial of his passion and resurrection."

"The purpose will be accomplished if the celebration takes into account the nature and circumstances of each assembly and is planned to bring about conscious, active, and full participation of the people, motivated by faith, hope, and charity. Such participation of mind and body is desired by the Church, is demanded by the nature of the celebration, and is the right and duty of Christians by reason of their baptism" (ibid., §3).

After paragraph 1 of chapter 1 of the *General Instruction* has described the meaning of the Mass as center and high point of Christian life, paragraphs 2 and 3 (just cited) give closer attention to its structure.

On the Structure of the Eucharistic Celebration

The Mass is "the Lord's Supper" and "sacrifice of the body and blood of Christ." There are good reasons why paragraph 2 speaks of the meal character of the Mass before describing it as a sacrifice: The fundamental structure of the Mass, which is the subject of these two articles, is a ritual derived from a meal, not a sacrificial rite. As a memorial of his pasch, the Lord left us the Eucharist—that is, a thanksgiving spoken over the components of a meal, bread and wine—and instructed the Church to do *this* in his memory. He did not order a sacrificial rite which, at least in religious-historical terms, would consist of the destruction, burning, or burial of a sacrificial object. He desired instead, under the form of bread and wine as his "sacrificed" body and blood "poured out for us" and "for the forgiveness of sins," to remain present to his community. It is important, therefore, that we be attentive to this proximity to the form of a meal in the Eucharist as the memorial of the Lord is carried out.

However, behind and above this structure of a meal is always the reality of Christ's sacrifice and that of the Church; in this context, "sacrifice" refers to its proper meaning as donation or self-surrender, and not primarily to the carrying out of a sacrificial rite. In the history of religions, and also in the old covenant, sacrifice meant the giving of things that human beings need to sustain life, which therefore have a great deal of existential importance for them, but which they nevertheless surrender to God by definitively renouncing these objects for personal use. From this point of view, the sacrificial action is more a symbol for the surrender of one's own life; that alone constitutes the genuine sacrifice. Otherwise, sacrifice could easily become merely a "satisfaction for the gods," an absolving of one's religious duties that evades ultimate seriousness: in the end, it would be hypocrisy and pure works-righteousness, something the Old Testament prophets repeatedly found themselves called upon to attack.

Thus Christ's death on the cross is a real symbol and the ultimate consequence of his own lifelong obedient surrender to the will of the Father, which was the true "sacrifice of his life."

The Letter to the Hebrews (10:5-7), which interprets Christ's saving action as a high-priestly sacrifice of expiation, therefore places these words of Psalm 40:7-9 on the lips of Christ: "Consequently, when Christ came into the world, he said, 'Sacrifices and offerings you have not desired, but a body you have prepared for me; in burnt offerings and sin offerings you have taken no pleasure. Then I said, "See, God, I have come to do your will, O God" (in the scroll of the book it is written of me.'" In the Eucharist, the Church enters into this total surrender of Christ, and so do we ourselves, with all the strength we can muster. Therefore the Mass is also our sacrifice, the expression of our complete surrender to God and God's will. A mere recitation of or attendance at Mass without this ultimate and completely serious dedication of our lives to God would be hypocrisy. Therefore Paul writes in 1 Cor 11:27-28: "Whoever . . . eats the bread or drinks the cup of the Lord in an unworthy manner will be answerable for the body and blood of the Lord. Examine yourselves, and only then eat of the bread and drink of the cup."

The Celebration of the Mass as the Church's Celebration

It is in the dimension just described that we find the "conscious, active, and full participation of the people" called for by the *General Instruction*, paragraph 3; in fact, this is what makes possible "a participation in body and spirit that is conscious, active, full, and motivated by faith, hope, and charity." Only in a secondary sense does it reside in the correct performance of ritual, no matter how necessary that certainly is, because the human being is a whole person made up of body and soul, and because every sacramental sign, that is, the outward side that is evident to the senses, is meant to show what the sacrament effects, in order thus to effect that for which it is a sign. Sacraments always live from faith and repentance; without these their recipients would find them empty. It is true that, on the one hand, the Church clearly teaches the objective certainty of the conferral of grace in the sacrament; but on the other hand, it affirms with equal seriousness that the sacraments' effectiveness is proportioned to the disposition and attitude—the faith, hope, and love—of the recipient.

Christians are members of the Church not through an abstract "spiritual" attachment, or simply in the feeling of belonging, but in the communion of the concrete local Church of the diocese and the community united with its bishop. "In the local Church, first place should be given, because of its meaning, to the Mass at which the bishop presides surrounded by the college of presbyters and the ministers and in which the people take full and active part. For this Mass is the preeminent expression of the Church." (*GI,* 74). However, the Church is also present in the parish Mass: "Great importance should be attached to a Mass celebrated by any community, but especially by the parish community, inasmuch as it represents the universal Church gathered at a given time and place. This is particularly true of the community's celebration of the Lord's Day" (*GI,* 75). Although even at the present time it is occasionally desirable to celebrate Mass for special categories of persons within our pastoral care (children, youth groups, students, family groups, etc.), still it is the local Church, particularly in the parish liturgy incorporating all ages and states of life, that is the visible and tangible, and therefore the concrete, manifestation of the whole Church. "The parish is the primary, structured community recognized by the diocesan Church and by virtue of that is, as the Council teaches, in communion with the universal Church. The parish is our first and normal spiritual family, developed not so much out of the homogeneity of the members (who in many cases are quite different from each other) but in virtue of a specific pastoral ministry and of the cohesive influence of the one faith and the one charity. . . . The parish is the school of God's word, the table of the eucharistic bread. It is the home of the community's love. It is the temple of shared prayer; in a certain sense, as the Council says, it is the visible Church established concretely in all parts of the earth" (Address of Pope Paul VI, 7 September 1969: *Osservatore Romano,* 8–9 September 1969. English: ICEL, *Documents on the Liturgy, 1963–1979* [Collegeville: The Liturgical Press, 1982]).

Paragraph 2 of the *General Instruction,* cited above, speaks initially of "fruitful" participation, urging that the people should "gain . . . more fully" the saving "fruits" of the memorial celebration of Christ's death and resurrection. That is the meaning and effect of every sacrament, but of the Eucharist most particularly. The other sacraments address specific situations in human life: the person's unique incorporation in the Church through baptism and confirmation; healing, when necessary, through reconciliation and anointing; the state of life in marriage or orders; but the Eucharist is

The principal characteristic of the liturgy of the Mass is therefore its common celebration, the gathering of Christians in the name of Jesus and the active participation of the people of God in the Eucharist. In this, the fundamental axiom is that each should do "solely and totally what the nature of things and liturgical norms require" of him or her (*SC* 28).

our "daily bread," the sacrament received most often, and to that extent the center and high point of the Christian life (§ 1). Thus the "sacramental praxis" of a Christian is largely determined by the nature of his or her participation in the Sunday Eucharist. This "church attendance" is in fact, and at all times, in a high degree the measure of her or his entire Church identification. Therefore paragraph 3 makes a second demand: that participation be conscious. In its emphasis on the objective effectiveness of the sacrament (particularly in medieval scholasticism and in post-Tridentine theology, in deliberate opposition to those who denied it, with the result that the arguments appear somewhat overdrawn) it may well be that Catholic sacramental teaching had become somewhat one-sided: it came to seem that the sacrament worked almost without human participation, as if it were "magic." In addition, a one-sided perspective on the liturgy as an "objective" action of the Church, conducted according to official books and ritual directives with obligatory instructions and rubrics, and even performed in a language understood by very few, could easily give the impression that the subjective activity of minister and recipient were secondary and therefore less important. But sacraments are always something related to humans as rational beings, that is, as conscious persons capable of thought.

That is why the liturgy, especially now, demands conscious and knowledgeable participation. The introduction of the vernacular is a valuable aid in this; the unfortunate language barrier has happily fallen. Nevertheless, the liturgy lives not solely from the word, but also and still more from signs, and these must be appropriate and comprehensible to modern people, and something they themselves can carry out. A number of signs have been added to the liturgy in the course of history and for that reason they are subject to change. Others can be substituted, or, depending on the cultural and social situation (for example, in missionary fields or where there has been a transition from agrarian to industrial culture), new ones may have to be found. The celebration itself, as paragraph 3 says, should be shaped by taking into account "the nature and circumstances of each assembly." This means that liturgical signs should always proclaim; they should never cloak something in mystery. It is noteworthy and helpful for us today that the fundamental signs of the seven sacraments are very few and are applicable almost everywhere even now: water and oil, bread and wine, imposition or extension of hands. But even beyond this, modern people—in spite of many opinions to the contrary—are still aware of symbols, for example in advertising, social status, forms of grouping, abstract painting, and technical formulae, even though our daily lives and work are more sharply rationalized and verbalized than in earlier cultures. In the interest of a humanizing and more universally humane shaping of our lives, in our own times the genius of the world of symbols is thoroughly desirable, and it is certainly the task of all types of educational effort to vivify symbolism in the face of abbreviated, dried up, and impoverished social trends and individual styles of life.

Romano Guardini pointed out seventy years ago in two books that are still important today (*Liturgische Bildung* [Rothenfels, 1923] and *Von heiligen Zeichen* [Rothenfels, 1922/23; 2nd ed. Mainz 1927]) that human beings need symbolic experiences, not only for the sake of the liturgy, but for the sake of their own humanity. If there is to be fully conscious participation in liturgy, there is a need for deliberate pastoral efforts to give resonance to the word that is preached and to enable the people to grasp the sacramental signs. Therefore the Constitution on the Sacred Liturgy says in article 19: "With zeal and patience, pastors of souls must promote the liturgical instruction of the faithful, and also their active participation in the liturgy both internally and externally. The age and condition of their people, their way of life, and degree of religious culture should be taken into account. By so doing, pastors will be fulfilling one of the chief duties of a faithful dispenser of the mysteries of God; and in this matter they must lead their flock not only in word but also by example."

Celebrating the liturgy in a genuinely human way is an important task. Our goal must be to eliminate the need for an explanation of the Mass outside the Mass itself; instead, liturgy must be more clearly and obviously a conscious self-realization of the community. The Mass, by its nature as a deliberate dialogic action between God and human beings, requires active participation. We cannot simply accuse previous eras of encouraging pure passivity in attendance at Sunday Mass. Even then—with some exceptions—personal prayer always formed a part of the Sunday service. But people for the most part prayed "during Mass"; they did not pray "the Mass," and the Mass is not the sum total of many personal prayers; it is a well-structured whole consisting of action, prayer, and singing, with the various tasks shaped in relation to one another. Neither one person alone nor all together should do everything. Like every community, the one celebrating Eucharist is made up of different members. In the first place, there is the distinction between presider and congregation. These two principal initiators of the action each carry out or delegate their parts: The presider (priest or bishop) leads the assembly; he acts in the name of Christ when he says the prayers that are proper to his office. But at the same time he is a member of the people of God and prays on their behalf when he articulates the thanksgiving and petitions of the community, which they acknowledge and make their own by saying "amen." He is the official proclaimer and interpreter of the word of God; according to the situation he can receive support from concelebrants, a deacon, and ordinarily from a lector as well.

The congregation, in turn, acts together in word and song, response and acclamation, or allows itself to be represented—especially for ministries that are difficult for a large group to carry out—by members of the community delegated for these purposes. These might include more demanding types of song that require a good deal of training and preparation and are sung by the choir or schola (the Greek word *scholé* means zeal or study) with its cantor; the procession with the gifts or tasks like the bringing forward of the liturgical vessels (performed by the servers); support of the community singing by a cantor or organist. Even modest services like the cleaning and decorating of the room, the laying out of hymnals and other liturgical aids, helping handicapped persons to their places, taking up the collection, and many others are ultimately liturgical tasks.

We speak, in this context, of a distribution of liturgical roles: Each contributes to the celebration what corresponds to his or her office or abilities. In order that such services not be left to chance or supplied in makeshift fashion, previous meetings and practices are required; ideally these should be the responsibility of a group such as the parish liturgy committee that exists in many places. They are also responsible for a purposeful development of the community's consciousness of liturgy: The aim is not to carry out a single concept or recipe that is valid always and everywhere, but to see that a concrete community with its own abilities and limitations assembles to celebrate *its own* Eucharist.

What is required in addition is full participation by the whole person. Human beings depend on their senses. Spiritual things can only be expressed in sensible forms. There never exists a conversation of soul with soul; such conversation can only be mediated by comprehensible words, gestures, or indications that are conveyed by the senses. It is characteristic of all sacraments and all liturgy that the externals correspond to something internal; the visible signs are conformed to a divine gift that is, for the most part, invisible. The human body is something expressive: its postures and gestures, words and expressions testify to the person's thoughts; in turn, physical attitudes such as standing and kneeling, sitting and walking, are aids to mental and spiritual movement or meditation.

For an experience of unified community, a common external attitude—though certainly not a rigid drill—is desirable. Before everything else, participation must be devout. While the characteristics here described are mentioned in article 14 of the Constitution on the Sacred Liturgy, paragraph 3 of the *General Instruction* deliberately speaks of "faith, hope, and charity." Together, these constitute a description of the Christian life and its realization in personal and liturgical piety. All the symbolism of externals aims at the one essential thing. Liturgical reform does not mean simply a reform of the signs, but primarily an intensification of faith. Just as every symbol derives its life from the living pre-understanding of the group, but remains empty and exhausted if that pre-understanding gradually disappears, the same is true of liturgy without faith, hope, and charity. In recent years much has been achieved in regard to externals, which have been made better and more appropriate. But if we confuse the *means* of reform of symbols and the more expansive proclamation of the message of salvation with the *purpose*, namely the renewal of the people of God that the Council wanted to bring about, we will achieve a more magnificent routine of churchly life, but in the end we will have attained nothing. It is vital that the improved opportunities for expression of sacramental life should be made our own internal reality, a genuine self-expression of the People of God in its liturgy.

Notes

[1] *Sacrosanctum Concilium,* hereafter abbreviated *SC.* Quotations from this and other conciliar documents are taken from Walter M. Abbott, S. J., ed., *The Documents of Vatican II* (New York: Guild Press, 1966).

[2] Quotations from the *General Instruction* (hereafter abbreviated *GI*) are taken from *The Sacramentary* (Collegeville: The Liturgical Press, 1974, 1985).

Part One

THE FUNDAMENTAL
STRUCTURE OF THE MASS
THROUGH THE AGES

Chapter One

Fundamental Structure of the Mass

A. The Eucharistic Celebration

The Church celebrates the Eucharist because the Lord commanded it at his Last Supper: "Do this in remembrance of me" (Luke 22:19; 1 Cor 11:24). The command is twofold: it embraces an action and a memorial, or more precisely, a memorial carried out in and through an action. Therefore the memorial is first of all not something static and objective, but something dynamic, an action; moreover, it is a community action. In addition, the action is something perceptible to the senses, not something that is purely spiritual or mental; we can therefore speak of an expressive action that presents and effects its spiritual meaning in sensible terms. This means that the characteristics of the sacramental, that is, of the liturgy, are from the very beginning the fundamental, structural laws for this memorial action commanded by the Lord.

The celebration of this act consists in the imitation of a model initiated and instituted by the Lord himself. It was an action done within the course of a meal, namely the blessing of the bread and cup. This action is relatively independent; it could be, and in fact very soon was detached from the event surrounding it, when the meal itself—as one of the elements that simply served as a framework for the action itself—acquired elements that were inappropriate and disruptive, even contradictory to the action (including, for example, gluttony, drunkenness, and divisions). Christ coupled this blessing of bread and cup, the "thanksgiving and praise" of God (Greek *eucharistia*, Latin *gratiarum actio* or *benedictio*) with explanatory words that declared that the gifts of bread and wine to be consumed

were not merely his body and blood, but also, in Jewish sacrificial terminology familiar to his table companions, Jesus' "sacrificed" body and blood
"poured out," an expiatory sacrifice "for you," or "for all."

1. The Nature of the Eucharist According to the Accounts of Its Institution

Christ's institution of the Eucharist has been handed down to us in the so-
called institution narratives, almost identical (with minor variations) in the
first three gospels: Mark 14:22-24; Matt 26:26-28; Luke 22:19-20. Very close
to them is 1 Cor 11:23-25, in which Paul recalls for the Corinthians the
legacy received from the Lord. The Lukan text, relatively the most extensive,
reads: "Then he took a loaf of bread, and when he had given thanks, he broke
it and gave it to them, saying, 'This is my body, which is given for you. Do
this in remembrance of me.' And he did the same with the cup after supper,
saying, 'This cup that is poured out for you is the new covenant in my
blood.'" Matthew and Mark omit the interpretive relative clause at the
bread-breaking, "which is given for you," but Paul includes it (1 Cor 11:24).
The blessing of the cup is more variable in the four accounts: Luke and Paul
(in 1 Cor 11) appear to put special emphasis on the cup, the container of the
wine, as a symbol of the new covenant, while Mark and Matthew speak expressly of the "blood of the covenant, which is poured out for many" (cf.
Mark 14:24; Matt 26:28). In the four eucharistic prayers of the Mass we have
a text that assimilates the four accounts rather strongly: "The day before he
suffered he took bread in his sacred hands and looking up to heaven, to you,
his almighty Father, he gave you thanks and praise. He broke the bread, gave
it to his disciples, and said: Take this, all of you, and eat it: this is my body
which will be given up for you. When supper was ended, he took the cup.
Again he gave you thanks and praise, gave the cup to his disciples, and said:
Take this, all of you, and drink from it: this is the cup of my blood, the blood
of the new and everlasting covenant. It will be shed for you and for all so that
sins may be forgiven. Do this in memory of me" (Eucharistic Prayer I).

The four traditional texts that New Testament exegesis calls the "institution narratives" are not just stenographic reports of the words of Jesus. At the
time they were written (1 Corinthians as early as 55 C.E., the three gospels in
the 70s), people had already been celebrating the Eucharist for a generation or
longer. Thus the accounts also give us a picture of the apostolic community
Eucharist, whose history we will have to survey later. However, they attempt
to retain the tradition that has been handed down, and they are convinced
that they are following Jesus' institution exactly, both in form and intention,
even though—as we now know—they reflect a developed stage of the cele-

bration, by which time the blessings of bread and cup had been placed more clearly in parallel. In addition, it is probable that explanatory, interpretive expressions had been introduced; these are not really new, but can be derived, without forcing, from Jesus' intention and proclamation: What is presumed there is stated more explicitly and developed for our understanding.

We can, then, speak of a "theologizing" of the text, an explanatory interpretation of something the community had been doing for a long time more or less simply and without reflection: The celebration of the Lord's instruction and institution ("Do this . . .") is older than its fusion with theological interpretation. Nevertheless, the latter also goes back to those who were present at the institution; it reveals especially the world of ideas nourished by the Old Testament (and by no means obsolete) in which Christ and the apostles lived and thought as a matter of course. Moreover, we should not fail to recognize that the biblical authors, with this report, also intended to present something normative for their contemporaries and those to come: Thus, and in no other way, is the Lord's memorial to be celebrated. Paul emphasizes this clearly in 1 Cor 11:23. Therefore the institution narratives present not simply a report of an event, but a reflection that is both theological and liturgical in its intention.

Examination of these accounts has allowed us to discover and distinguish three strands of tradition: (1) the oldest text in Mark, which reveals the Old Testament thought world of a community consisting mainly of Jewish Christians, and which is discernible under the later redaction by Matthew and Luke; (2) a tradition based on the paschal theology that influenced Luke in particular (Luke 22:7-23) to consciously combine older textual witnesses according to this schema, although these traditional elements also appear clearly in the other accounts; and (3) the Johannine account (John 13:1-17, 26, which should be expanded by the addition of the so-called "discourse of promise" in 6:51-58), in which a later stage of reflection appears. We have no common primitive account (which would have been in Aramaic), and yet such a report is evident behind the Markan account in particular.

We will do best to turn, first of all, to the Lukan account quoted above. It is the most detailed; it reflects the Old Testament traditions derived from Markan theology; and it combines these with a paschal theology.

(a) The new covenant in the atoning blood of Christ

Reference to Old Testament ideas appears with special clarity first of all in the words of Jesus over the cup: "This cup that is poured out for you is the new covenant in my blood" (Luke 22:20). Here Mark 14:24 is taken up with a slight variation: "This is my blood of the covenant, which is poured out for many." This idea of covenant, which is somewhat pallid for us today even though we very often speak about the "new covenant" or "new testament," was for Jews constitutive for their whole religious thought and action: The Jews had been chosen by God through God's covenant with the people, and they continued to live in a covenant relationship with God. Their whole religious, social, and national existence was bound up with their fidelity to the covenant.

Exodus 24 describes the formation of this covenant, which was and is vividly present to every religious Jew, and therefore to Christ and the apostles. There we read: "And Moses wrote down all the words of the Lord. He rose early in the morning, and built an altar at the foot of the mountain, and set up twelve pillars, corresponding to the twelve tribes of Israel. He sent young men of the people of Israel, who offered burnt offerings and sacrificed oxen as offerings of well-being to the Lord. Moses took half of the blood and put it in basins, and half of the blood he dashed against the altar. Then he took the book of the covenant, and read it in the hearing of the people, and they said, 'All that the Lord has spoken we will do, and we will be obedient.' Moses took the blood and dashed it on the people, and said, '*See the blood of the covenant* that the Lord has made with you in accordance with all these words'" (Exod 24:4-8, emphasis added).

These words of Moses about the blood of the covenant (Exod 24:8) are replicated literally in the Last Supper account. Thus we are dealing here with an apparent parallelism between the old covenant and the new covenant proclaimed by Christ: As Moses proclaimed the old covenant, so Christ the new. The old people of God, with its twelve tribes, corresponds to the new, represented by the twelve apostles, to whom Christ gives authority in the reign of God (in close connection with his own actions): "You are those who have stood by me in my trials; and I confer on you, just as my Father has conferred on me, a kingdom" (Luke 22:28-29). Both the old and the new covenants are sealed and ratified in the blood of the covenant that is poured out—formerly the blood of the sacrificial animals and now the blood of Christ that is shed. Later, this mediating function of Christ and his blood of the covenant will pervade the whole letter to the Hebrews; nevertheless, this mediation by Christ infinitely surpasses the old: "he entered once for all into the Holy Place, not with the blood of goats and calves, but with his own blood, thus obtaining eternal redemption" (Heb 9:12).

It is worth noting in addition that there was a feast in connection with, or more precisely as a final stage of, the making of the old covenant.

In Exod 24:11 we read: "and [the Israelites] ate and drank." The awareness of the atoning power of the blood of the covenant was a matter of course for Jews. It pervades the whole of the Old Testament. In addition, the regular bloody sacrifices in the Temple were based on it, for they were simply the fulfillment of the covenant obligation. A reference to the blood of the covenant that is highly significant for our context is found in the prophet Zechariah (Zech 9:9-11). All four evangelists wove this passage into the story of Jesus' passion, beginning with his entry into Jerusalem. Matthew 21:5 and John 12:15 give a direct quotation from the promise of Zechariah: "Rejoice greatly, O daughter Zion! Shout aloud, O daughter Jerusalem! Lo, your king comes to you; triumphant and victorious is he, humble and riding on a donkey, on a colt, the foal of a donkey" (Zech 9:9). In Mark 11:2-8 and Luke 19:29-36 the sense of the passage is recalled. The continuation of this promise of the entry of the king of peace contains the word of consolation: "As for you also, because of the blood of my covenant with you, I will set your prisoners free from the waterless pit" (Zech 9:11).

For those who lived within the world of the Old Testament promises, the formation of a new covenant was also part of the hope of salvation that was fulfilled in Christ. Jeremiah had promised that this new covenant would be realized in the eschatological time of salvation ("the days to come"): "The days are surely coming, says the Lord, when I will make a new covenant with the house of Israel and the house of Judah. It will not be like the covenant that I made with their ancestors when I took them by the hand to bring them out of the land of Egypt—a covenant that they broke, though I was their husband, says the Lord. But this is the covenant that I will make with the house of Israel after those days, says the Lord: I will put my law within them, and I will write it on their hearts; and I will be their God, and they shall be my people. No longer shall they teach one another, or say to each other, 'Know the Lord,' for they shall all know me, from the least of them to the greatest, says the Lord; for I will forgive their iniquity, and remember their sin no more" (Jer 31:31-34). Thus this covenant is promised as one of the greatest possible intimacy: It will not be written on stone, like the old tables of the law, but on the heart (Jer 31:33). Christ fulfilled this promise as the one teacher in a community of brothers and sisters (Matt 23:8), revealing himself especially to the marginal and the disenfranchised (Matt 11:25). The enduring real presence of Christ among his people in the Eucharist is the complete fulfillment of the promise of Emmanuel (God with us) in the midst of the people (Jer 31:33); in baptism and reconciliation human beings, through the saving action of Christ, obtain complete freedom from sin and guilt (Jer 31:34).

The power of this initiation of a new covenant to eradicate sin is again emphasized and further exemplified in the twofold "for you" of the "body that is given up" and of the "blood that is shed." Behind this is the martyrdom theology of contemporary Judaism in which one person stands as a representative and expiation for others. This is the theology of the so-called "servant song" (the song of the *'ebed YHWH'*) in Isa 53:1-12, which Jesus, according to Mark 10:45, applies to himself: "For the Son of Man came not to be served but to serve, and to give his life a ransom for many." The "for" in the last phrase stands logically for "in the place of" or "as a representative of." One acts *for* others or *for* many (or *for* all: *many* and *all* are merely alternative translations of the Hebrew word *rabim*); the others are then free. To summarize with an obvious example: Maximilian Kolbe went into the starvation bunker *for* a fellow prisoner who had been assigned a gruesome lot and he died; the other was free and survived. Kolbe is a *martyr* in this sense, that he suffered in place of another. This is the function that the servant of God in Isaiah 53 fulfilled *for* his people.

Hence it is unimportant at this point to know who, from the point of view of the inspired Old Testament author, this servant of God was: whether he stands for all Israel collectively, or for an ideal Israel as the "sacred remnant," or is an individual, concrete person, either a historical king or a revivified Moses or an ideal of the eschatological prophet who will appear in the future. What is essential here is only that the text refers to one who will affect atonement as a representative and whose death is understood as analogous to a cultic sacrifice. The text of Isaiah is familiar to us from the Good Friday liturgy, but it should be cited in full here so that the context may be made clear:

> Who has believed what we have heard?
> And to whom has the arm of the LORD been revealed?
> For he grew up before him like a young plant,
>   and like a root out of dry ground;
> he had no form or majesty that we should look at him,
>   nothing in his appearance that we should desire him.
> He was despised and rejected by others;
>   a man of suffering and acquainted with infirmity;
> and as one from whom others hide their faces
>   he was despised, and we held him of no account.
> Surely he has borne our infirmities
>   and carried our diseases;
> yet we accounted him stricken,
>   struck down by God, and afflicted.

But he was wounded for our transgressions,
>   crushed for our iniquities;
upon him was the punishment that made us whole,
>   and by his bruises we are healed.
All we like sheep have gone astray;
>   we have all turned to our own way,
and the LORD has laid on him the iniquity of us all.
He was oppressed, and he was afflicted,
>   yet he did not open his mouth;
like a lamb that is led to the slaughter,
>   and like a sheep that before its shearers is silent,
>   so he did not open his mouth.
By a perversion of justice he was taken away.
>   Who could have imagined his future?
For he was cut off from the land of the living,
>   stricken for the transgression of my people.
They made his grave with the wicked
>   and his tomb with the rich,
although he had done no violence,
>   and there was no deceit in his mouth.
Yet it was the will of the LORD to crush him with pain.
When you make his life an offering for sin,
>   he shall see his offspring, and shall prolong his days;
through him the will of the LORD shall prosper.
>   Out of his anguish he shall see light;
he shall find satisfaction through his knowledge.
>   The righteous one, my servant, shall make many righteous,
>   and he shall bear their iniquities.
Therefore I will allot him a portion with the great,
>   and he shall divide the spoil with the strong;
because he poured out himself to death,
>   and was numbered with the transgressors;
yet he bore the sin of many,
>   and made intercession for the transgressors (Isa 53:1-12).

Jesus is now this servant of God portrayed by Isaiah, who suffered as a *representative for* his people: "The Lord has laid on him the iniquity of us all" (Isa. 53:6). "But he was wounded for our transgressions" (Isa 53:5, and frequently). Nevertheless, this representation is *atoning:* "upon him was the punishment that made us whole, and by his bruises we are healed" (Isa 53:5); "he bore the sin of many, and made intercession for the transgressors" (Isa 53:12). This atonement is made as if by a cultic atoning sacrifice: Jesus suffered "like a lamb that is led to the slaughter" (Isa 53:7), "his life [became] an offering for sin" (Isa 53:10). Jesus' surrender of his life as a true sacrifice in his "body given for many" and his "blood shed for many" is thus by no means a later interpretation; it is already clearly evident in the accounts of the institution of the Eucharist as a reality behind Jesus' action and institution of the sacrament: He had not come to be served, but to serve, and to give his life as ransom for many (cf. Mark 10:45).

The adjectival attributes of the body "given" and the blood "shed" also belong within this context of an atoning sacrifice. Christ is now the true servant of God "like a lamb that is led to the slaughter" (Isa 53:7), whose life is made "an offering for sin" (Isa 53:10). In the old covenant, one who was not a Levite completed the sacrificial action by "giving" or "handing over" the sacrifice; the Levite took it, slaughtered it, and "poured out" its blood at the foot of the altar. These two actions, the handing over of the sacrificial animal and the pouring of the blood, constituted the sacrifice. Jesus is thus the ritual atoning sacrifice of the new covenant. "For our paschal lamb, Christ, has been sacrificed" (1 Cor 5:7). The saving and atoning merit of the Lord's death was applied to his disciples even before his physical death, at the last supper; the community experiences it in the Eucharist.

Jesus fully accepts this task of suffering as atonement, which was given him by the Father. He goes deliberately to his death. He is conscious that this is his last meal, and he says so. Luke reports his prediction of his death immediately before the institution of the Lord's memorial in a double saying: "He said to them, 'I have eagerly desired to eat this Passover with you before I suffer; for I tell you, I will not eat it until it is fulfilled in the kingdom of God.' Then he took a cup, and after giving thanks he said, 'Take this and divide it among yourselves; for I tell you that from now on I will not drink of the fruit of the vine until the kingdom of God comes'" (Luke 22:15-18; cf. Mark 14:15; Matt 26:29, after the words over the cup). However, this double prophecy of his death is "saturated with hope" (Heinz Schürmann): his fate is his "unique death," which is not the end, but the beginning of something new, the dawning of the reign of God. For his resurrection is already contained in his death. Jesus' command of repetition: "Do this in remembrance of me" (Luke 22:19; 1 Cor 11:24) should be seen against this background: The command points already to the future, the time of the Church and the actions of the eschatological community of Christ. He institutes the sacrament: the Church's Eucharist.

Let us briefly summarize this initial complex of theological statements in the institution narratives, arising out of Jewish ideas and ways of thinking regarding the meaning and nature of the eucharistic meal: The Lord who is present under the forms of bread and wine is the new Moses, the new covenant mediator, who constitutes the new Israel; he ratifies this new covenant promised by Jeremiah for the end time not in the blood of sacrificial animals, but in his own blood. With the surrender of his body and the shedding of his blood, he becomes the true servant of God, the atoning sacrifice for the guilt of the many. He accepts his death deliberately, as total surrender of his life to the Father, but at the same time he is conscious of hope for a "new eating and drinking" in the reign of God, and with his command to repeat his actions he points to the time after his death and resurrection, the time of the Church and the sacraments.

(b) The Eucharist as Passover of the new covenant

Another strand of interpretation, also resting on Jewish ideas and liturgical practices, explains the Eucharist as a "new Passover," or more precisely as a "re-instituted Passover." This is especially clear in the Lukan account (Luke 22:7-20), where he redacts the traditional materials consistently in terms of an account of a Passover meal. It is true that the paschal context is also evident in Matthew (Matt 26:17-19) and Mark (Mark 14:12-16); moreover, in all the accounts the interpretive words over the bread and wine point to a paschal custom that is unusual in other contexts. Known foods or drinks are particularly named only when they have a special meaning beyond what is apparent. Luke's composition and redaction are entirely guided by this context: In 22:7-13 he first gives a detailed account of the preparation of the Passover meal (almost identical with Mark 14:12-16).

Then he makes use of an old piece of tradition (Luke 22:15-18; according to Heinz Schürmann this appears to be a very old "last supper account" in the form of a rigidly symmetrical double saying; however, probably because of the awkwardness of the action with the bread, it was not received as such). In this way he introduces the "first cup" of the Passover meal (with its blessing of the "fruit of the vine," Luke 22:18), and he sets the paschal words of interpretation in parallel with Jesus' words of institution, thus approaching the description of a Passover as described in the Haggadah, the liturgical ritual for Passover. Of course, nothing is said about the slaughtering and eating of a paschal lamb; we must imagine a Passover without a lamb. In this case, "Christ our paschal sacrifice" (1 Cor 5:7) would already be present in the meal of institution.

The dating of this Passover also offers some difficulties. According to the first three evangelists, it is perfectly obvious that Christ would have celebrated the meal with his apostles at the usual time. But according to John,

Jesus died at the time when the paschal lambs were being slaughtered; for according to John 18:28b, the Jews did not want to enter the praetorium of the Roman governor "so as to avoid ritual defilement and to be able to eat the Passover." Therefore they ask Pilate to come out to them. The dating thus differs by one day. However, it appears that John also knows the tradition of a Passover theology: He appears to see in the fact that Jesus' legs were not broken after his death (John 19:36) the fulfillment of the command in Exod 12:10 "not to break any bone" of the paschal lamb. Thus for John also, Jesus is the new pasch, the fulfillment of the old (as in 1 Cor 5:7). However, we cannot exclude the possibility that he simply intends to cite Ps 34:21, especially since the piercing of Jesus' side (John 19:34) is understood as a fulfillment of Zechariah's prophecy (Zech 12:10). In both cases, then, we would find here a description of God's rescue of the one who suffers.

It is appropriate at this point to describe, in brief, the meaning and procedure of a Jewish Passover. In this way we can better appreciate the New Testament paschal theology, especially evident in Luke.

The Jewish Passover was a memorial feast, the supreme religious and political festival. Every year, at the first full moon of spring, they celebrated (and made present) God's great deeds on behalf of the people on their departure from Egypt, beginning with the gracious "passing over" (pasch, *pesach*) of the houses of the Israelites at the time when all the firstborn of the Egyptians were slain (Exod 12:29), through the rescue in the passage of the sea, the covenant at Sinai in the blood of the peace offerings and the covenant meal (Exod 24:4-11), to the possession of the promised land of Canaan. These facts, taken together, were constitutive of the making of the covenant and the existence of Israel as God's covenant people.

The Passover was regarded as having been instituted and commanded by God, and is described in Exod 12:1-14, 21-28. This pericope comes from the deuteronomic and priestly laws. In common with the Last Supper institution accounts, it both describes the institution and reflects the celebration as it took place after the entry into the land: The taking of the lamb four days before the feast (Exod 12:3), for example, clearly reflects the ritual of a repeated celebration. Thus the first festival and its repetition are combined in the account.

Let us begin by reading the text of Exod 12:1-14, 21-28, which narrates the context of the institution of the Passover:

> The LORD said to Moses and Aaron in the land of Egypt: This month shall mark for you the beginning of months; it shall be the first month of the year for you. Tell the whole congregation of Israel that on the

tenth of this month they are to take a lamb for each family, a lamb for each household. If a household is too small for a whole lamb, it shall join its closest neighbor in obtaining one; the lamb shall be divided in proportion to the number of people who eat of it. Your lamb shall be without blemish, a year-old male; you may take it from the sheep or from the goats. You shall keep it until the fourteenth day of this month; then the whole assembled congregation of Israel shall slaughter it at twilight. They shall take some of the blood and put it on the two doorposts and the lintel of the houses in which they eat it. They shall eat the lamb that same night; they shall eat it roasted over the fire with unleavened bread and bitter herbs. Do not eat any of it raw or boiled in water, but roasted over the fire, with its head, legs, and inner organs. You shall let none of it remain until the morning; anything that remains until the morning you shall burn. This is how you shall eat it: your loins girded, your sandals on your feet, and your staff in your hand; and you shall eat it hurriedly. It is the passover of the LORD. For I will pass through the land of Egypt that night, and I will strike down every firstborn in the land of Egypt, both human beings and animals; on all the gods of Egypt I will execute judgments: I am the LORD. The blood shall be a sign for you on the houses where you live: when I see the blood, I will pass over you, and no plague shall destroy you when I strike the land of Egypt.

This day shall be a day of remembrance for you. You shall celebrate it as a festival to the LORD; throughout your generations you shall observe it as a perpetual ordinance. . . .

Then Moses called all the elders of Israel and said to them, "Go, select lambs for your families, and slaughter the passover lamb. Take a bunch of hyssop, dip it in the blood that is in the basin, and touch the lintel and the two doorposts with the blood in the basin. None of you shall go outside the door of your house until morning. For the LORD will pass through to strike down the Egyptians; when he sees the blood on the lintel and on the two doorposts, the LORD will pass over that door and will not allow the destroyer to enter your houses to strike you down. You shall observe this rite as a perpetual ordinance for you and your children. When you come to the land that the LORD will give you, as he has promised, you shall keep this observance. And when your children ask you, 'What do you mean by this observance?' you shall say, 'It is the passover sacrifice to the LORD, for he passed over the houses of the Israelites in Egypt, when he struck down the Egyptians but spared our houses.'" And the people bowed down and worshiped.

The Israelites went and did just as the LORD had commanded Moses and Aaron.

In Exod 12:43-50, the Passover is explicitly restricted to Israel. Verse 46c also prescribes that no bone of the paschal lamb shall be broken (see above; cf. John 19:36). Jews celebrated, and still celebrate, the Passover on the fourteenth day of the month of Nisan, the first month of spring (March or April in our calendars). Because the lunar month of 28 days always begins with the new moon, the full moon occurs on the fourteenth day. Making this the first month of the year is traced in this passage to God's, or Moses,' command, but it corresponds to the Babylonian calendar from the time of Hammurabi. The festival itself was already, even before Moses, a nomadic celebration connected with the shifting of pastures; in a ritual shepherds' meal one of the new lambs was sacrificed, roasted on the fire, and eaten. That is the reference of the prohibition in Exod 12:9 against eating the lamb raw or boiled.

The original character of a nomadic meal, in contrast to the customs of hunters and farmers, is thus deliberately preserved. The same is true of the unleavened bread (*matza,* pl. *matzoh*). These are unleavened flat breads, baked on flat, heated stones; in terms of cultural history they represent a more advanced stage than eating raw grain (cf. the disciples' plucking grain on the sabbath in Matt 12:1; Mark 2:23; Luke 6:1) or roasting kernels and ears of grain over the fire (Lev 23:14; Josh 5:11, and frequently), because in this case the starch in the grain is released by beating or grinding, dampening and heating, and thus becomes more digestible for the human body; in this way, grinding the grain in one's teeth and mixing it with saliva is in some sense obviated. But this unleavened flat bread of the nomads was much older than the customary leavened bread of farmers, baked in ovens. The unleavened bread was more primitive and less palatable, the "bread of tears" (in the terms of the paschal ritual). In the time of Jesus, people normally—except at Passover—ate the bread of settled farmers (cf. the parable of the reign of God as yeast in Matt 13:33: "The kingdom of heaven is like yeast that a woman took and mixed in with three measures of flour until all of it was leavened;" cf. Luke 13:21). Hence meat roasted on the fire and the bread of nomads were impressive signs for Israelite farmers, pointers back to the time when Israel was still a wandering nomadic people and strangers to the land of Canaan.

At the first celebration in Egypt the place for eating the Passover was obviously the house of the Israelite family; after the cultic centralization and reform of Josiah it could only be eaten in Jerusalem. The directions in Deut 16:5-6 reveal the process of this development, projecting the later custom into the past era of the wilderness wandering. "You are not permitted to offer the passover sacrifice within any of your towns that the

Lord your God is giving you. But at the place that the Lord your God will choose as a dwelling for his name [= Jerusalem], only there shall you offer the passover sacrifice, in the evening at sunset, the time of day when you departed from Egypt." Therefore after the return from exile Passover was celebrated only in Jerusalem (Ezra 6:20; cf. also the custom of Jesus' parents in Luke 2:41). Christ himself, with his apostles, holds strictly to this custom: He sends the disciples into Jerusalem to prepare the meal (Matt 26:18; Mark 14:13; Luke 22:8); then, in the evening, he enters the city, sits at table (Matt 26:20; Mark 14:17-18; Luke 22:14), and leaves the city again after the meal (Matt 26:30; Mark 14:26; Luke 22:39; John 18:1). After the final destruction of the Herodian temple, and to the present time, the people returned to celebrating the meal at home, in their residences throughout the diaspora.

The course of the Passover meal at the time of Jesus was strictly regulated by the pericope quoted above (Exodus 12) and by customary rules (cf. m. 2 Seder Mo'ed; 3 Pes.). The Passover consisted of the preparatory rituals and the meal itself. The preparation began with the choice of the lamb, four days before the feast (on the 10th Nisan), the baking of the unleavened bread and the ceremonial removal—sometimes even the burning—of all leavened bread before noon on the feast day (cf. 1 Cor 5:7: "Clean out the old yeast so that you may be a new batch, as you really are unleavened. For our paschal lamb, Christ, has been sacrificed"). Just before sunset on the 14th Nisan, the first day of Passover, the lambs were slaughtered in the temple according to the sacrificial ritual: The lamb that was "given" was slaughtered by the head of the household; the priests captured the blood and "poured" it at the foot of the altar of sacrifice. The head of the household then took the lamb home, where it was roasted on the spit and prepared for the family's consumption. Pilgrims were either invited to the homes of their relatives or friends, or, if there were too many of them to be received into one house, they combined themselves into "fellowships" (haburoth; sg. habura); in those cases, the oldest or most honored among them took the role of the head of household. Such a situation is apparently envisioned in Luke 22:7-13 (Matt 26:17; Mark 14:12-16): Jesus is the head of his household of disciples.

If possible, the meal was eaten in a beautifully decorated and lighted room. According to Luke 22:12 (Mark 14:15), Jesus and his disciples used an upper chamber outfitted with couches. While at the beginning, according to Exod 12:11, the meal was eaten standing and in traveling costume, in haste as before the flight from Egypt, at the time of Christ the custom of reclining at table—as in Hellenistic symposia—had long dominated, although this did great damage to the symbolic nature of the meal and its memorial character. The table companions on their couches faced toward the central, flat table (or sometimes merely a mat or similar floor covering), on which the food was placed; they rested on the left elbow and ate with the free right hand. The circle around the table was not completely closed: one side of the table was open to make it easier for the food to be placed on it. The head of the household had the place of honor, either in the center or at the end of the three-quarter circle of those reclining at table. The place to the head's right hand (so that the one occupying it could "recline on the breast" of the head of household [cf. John 13:25; 21:20]) was next in honor, because the presider at table could most easily converse with the one occupying that place.

This custom of reclining at table was expressly authorized by the Mishna, because of the festal character of the meal. Even the poorest people should be allowed to recline, and should receive four cups of wine (m. Pes. 10, 1).

The meal then proceeded in this fashion: the head of the household first took a cup containing the "fruit of the vine" (cf. Luke 22:17-18), gave thanks and blessed it, and all drank from it; then the unleavened bread and "bitter herbs" were brought (the latter is the so-called *maror*, a type of leek, dipped in salt water and vinegar). It was unusual to begin a meal with this kind of dish; a Jewish meal would otherwise begin with the ritual breaking of bread and thanksgiving (a kind of grace before meals). Then, after the meal itself was served, the people began the memorial ritual itself, with the narrative and the praising of God's saving deeds for the people. This ritual anamnesis made the whole meal a Passover. The post-Talmudic redactions in use today reveal a number of ritual elements that are probably more recent: the hiding of the bread, washing of hands, reshaping of part of the Passover narrative into an epic hymn (*dayyenu*), and very likely also the placing of the interpretive word about the "bread of tears" at the beginning, together with a perspective that is certainly newer: "In this year, in entering into the land of Israel, in this year we are servants; in the year to come we will be children of freedom." In other modern redactions this is recited, or repeated, at the end of the meal. Nevertheless, the fundamental structures (especially those drawn from Exodus 12 and the Mishna tractate Pesahim) can still be clearly discerned. The narrative (*haggada*) that shapes the ritual, recited by the head of the household, is initiated by the question of the youngest: "Why is this night different from all other nights?" (cf. Exod 12:26). The household head gives the meaning of the celebration: "We were slaves of Pharaoh in Egypt, and the Lord our God led us out from there with a strong hand and an outstretched arm. For if God, the Holy One, blessed be he, had not led our ancestors out of Egypt, we and our children and our children's children would still be the slaves of Pharaoh in Egypt. . . ."

The account continued to the taking possession of the land. Especially characteristic of this account were the interpretive words spoken over the food specific to this meal, unusual otherwise: Thus it is said over the paschal lamb itself, "It is the passover sacrifice to YHWH, for he passed over the houses of the Israelites in Egypt, when he struck down the Egyptians but spared our houses" (Exod 12:27); the unleavened bread that the people of Israel took with them in haste, before it was leavened (Exod 12:34) is called "the bread of tears that our ancestors ate in Egypt," and the bitter herbs are eaten "because the Egyptians made the lives of our ancestors bitter." In this account, words and symbols enhance each other in a most impressive way. While speaking the words of interpretation over the *matzoh*, the unleavened bread, the head of the household lifted it a handsbreadth. Then the second cup was poured. The head of the household continued the story of the exodus with praise for God's saving deeds, culminating in the first part of the great *hallel* (Pss 114 and 115:1-8). In contrast to the account of bitterness in the first part of the *haggada*, the cup hymn had an altogether joyous character and emphasized the continuing and joy-bringing care and protection of God. Then the second cup was drunk and the *matzoh* eaten. This completed the essentials of the memorial ritual; it was followed by the meal itself, with the lamb. At the end of the meal, the third cup was poured, again with a blessing that was an expanded form of the usual prayer after meals, augmented by paschal elements. Finally, the second part of the *hallel* was sung (Pss 115:9ff., 116, 117). This was probably the original conclusion of the meal.

It appears that at the time of Christ the "fourth cup" of later custom, which served as transition to the post-prandial festivities, was not yet part of this joyful feast, because "after the singing of the hymn" (the *hallel*) the Lord immediately went out to the Mount of Olives (Mark 14:26; Matt 26:30; Luke 22:39). The Passover was generally supposed to end by midnight.

The Passover meal clearly consists of two fundamentally independent elements, a festival banquet and a memorial ritual *(anamnesis)*. The banquet contains all the elements that were and are to be expected at a normal meal: meat (the paschal lamb), carbohydrates (bread, rather than potatoes or pasta; in this case the bread is unleavened), vegetables (leeks or bitter herbs), relish *(haroseth)*, and wine. The memorial, on the other hand, is aimed at the most impressive possible depiction of liberation, from the exodus from Egypt to the taking possession of the land: Even when the originally graphic elements (standing in clothes suited to travel or flight, and eating in haste) had been replaced by reclining on couches or pillows, still the contrast between the bread of tears and the bitter herbs on the one hand and the cup of wine on the other (as symbol of the covenant and its fulfillment by God in the form of possession of a fruitful agricultural country that produced wine, the symbol of rejoicing and festival) served quite clearly as a "transparent symbol." The contrast between slavery and freedom, bitterness and joy, suffering and rescue, dominates the entire ritual. This anamnesis is, as we have said, the overarching, specifying factor in this festival banquet and gives it its name; at the same time it is an independent symbol in itself and can be detached from the meal.

This paschal ritual in the narrower sense, as a memorial meal, meant more to the Jews than simply a remembrance of something past: it was a making present, a calling into present reality of God's ongoing and enduring fidelity to the covenant. Even Exod 13:4 speaks of "today," and m. Pes. 10, 5 specifically emphasizes that at this celebration "in every age, each one shall regard himself or herself as one who has come out of Egypt." Thus at Passover God's saving deeds in the past again become a gracious and enduring present; at the same time, however, there is an echo of the expectation of the final, eschatological liberation. When Jews today conclude their Passover with the simple words, "this year still slaves, but next year free people in a restored Jerusalem," the statement corresponds to Paul's intention in speaking of "proclaim[ing] the Lord's death until he comes" (1 Cor 11:26), a phrase that is taken up in the people's acclamations in the new eucharistic prayers. The Jewish Passover is "sacramentally structured" (cf. Thomas Aquinas, S. T. III 60 ad 2: a "sacrament of the old covenant") by this relationship of symbol and saving event/expectation. In the Hebrew *zikkaron* (corresponding to *anamnesis*, memorial) this theology of presence, founded on the transcendence of God's eternity beyond the passage of created time, is emphatically sensed. Ultimately, our Christian understanding of sacraments is grounded also in this truth that was already familiar to Judaism.

Against this background of the sacramental interpretation of Passover by Jesus' contemporaries and the symbolic character of the lamb, bread, and wine, Christ's action becomes fully clear and understandable for us. Christ institutes a new covenant and gives the symbols of the new Passover, no longer the bread of tears and the cup of the covenant, but himself, under the forms of bread and wine. If we consider as well that his surrender to death occurred on the same day as the paschal supper (in ancient reckoning, the old day ended and the new day began at sunset, so that "Holy Thursday" evening and "Good Friday" afternoon are parts of the same day), we will comprehend still more urgently that Christ himself is "our paschal lamb" (1 Cor 5:7). If this "paschal sacrifice of Christ" at the end of the Passover day, before sunset, is his real and "historical" surrender of his body and his atonement "for us," the last supper is already the making present, the symbolic and sign-rich anticipation. Our eucharistic celebration, on the other hand, is the posterior, real making-present and memorial under the same signs, until the Lord returns. Thus the last supper and the Mass are rooted in the same reality of sacrifice and are shaped by the same signs that make present what they signify.

It is difficult to determine at the present time whether Jesus' final meal was really a Passover or whether the Passover was simply introduced by the first three evangelists as a "sacramental interpretation." Paul merely gives the time as "on the night when he was betrayed" (1 Cor 11:23). John, as we have said, depicts Christ as dying at the time when the lambs were being slaughtered, so that the meal was celebrated on the day before the Passover itself. Nevertheless, the accounts of the supper, the pre-understanding of the memorial celebration, and the otherwise unusual words of interpretation over the food and drink are best explained if we suppose that this really was a Passover: The meal is eaten in Jerusalem (as prescribed by Deut 16:5-6), although, at this time, the Lord otherwise spent the night in Bethany (Mark 11:11) or on the Mount of Olives (Luke 22:39), and it is said that he went there after the meal (Mark 14:26; John 18:1), although he could easily have eaten an ordinary supper in that place.

There are also the ritual number of participants for a Passover; the celebration beginning after sundown, during the night, as Exod. 12:8 commanded; the breaking of the bread "while they were eating" (Mark 14:22; Matt 26:26), something that happened only at Passover, because otherwise the bread was broken before the meal, during the opening prayer; the hymn at the end of the meal (Mark 14:26; Matt 26:30) instead of the usual prayer over the cup; and especially, as we have said, the interpretive words, unusual at any other than a Passover meal.

We should note one thing in particular: This form of the "Lord's supper," (1 Cor 11:20) instituted by Christ for the Church's future is constitutive for the fundamental shape of the Mass. Every meal is a foundation for community, belongingness, communion. This was especially evident in the room of the last supper in the eating of the bread that was broken and the drinking from the one cup that circulated, as well as in the eating of food from a common dish (John 13:26) at the one table (Luke 22:21). Paul emphasizes in 1 Cor 10:16-17: "The cup of blessing that we bless, is it not a sharing in the blood of Christ? The bread that we break, is it not a sharing in the body of Christ? Because there is one bread, we who are many are one body, for we all partake of the one bread." Hence Christ emphasizes the ethos of this table fellowship: Although he presides, he is the one who serves (Luke 22:27), who washes the feet of the others (John 13:1-17), and who settles the quarrel about rank that breaks out during the meal (Luke 22:24-27) with a reference to his own attitude: "I have set you an example, that you also should do as I have done to you" (John 13:15). The rediscovery of the meal context has undoubtedly been of fundamental significance for the revival of our celebration of the Mass. It is no accident that the *General Instruction* of the new missal (1, §2) speaks of the Mass as the Lord's supper before emphasizing its character as eucharistic sacrifice.

(c) The bread of life

The last of the four gospels to be written (ca. 100 C.E.), the gospel according to John, no longer contains an institution account. Apparently its interest in the Lord's supper is less liturgical than theological: The community's eucharistic celebration had already assumed its more or less fixed form. It is true that John describes a farewell supper (John 13:1-17:26), but mentions it only in passing in 13:2, and speaks of the washing of feet during the meal (13:4) and of table fellowship with the betrayer (13:26). The atoning power of the blood of the covenant that was so important in the first three evangelists' understanding of the Eucharist scarcely plays any role for the fourth.

It is true that the connection with Passover is conveyed (in John 18:28 the Jews refuse to enter the governor's praetorium so they may preserve their ritual purity and be able to eat the Passover meal in the evening), but for this evangelist it is no longer constitutive for the Eucharist. Time has passed, and other problems and theological cruxes in the gospel preaching are more central and urgent, especially in Hellenistic Asia Minor, where the Jewish population is smaller. Moreover, gnosticism is making its appearance, with a devaluation of the "flesh" and thus, in the final analysis, a denial of the genuine "word made flesh" and the reality of our redemption by Jesus. Therefore, right at the beginning of the gospel (John 1:14) we find the succinct statement that "the word became *flesh* and dwelt among us." We should note here that "flesh," and "body" are simply alternative translations (stemming from the same Hebrew word, *basar*), and therefore ultimately mean the same thing.

While the synoptic authors and Paul repeat the words of institution as "This is my body" (Matt 26:26; Mark 14:22; Luke 22:19; 1 Cor 11:24), John always speaks of Jesus' "flesh," and combats gnosticism by adopting its own terminology, even though this gospel's teaching is not different from that of the other evangelists. Proclamation never takes place in a spatial or temporal vacuum; it is always subject to the concrete conditions of the particular sociocultural situation; this is equally true even within the relatively short time span within which the New Testament texts were written.

Johannine eucharistic theology is not contained in a so-called "institution narrative," but is presented in the sixth chapter, as part of the "discourse that promises the bread of heaven," especially in vv. 48–58:

> "I am the bread of life. Your ancestors ate the manna in the wilderness, and they died. This is the bread that comes down from heaven, so that one may eat of it and not die. I am the living bread that came down from heaven. Whoever eats of this bread will live forever; and the bread that I will give for the life of the world is my flesh." The Jews then disputed among themselves, saying, "How can this man give us his flesh to eat?" So Jesus said to them, "Very truly I tell you, unless you eat the flesh of the Son of Man and drink his blood, you have no life in you. Those who eat my flesh and drink my blood have eternal life, and I will raise them up on the last day; for my flesh is true food and my blood is true drink. Those who eat my flesh and drink my blood abide in me, and I in them. Just as the living Father sent me, and I live because of the Father, so whoever eats me will live because of me. This is the bread that came down from heaven, not like that which your ancestors ate, and they died. But the one who eats this bread will live forever."

What is especially important to John, as a theologian, is first of all the real identity of the bread and wine with Jesus' flesh and blood: Under these forms he is really and genuinely present. Hence there is a strikingly frequent use of the verb "to be": "I *am* the bread of life" (6:35, 48, 51); the bread "for the life of the world *is* my flesh" (6:51c), etc. In the Aramaic that we must presume stands behind Jesus' words of institution, there is no equivalent of "to be," so that they would simply say "this—my body," "this—my blood." Of course, the identity of subject and predicate noun is just as clearly expressed in this way, and the wording of the Greek and canonical version of the New Testament is quite correct in inserting the copula "is." But apparently John places a special emphasis on the equation of bread and flesh. Weakening the "is" to "means" or "represents" or "symbolizes" or some other expression is simply impossible: The bread *is* Jesus' flesh, and the wine *is* Jesus' blood.

Beyond this, the character of the Eucharist as *food* is important for John. The very fact that Jesus' discourse on the bread of life is placed immediately after the feeding of the five thousand (John 6:1-15) speaks clearly: "for my flesh is true food and my blood is true drink. Those who eat my flesh and drink my blood abide in me, and I in them" (John 6:55-56). Even in face of the clear opposition of the hearers (John 6:52), Jesus continues to emphasize this eating and drinking, and retracts nothing of the sharpness of his proposal, not even for the disciples (John 6:67-68), whose statement of faith he accepts (John 6:68).

Thus this bread is the bread of believers. There is only one faith in Jesus himself and in this bread: both have "come down from heaven."

The significance of this bread is "for the life of the world" (John 6:51c), so that "whoever eats of this bread will live forever" (John 6:51b). "Life" is a key word in John's gospel. It is the "life of Jesus," his very specific way of being as divine and human, that is given to believers in the Church through the sacraments. "Life" is nearly identical with what we call "grace."

Also important for John is the eschatological significance of the Eucharist: "eternal life" (John 6:51-58) and "being raised up on the last day" (John 6:54). The Eucharist is the food of the community through the whole time of the Church, until the Lord comes again.

2. The Eucharist in Its Basic Form

It is popular today to speak of the Mass as a meal. However, this is often done in an undifferentiated fashion. Holy Mass obviously has something to do with a meal, but it is not simply that. The basic form of the Mass is the Eucharist, that is, the prayer of thanksgiving and praise over the elements of bread and wine, which, of course, are intended for "symbolic," sacramental consumption. A meal to satisfy hunger *can* be connected with it, as it was in the early years of the Church, in the form of the *agape,* and as it sometimes is today in the context of a home Eucharist. But throughout most ages, as we will see, elements of proclamation—a service of the word—were joined with it, and even the administration of other sacraments, as happens today at baptism, confirmation, ordination and marriage, and sometimes when the sick are anointed. In these cases, the particular sacrament, as the dominant event, determines the character of the service of the word, in the readings and prayers; it is thus united with the Eucharist as the source, center, and high point of Christian life. This tradition is ancient and legitimate. As early as the second and third centuries we find baptism coupled with the Eucharist (taking the place of a service of the word): this is attested in Justin and Hippolytus, and in the latter case it is also found in connection with the consecration of a bishop. The ordination of priests likewise occurred almost exclusively within an ordination Mass.

Although Paul speaks of the Eucharist as "the Lord's supper" (1 Cor 11:20), he at the same time distinguishes it very clearly from any other meal, for what the Corinthians are doing in an unloving way at their gatherings (1 Cor 11:21-22) is no longer the Lord's supper; it is "eating the bread and drinking the cup of the Lord in an unworthy manner" and makes them "answerable for the body and blood of the Lord" (1 Cor 11:28). The Mass is not just eating and drinking in community, a meal that Jesus' disciples consume together; it is the continuation of his Eucharist, the very specific giving of thanks over the elements of bread and wine. As we have already seen, at Passover the ritual thanksgiving was also embedded in a full meal, but the meal was not the Passover itself; it became such only through the specific ritual during the meal. When the earliest community continued to celebrate this memorial of Christ in the context of meals, the so-called *agapes,* it was obviously not the *agape* that was the Lord's memorial, no matter how much fellowship and concern for the members of the community present there may have been included; it was the grateful and "consecrating" praise over bread and wine. The earliest history of the Mass shows us clearly how the two elements of meal and sacramental eucharistic rite very quickly separated, because of the many inappropriate things that intruded.

If Christ's last meal was a Passover meal (which is indeed possible, even probable, but by no means certain), it is striking that the interpretive rituals of Passover that were not instituted at that meal were removed from this new "Christian Passover" very quickly. Nothing favors the idea that the earliest communities continued to maintain any Jewish Passover form for their meal, or even that they retained the unique Passover date for an annual celebration of the Lord's memorial. It is uncertain, of course, whether Acts 2:46 refers to eucharistic celebrations, as such, when it reports: "Day by day, as they spent much time together in the temple, they broke bread at home and ate their food with glad and generous hearts." However, the reference to "breaking bread" as a Jewish ritual, even at ordinary meals, is an important indication of the earliest form of the Eucharist.

It is characteristic of every Jewish meal, and especially a cultically shaped occasion such as the eve of the sabbath, that it begins and ends with a thanksgiving *(berakah)*, a blessing over the bread at the beginning and the wine at the end. Of the two blessings, that over the bread is by far the shorter and simpler: "Blessed are you, Lord, our God, ruler of the universe, who brings forth bread from the earth." In contrast, the blessing of the cup at the end of the meal is more extensive and solemn. It begins with dialogic forms intended to draw attention away from the meal and concentrate it in prayer:

> *Presider:* (My friends), let us bless the Lord.
>
> *All:* May the name of the Lord be praised henceforth now and forever.
>
> *Presider:* Blessed be our God, from whose gifts we have eaten and from whose goodness we live.
>
> *All:* Blessed be God and blessed be God's name.

Then follows the grace proper, in four parts: (1) thanksgiving to the creator and sustainer, who (2) provides and preserves the land, (3) the temple, and (4) all that is good.

(1) Blessed are you, O Lord, our God, ruler of the universe, who nourishes the world in kindness, friendship, and compassion. Blessed are you, O God, who nourishes the world.

(2) We thank you, O Lord, our God, because you have made us to inherit a good land (that we may eat of its fruits and be filled with your kindness). Blessed are you, O Lord, our God, for the land, and for our food.

(3) Have mercy, O Lord, our God, on your people Israel and your city of Jerusalem and Zion, the place of your glory, your altar, and your sanctuary. Blessed are you, O God, who builds up Jerusalem.

(4) Blessed are you, O Lord, our God, ruler of the universe. You are good and you give us all good things.

This blessing after meals praises the goodness of God, on the one hand as the Lord and creator of the world, on the other hand as the God of the covenant who proves faithful to the people by giving them the land and dwelling among them: God is both the universal creator and the author of salvation history. The stronger petitionary character of the third section—apparently given this form after the destruction of the temple—does not contradict the schema of thanksgiving: God is the powerful one who even knows how to turn disaster into salvation.

Many later Jewish redactions of the blessing after meals reveal expansions of this schema, but without changing the structure. Such an expansion, for example, is the household head's blessing of the so-called "third cup" at Passover (see above); however, its elements are in complete agreement with the basic schema, because, basically, this third cup ended the meal itself (when the lamb was eaten). What followed were merely a few more fragments of religious tradition (the second part of the *hallel*) and the domestic feast associated with the so-called "fourth cup." We may today regard it as certain that, from the form-critical point of view, the blessing after meals, whether at Passover or other meals with cultic character, was the starting point for the Eucharist of the Christian communities.

We do not know the exact wording of the earliest Christian "blessing over the bread" (before the meal). However, it must have been a very specific expansion of the Jewish model, possibly going back to Jesus himself, for the Emmaus disciples, on the evening of the first Easter day, knew the Lord by the way he "broke the bread" (Luke 24:30-31, 35), that is, not the way he divided and gave it, but his special blessing before the meal. For Jews, "breaking bread" does not refer so much to the manual act of "breaking," as to the words, the prayer of thanksgiving, spoken while the bread is divided. It seems to me to be certain, or at least highly probable, that from the beginning the Christian "breaking of bread" not only praised, over the broken loaf, the one "who brings forth bread from the earth," but contained an unmistakable christological aspect that in some way probably also contained Christ's words of interpretation.

This kind of Christian expansion of the Jewish table blessing over bread and wine is attested by the Didache, the "teaching of the twelve apostles," a writing probably from Syria, stemming from the first half of the second century. It was very popular in ancient times, but then disappeared until it was rediscovered in Constantinople, a century ago, by Patriarch Briennios of Nicomedia. Besides its catechetical elements, the Didache contains directions for the administration of the sacraments, and in chapters 9 and 10 directions for the thanksgiving (= Eucharist?). This writing, at least as far as its origins are concerned, appears very ancient: the table blessing and eucharistic prayer are still not clearly differentiated. However, the christological interpretation of the Jewish models for thanksgiving for God's creation and saving deeds completely dominates this text. Even though its specific use is still disputed today and has not been fully clarified, it is still highly interesting for the early period and should therefore be quoted here:

9. Now about the Eucharist: This is how to give thanks: First in connection with the cup: "We thank you, our Father, for the holy vine of David, your child, which you have revealed through Jesus, your child. To you be glory forever." Then in connection with the piece [broken off the loaf]: "We thank you, our Father, for the life and knowledge which you have revealed through Jesus, your child. To you be glory forever. As this piece [of bread] was scattered over the hills and then was brought together and made one, so let your Church be brought together from the ends of the earth into your Kingdom. For yours is the glory and the power through Jesus Christ forever." You must not let anyone eat or drink of your eucharist except those baptized in the Lord's name. For in reference to this the Lord said: "Do not give what is sacred to dogs" [Matt 7:6].

10. After you have finished your meal, give thanks in this way: "We thank you, holy Father, for your sacred name which you have lodged in our hearts, and for the knowledge and faith and immortality which you have revealed through Jesus, your child. To you be glory forever. Almighty Master, 'you have created everything' [Wis 1:14; Sir 18:1; Rev 4:11; 10:6] for the sake of your name, and have given [human beings] food and drink to enjoy that they may thank you. But to us you have given spiritual food and drink and eternal life through Jesus, your child. Above all, we thank you that you are mighty. To you be glory forever. Remember, Lord, your Church, to save it from all evil and to make it perfect by your love. Make it holy, 'and gather' it 'together from the four winds' into your Kingdom which you have made ready for it. For yours is the power and the glory forever. Let grace come and let this world pass away. Hosanna to the God of David [Matt 21:9]. If anyone is holy, let him or her come. If not, let him or her repent. Maran atha ["Our Lord, come;" cf. 1 Cor 16:22]. Amen." In the case of prophets, however, you should let them give thanks in their own way [or: as long as they wish].

Chapter 14 of the Didache certainly speaks of the Sunday Eucharist. It is true that the text of the prayer of thanksgiving is not included there, but it may be the same as that in chapters 9 and 10. What is emphasized here especially is the fraternal spirit and readiness to forgive that are preconditions for the celebration, but also characteristic of it as fulfillment of the pure, eschatological sacrifice promised by the prophet Malachi (1:11).

14. On every LORD's day, . . . come together and break bread and give thanks, first confessing your sins so that your sacrifice may be pure. Anyone at variance with [his or her] neighbor must not join you, until they are reconciled, lest your sacrifice be defiled. For it was of

this sacrifice that the LORD said: "Always and everywhere shall a pure offering be brought; for I am a great ruler, says the LORD, and my name is reverenced among the nations" (Mal 1:11, 14).[1]

We must suppose that in the very earliest times the eucharistic celebration, with the "blessing" of bread and cup, was still divided by the length of the meal; very soon, however, this was felt not to be an ideal arrangement. Hence the two blessings were put together and formed into a unified, twofold action, and the two parts were placed clearly in parallel, much more strongly than in the two Jewish table prayers. Probably because the blessing of the cup was far longer, more solemn, and had more content, it drew the prayer over the bread to itself; that is, to the end of the meal. This must have happened very quickly, probably in the 40s, because Paul's account in 1 Cor 11:23-25, which must be dated around 55 C.E., describes this new arrangement as something accepted, even though he still expressly mentions, in connection with the blessing of the cup, that it is spoken "after the supper," and thus originally was not immediately connected with the blessing of the bread (cf. also Luke 22:20). As we have already seen, this arrangement of the Eucharist then became the completely normal situation for the three earliest evangelists (in the 70s). It was regarded as the practice of the apostles.

If this close connection of the two thanksgiving prayers and their displacement to the end of the meal was the principal characteristic of the apostolic community celebration, in contrast to Jesus' Last Supper, the next step was the separation of this celebration from the community meal. This is characteristic of the post-apostolic period: The meal context was abandoned, and the Eucharist was connected to a service of the word composed of reading, sermon, and prayer. Thus began a new era in the discovery of the obligatory fundamental shape of our Mass: the service of the word and the Eucharist were tightly combined into a single liturgical celebration.

B. The Liturgy of the Word

1. Reasons for Its Institution

The combination of meal and Eucharist probably led to disagreements from the outset. Because of it, even in the early apostolic period, as we have seen, the Eucharists over bread and cup, originally separated by the whole course of the meal, were brought together at the end of the meal in order better to "discern . . . the [Lord's] body" (1 Cor 11:29). Yet apparently that was not sufficient, because the full meal, with all its possible negative complications, still preceded the Lord's memorial and was an irritation to the "Lord's supper."

Thus Paul complains of the course taken by the celebration in Corinth (1 Cor 11:17-22):

> Now in the following instructions I do not commend you, because when you come together it is not for the better but for the worse. For, to begin with, when you come together as a Church, I hear that there are divisions among you; and to some extent I believe it. Indeed, there have to be factions among you, for only so will it become clear who among you are genuine. When you come together, it is not really to eat the Lord's supper. For when the time comes to eat, each of you goes ahead with your own supper, and one goes hungry and another becomes drunk. What! Do you not have homes to eat and drink in? Or do you show contempt for the Church of God and humiliate those who have nothing? What should I say to you? Should I commend you? In this matter I do not commend you!

The image of this community gathering is rather pathetic. Corinth was a port city and thus scarcely the most moral place on earth. Paul's advice that an incestuous man should be expelled from the congregation (1 Cor 5:1-5) is a clear enough hint. But even here, in the context that concerns us, he condemns loveless behavior, antisocial attitudes, and divisions, as well as greed and excessive drinking. Uneasiness about ethnic discrimination is reflected in an early report of the Jerusalem community: "Now during those days, when the disciples were increasing in number, the Hellenists complained against the Hebrews because their widows were being neglected in the daily distribution" (Acts 6:1). There a special diaconal service was substituted for table service in order to guarantee impartial behavior in the community. In other words, the *agape* meals revealed not only selflessness and love of neighbor, but also a generous portion of self-seeking.

The divisions in Corinth can easily be traced to the ancient custom of eating in groups, table by table. Ordinarily, people ate from the same dish, and often they drank from a single cup. A natural consequence of eating from the same dish was that a table group could not easily consist of more than a dozen persons or so, because otherwise individuals would be placed too far from the dish to be able to reach it with their hands. At that point the group would have to be divided. In the dining rooms of the monks in Egypt (for example, in the monastery of St. Simeon in Aswan), I found a series of tile circles built just above the floor as seating places, each about a meter across; the common dish would have been placed in the middle. The ten or twelve who ate in each group sat on the round tile bench, from which they could reach the dish. Hence the Corinthian congregational meals presumably were taken also by a number of table groups, perhaps five or six in a community of fifty or sixty members.

We need not be surprised if the groups quickly sorted themselves out by social status or by other interests, whatever they might be, and became "institutionalized" by the regularity of the gatherings. In Corinth there were rich business owners (like Aquila and Priscilla, the tentmaking couple with whom Paul worked: Acts 18:2-3), but certainly slaves as well, and other poor people. If the poor and rich sat in separate groups, the difference between their meals surely became quite noticeable in a very short time. And if the "charity soup" was not opulent enough for the rich, they may well have begun to eat at home beforehand, thus leaving themselves more time and occasion for drinking: "one goes hungry and another becomes drunk" (1 Cor 11:21). Unhappiness and divisions within the community were almost inevitable results.

Thus nothing was more natural than to separate the meal completely from the Eucharist. Since, in the Mediterranean, it is the custom even today to eat the main meal in the evening—in Spain, for example, you cannot get a menu in a restaurant before 8 p.m.—the common meal was still taken in the evening, both as provision for the poor and as a celebration of community fellowship. The Eucharist, on the other hand, was transferred to the morning, where the likelihood of sobriety, especially in terms of an absence of intoxicating drink, was much greater: for example, on Pentecost Peter very easily dismissed the suspicion of drunkenness on the part of those filled with the Spirit by saying: "it is only nine o'clock in the morning" (Acts 2:15).

The separation of Eucharist and meal brought important consequences in its wake: first of all in the use of space. While previously the squatting groups of those sharing the meal were scattered throughout the allotted space, one circle around each low table or mat on which the common dish was placed, there now remained only a single table on which the eucharistic gifts were placed. But the "many tables previously" and the "one table thereafter" were very different. While the "many tables" were simple boards or planks laid on the floor, the "one table" was higher, suitable for the presider to stand behind it. As a consequence, the individual meal groups were reshaped into a single, larger group of co-celebrants, standing and facing the "liturgist" in a semi- or three-quarter circle, with the table constituting the spatial and ideal center until—probably in short order—it was moved from the middle of the space and placed against a wall. We may presume that they were standing, rather than reclining or squatting as before, because that posture would even then have been thought appropriate. At the same time, through the elimination of the meal for satisfaction of hunger, the shape of the Eucharist itself would have become more obvious: it consisted of the consumption of the "signs" of bread and wine that, through the prayer of thanksgiving, had been changed into the body and blood of Christ.

However, there must have been a feeling that this reduction had impoverished the celebration: such a symbolic meal consisting of the preparation of the gifts, the thanksgiving, and consumption of the elements would have been relatively brief—too brief and unsatisfactory to the group's feelings of community and religious emotions. Not only the social atmosphere of the meal had been eliminated, but also the open possibilities for preaching, reading, response, explanation, song, etc. We may suppose that at those community meals there had also been reading of letters, communications, and greetings from neighboring communities, and especially from the founders of the community, the apostles and missionaries. For example, the letters of the apostle Paul usually conclude with prayers of praise that sound very much like a transition to a meal or eucharistic celebration. Significantly, the formulae of greeting for the beginning of Mass today are mainly taken from the concluding formulae of the Pauline letters.

Acts 20:7-8 presents this kind of situation in which teaching took place during the community meal: "On the first day of the week, when we met to break bread, Paul was holding a discussion with them; since he intended to leave the next day, he continued speaking until midnight. There were many lamps in the room upstairs where we were meeting. . . ." The text goes on to relate how a young man named Eutychus fell asleep while Paul was preaching and tumbled from the window: surely a comfort to preachers less gifted than Paul!

Thus, in order to reintroduce the fundamental features of a Christian worship service, such as reading, song, preaching, and prayer, Christians enriched the Eucharist by adding a service of the word, for which a ready-made cultic form already existed in the synagogue service. It is true that the Christian communities did not simply imitate that service; they reshaped and gave a new order to the elements of word and prayer that were already familiar from meal contexts like the symposium. John, for example, in describing the Last Supper tells us more about the elements of this kind of "service of the word" than about the "Eucharist." We may also understand the admonition in Eph 5:18-20 to mean that the time of the community gathering should be used rightly, not for dissipation, but for mutual enrichment: "Do not get drunk with wine, for that is debauchery; but be filled with the Spirit, as you sing psalms and hymns and spiritual songs among yourselves, singing and making melody to the Lord in your hearts, giving thanks to God the Father at all times and for everything in the name of our Lord Jesus Christ." These kinds of suggestions are more suited to the service of the word than to the earlier meal.

2. The Synagogal Liturgy as Model

The service of the word in the synagogue originated in some very serious thinking on the part of sensible Jewish men in the diaspora situation in Babylon, after the destruction of the first temple, which meant the loss of the central sanctuary and its sacrifices. We can scarcely exaggerate the culture shock experienced by the people of Israel after the catastrophic fall of Jerusalem. Was God unfaithful to the people of the covenant? Were the pagan gods more powerful than YHWH? It seemed that the culture and civilization of the victors were immensely more impressive than those of the little Palestinian nation of *fellaheen*. The magnificent religious festivals of the new rulers constituted an enduring temptation. Should one not simply acknowledge the situation as it was and follow these new, apparently mightier gods, assimilate oneself and vanish as quickly as possible, through intermarriage, into the foreign people? The intellectual leaders of Judaism at that period, the "scribes," that is, the "intellectuals," quickly perceived the demands of the moment: Israel, lacking its temple, must reconstitute itself around the words of "instruction" (later the "Torah," the five books of Moses, also called "the law") and the "expectation" of salvation promised by the prophets.

The division of the Old Testament writings with which we are familiar, into "Moses and the prophets" (cf. Luke 16:29) or "Moses and Elijah" (Matt 17:3-4; Mark 9:3-4; Luke 9:30, 33) corresponded then, and still corresponds, to synagogal usage. These contain the tradition and the history of salvation looking to its future fulfillment. The history of Judaism—even to the present day—is, apart from the relatively short period when it possessed a central sanctuary, the history of the synagogue. Through the synagogue, Israel survived. Nowadays "synagogue" and "Judaism" are nearly synonymous concepts to us, and rightly so. The word endures, while the temple cult (even according to Jewish belief) is suspended until "the holy city, the new Jerusalem" comes "down from heaven from God, prepared as a bride adorned for her husband" (Rev 21:2). The new liturgy at the coming of the Messiah in glory is the common hope of the old and the new Israel. Christian liturgy, too, is simply a stage on the journey toward it (*SC* §8). It is also worth remembering that the Greek words *synagoge* (= God's assembly of the people of the covenant) and *ek-klesia* (= calling together of a new covenant people from all the nations) mean almost the same thing. They both rest on a common original Hebrew concept. The Church, in this as well, is the heir of the synagogue.

The elements of a synagogue worship service were and are derived from the nature of the service itself and the course of a religious assembly: Greeting and reflection on what is to be done; the first reading from the "commandments of God" (in the books of Moses, called *parash*); song and reflection on what was heard, as the new scroll is brought forward; second reading (from the prophets, in anticipation of the future fulfillment of the promise, called *haftarah*); preaching as a concretization and actualization, in the context of "today," of the word of God given "at that time;" prayer, blessing, and dismissal.

The early Christian community was well acquainted with the synagogue service. Jesus regularly went to the synagogue on the sabbath. "When he came to Nazareth, where he had been brought up, he went to the synagogue on the sabbath day, as was his custom" (Luke 4:16). There he revealed himself as the Messiah promised by Isaiah (Isa 61:1-2). According to this pericope in Luke, Jesus was learned in the scriptures and rose for the second reading, the *haftarah* from the prophets, following it immediately with a sermon. "He stood up to read, and the scroll of the prophet Isaiah was given to him. He unrolled the scroll and found the place where it was written: 'The Spirit of the Lord is upon me, because he has anointed me to bring good news to the poor. He has sent me to proclaim release to the captives and recovery of sight to the blind, to let the oppressed go free, to proclaim the year of the Lord's favor.' And he rolled up the scroll, gave it back to the attendant, and sat down. The eyes of all in the synagogue were fixed on him. Then he began to say to them, 'Today this scripture has been fulfilled in your hearing.' All spoke well of him and were amazed at the gracious words that came from his mouth" (Luke 4:16-22).

Paul's mission (and probably that of other missionaries as well) customarily attached itself to the Jewish synagogue services in the diaspora. It was quite logical to follow the promise in the words of the prophets with a proclamation of the Messiah who had actually come. Paul followed this pattern in Pisidian Antioch (Acts 13:14-41), Iconium (Acts 14:1), Philippi (Acts 16:12), Thessalonica (Acts 17:1), and frequently elsewhere. He was ready and willing to accept the opportunity to preach to his fellow Jews, for it was the custom of the synagogue to invite visitors learned in the scriptures to speak. "Brothers, if you have any word of exhortation for the people, give it" (Acts 13:15). The opportunity to preach was by no means reserved to priests from the tribe of Levi; it was, in principle, open to all those who were capable, if the president of the synagogue, as leader of the assembly, invited them to speak. Paul was not a Levite but a member of the tribe of Benjamin (Rom 11:1; Phil 3:5). Jesus himself was not a "priest" under the Old Testament law, but a "layman" from the house of David and the tribe of Judah (Matt 1:3). The synagogue worship service was essentially the worship of the laity, even though Levites had certain privileges, for example the right to speak the concluding blessing.

At the time of Jesus, the Jewish service of the word had a long tradition, through which it had differentiated certain functions and developed a particular internal arrangement of the assembly room. The president of the synagogue *(archisynagogos)* had an established place on the "seat of Moses" (Matt 23:2), in the midst of the group of presiding elders *(archisynagogoi)*, facing the congregation; the *archisynagogos* named the presider and the preacher, when not assuming those functions in person. Occasionally, the *archisynagogos* was assisted by a master of ceremonies *(hazzan)*. Usually, the presider's chair and the ambo were elevated, as shown by archeological excavations of synagogue buildings. The congregation sat on three sides of the room, in an open three-quarter circle around the lectern and presider. It is uncertain whether there was already a kind of schola for the responsorial or antiphonal singing of the psalms, but it is not unlikely. Also noteworthy is the "hierarchical contrast" between leader and congregation. The very earliest church buildings, such as that in Dura Europos on the middle Euphrates, dating from the middle of the third century C.E., are very similar to the contemporary synagogues. The similar course of the worship services apparently demanded similar worship spaces as well.

3. The Basic Form of the Liturgy of the Word

The earliest Christian liturgies of the word were similar to those of the Jewish communities. The first accounts, such as those of Justin Martyr (around the middle of the second century: see below) report that there were two readings, a sermon, and a prayer concluding the service of the word. It is true that Justin says nothing explicitly about singing, but here, unexpectedly, a pagan witness comes to our aid. Pliny the younger, the governor of Bithynia in Asia Minor, in a letter to his friend, the emperor Trajan (*Ep.* 10.96, ca. 111–113 C.E.), writes that he sent someone to observe the Christian assembly. The observer reported that the Christians were accustomed to gather on a particular day before dawn *(stato die ante lucem)* and to sing, antiphonally, a hymn to Christ as their God; they also obligated themselves not to commit any crime. Then they separated and re-assembled at a later hour for an ordinary meal. This account from the period shortly after the year 100 also attests to the shift of the worship service to morning, and the related postponing of the full meal to a later time.

Both Jewish and Christian liturgies of the word reveal, even in their structure, the dialogical form of all liturgy. God initiates salvation and addresses humankind; God's word touches human beings and calls them to faith; in their listening, in silence, or in sung reflection on God's mighty deeds, the word thus heard can create a space for itself in the hearers; a vivid, actualizing proclamation by the preacher makes access to the word easier; only then can a human being turn back to God in faith, acknowledgment, and common prayer. This downward and upward movement of the word is tellingly illustrated by Isaiah in a beautiful parable (Isa 55:8-11):

> . . . my thoughts are not your thoughts, nor are your ways my ways, says the LORD. For as the heavens are higher than the earth, so are my ways higher than your ways and my thoughts than your thoughts. For as the rain and the snow come down from heaven, and do not return there until they have watered the earth, making it bring forth and sprout, giving seed to the sower and bread to the eater, so shall my word be that goes out from my mouth; it shall not return to me empty, but it shall accomplish that which I purpose, and succeed in the thing for which I sent it.

C. The Unity of the Liturgy of the Word and Eucharist

Probably as early as the first century, in the post-apostolic period, the basic form of the Mass that still endures today had already been shaped. This would not have happened simultaneously in every place and in the same way. However, in spite of the variety of liturgical customs we can recognize in the Church from the very beginning a tendency to approximate the essential rituals and forms of organization in the different communities to each other. Paul's account of the last supper (in 1 Cor 11) witnesses to this, as do the accounts in the gospels. Paul is interested in achieving an alignment in ritual, and the evangelists apparently desire to regulate the community celebrations and bring them into line with one another by applying the words of Christ, for not just anything is supposed to happen at the Lord's supper; instead, an explicit command is to be obeyed. The retrospective alignment of the actions in worship with their origins, although it should not be puristic and unhistorical, remains an enduring task of liturgy.

For the relative similarity of the celebration of the Mass in East and West we have testimony at the end of Justin's First Apology. Justin came from Flavia Neapolis (formerly Sichem) in Palestine and reached Rome by way of Ephesus in the reign of the emperor Antoninus Pius, after 138 C.E. There he was a teacher of philosophy. He was beheaded, with six companions, in about 165: hence he is usually called Justin Martyr. As a well-traveled man, he was acquainted with the liturgical customs of many congregations, which is why his account is so important. Justin describes the celebration of Mass twice in chapters 65–67 of his First Apology: first, in chapter 65, in connection with baptism, when the celebration of the sacrament replaced the liturgy of the word; in chapter 66 he makes some dogmatic statements about the nature of the Eucharist and then, in chapter 67, he gives a swift overview of the Sunday worship service.

Chapter 65:

> After we have thus baptized [the one] who has believed and has given his assent, we take him to those who are called brethren where they are assembled, to make common prayers earnestly for ourselves and for [the one] who has been enlightened and for all others everywhere, that, having learned the truth, we may be deemed worthy to be found good citizens also in our actions and guardians of the commandments, so that we may be saved with eternal salvation.
>
> When we have ended the prayers, we greet one another with a kiss. Then bread and a cup of water and [a cup] of mixed wine are brought to the one who presides over the brethren, and [the presider] takes them and sends up praise and glory to the Father of all in the name of the Son and of the Holy Spirit, and gives thanks at some length that we have been deemed worthy of these things from him. When he has finished the prayers and the thanksgiving *(eucharistia)*, all the people give their assent by saying "Amen." "Amen" is the Hebrew for "So be it." And when the president has given thanks and all the people have assented, those whom we call deacons give to each of those present a portion of the bread and wine and water over which thanks have been given, and take them to those who are not present.

Chapter 66:

> And we call this food "thanksgiving"; and no one may partake of it unless he is convinced of the truth of our teaching, and has been

cleansed with the washing for the forgiveness of sins and regeneration, and lives as Christ handed down.

For we do not receive these things as common bread or common drink; but just as our Savior Jesus Christ, being incarnate through the word of God, took flesh and blood for our salvation, so too we have been taught that the food over which thanks have been given by a word of prayer which is from him, [the food] from which our flesh and blood are fed by transformation, is both the flesh and blood of that incarnate Jesus.

For the apostles, in the records composed by them which are called gospels, have handed down thus what was commanded of them: that Jesus took bread, gave thanks, and said, "Do this for the remembrance of me; this is my body"; and likewise he took the cup, gave thanks, and said "This is my blood"; and gave to them alone. . . .

Chapter 67:

. . . And on the day called Sunday an assembly is held in one place of all who live in town or country, and the records of the apostles or the writings of the prophets are read as time allows. Then, when the reader has finished, the president in a discourse admonishes and exhorts [us] to imitate these good things. Then we all stand up together and send up prayers; and as we said before, when we have finished praying, bread and wine and water are brought up, and the president likewise sends up prayers and thanksgivings to the best of his ability, and the people assent, saying the Amen; and the [elements over which] thanks have been given are distributed, and everyone partakes; and they are sent through the deacons to those who are not present. And the wealthy who so desire give what they wish, as each chooses; and what is collected is deposited with the president. He helps orphans and widows, and those who through sickness or any other cause are in need, and those in prison, and strangers sojourning among us; in a word, he takes care of all those who are in need.

And we all assemble together on Sunday, because it is the first day, on which God transformed darkness and matter, and made the world; and Jesus Christ our Savior rose from the dead on that day; for they crucified him the day before Saturday; and the day after Saturday, which is Sunday, he appeared to his apostles and disciples, and taught them these things which we have presented to you also for your consideration.[2]

This account is extraordinarily informative for us. It appears that by 150 C.E. at the latest the basic outline of the Mass was already the same as it is today. According to chapter 67, the framework elements of the Sunday service of the word were at least two readings presented by a lector, the presider's sermon, and the common prayer of the faithful. This common prayer was also present when baptism was administered in place of a specific service of the word (chapter 65); in that case, the mystagogical rites apparently replaced the readings. The eucharistic celebration, described twice in almost the same words in chapters 65 and 67, follows the rhythm of three in the actions of Jesus (chapter 66): taking, blessing, and interpretive words over bread and wine, presentation (that is, the bringing of the gifts), eucharistic prayer, distribution of the gifts. The true presence of the Lord in the bread and wine is affirmed. However, the common meal, the context within which the Eucharist was celebrated even in apostolic times, has faded away. The feeding of the poor from the gifts given by the wealthy during the Mass can take place at any time; in accordance with Mediterranean usage, it was probably in the evening.

Special emphasis is placed on the participation of the community. Although the presider, as the most active member, is in the foreground, the acclamatory "amen" is mentioned twice, both times with emphasis.

Sunday is deeply anchored in the community's life as the day for common assembly, as we already have seen from apostolic times. The Lord arose on the first day of the week (Matt 28:1; Mark 16:2; Luke 24:1; John 20:1), appeared on that day to the apostles in the upper room (John 20:19-23; Luke 24:36) and to the disciples at Emmaus (Luke 24:31). The assembly of the community on the first day of the week is explicitly attested in Troas (Acts 20:7) and also in Corinth (1 Cor 16:2: collection of money at the worship service on behalf of the Jerusalem community, much as in Galatia). In the Revelation of John (Rev 1:10) Sunday is already called "the Lord's day," as it is in the Didache (14:1) and in the letter from Ignatius of Antioch to the community of Magnesia in Asia Minor (Ign. *Magn.* 9:1).

To summarize: The point of origin for the Mass is Jesus' farewell meal with his disciples (probably a Passover meal), with his institutional words of interpretation over the elements of bread and wine that, as his "body given" and "blood shed," represent (that is: make present) his death and atoning sacrifice. The disciples are to celebrate Jesus' memorial, following his example, by giving praise and thanks *(berakah, eucharistia)* over bread and wine, in a manner comparable to the practice in Jewish table blessings and over the "third Passover cup." Still in apostolic times, the eucharistic actions, which had been separated by the length of the meal, were brought together, made parallel, and formed into a unified ritual at the end of the meal. In post-apostolic times, after the full meal, because of difficulties connected with it, had fallen away, the Eucharist was combined with a service of the word, the latter structured according to the synagogue model. This development was already in progress in the first century, and appears fully complete by the middle of the second century (ca. 150) in the testimony of Justin Martyr. This basic form remained obligatory for all subsequent orders of the Mass throughout the history of the Church, even till now.

Notes

[1]English translation adapted from Cyril C. Richardson, editor and translator, *Early Christian Fathers* (Philadelphia: Westminster, 1953).

[2]English translation from R.C.D. Jasper and G. J. Cuming, *Prayers of the Eucharist: Early and Reformed.* 3rd rev. ed. (New York: Pueblo, 1987; Collegeville: The Liturgical Press, 1990).

Chapter Two

The Continuing Identity of the Mass
Through Many Changes

A. Creative Beginnings

Even in considering the basic form of the Mass we have seen that Christ's command to celebrate his memorial under the forms of food and drink and in combination with the prayers said at meals was followed by apostolic and post-apostolic communities with fidelity, but not in slavish obedience. The concrete needs of the time made it necessary for the communities to find forms that were appropriate to the changing circumstances. As with most beginnings, that of the Mass was highly creative until a form was discovered that best fit changing needs, and yet could be altered to meet new demands in the course of history as long as the fundamental structure remained intact. A variety of elements from the sociocultural environment were tried again and again, and when appropriate, they were forged into the order of celebration of the Mass.

In the following chapter we will first briefly list the driving and formative forces in the history of the Mass. It is by no means my intention to offer a complete history of the liturgy. The historical facts, or a deliberate selection of them, will be mentioned only when they are, or could be, still useful for an explanation of the present liturgy or its celebration. However, if their importance was only fleeting and not enduring or if they have already been eliminated at an earlier time, they will not be mentioned here. Often, the real contemporary meaning of the forms and patterns of a particular age was later forgotten, and yet those forms have been retained and handed on until today; in such cases historical explanation can be helpful to us in grasping their real meaning and better understanding them, or possibly in restoring them. For that reason, they seem well worth explaining.

1. The Jewish and Hellenistic Dowry

Christ and the apostles, and the first communities as well, lived in the Jewish world of ideas and liturgical customs. For that very reason we may suppose that the first "enfleshment" of the Christian liturgy arose from the Jewish milieu. Research, particularly in the last half century, has made it clear that Judaism—especially in its "intertestamental" form, that is, in the period when the last books of the Old Testament and the first of the New Testament were being written—is the root and ground of Christian worship, much more so than Hellenism and its mystery religions, as was so often supposed in the last century.

Particularly Jewish in character, as we have already explained at length, is the idea of a real memorial that is fundamental to the Mass: God, as the true covenant God of the community, is graciously and "sacramentally" present when the memorial of God's saving deeds is celebrated. To that extent the Mass is always the "new Passover," whether Christ's last meal was really a Passover or not, whether its paschal character was really a historical fact or merely the theological interpretation of the synoptic evangelists, especially Luke. In any case, the Eucharist draws its life from the enduring *now*-ness of God's saving deeds. In addition, the eucharistic prayer, as the heart of the eucharistic worship service, takes its origin from the praises or blessings *(eucharistia, berakot)* in domestic Jewish worship. Apart from the wording of such prayers of praise and blessing, the *matter* of the eucharistic celebration is anticipated in Jewish worship in the food of the Passover. As bread was the epitome of human food, wine represents "what gives cheer to mortals" (Judg 9:13), "gladdens the human heart" (Ps 104:15), and characterized Jewish festive meals, in contrast to the water that was drunk at the normal, ordinary supper of Palestinian farmers. While in the Passover narrative spoken by the head of the household over the *matzoh*, the "bread of tears," the bitterness of Egypt took the foreground, it gave way to the telling of God's mighty deeds over the cup, culminating in the taking possession of the land under Joshua.

Even in Isaac's blessing of the firstborn, given to Jacob, the harvest of "grain and wine" (Gen 27:28) is the epitome of possession of the land. We should recall also the cultic value of the bread in the grain offering of the *minha* (cf. Lev 2:1-16, and frequently), the wine in the drink offering (Exod

29:38-41; Num 15:2-15; Lev 23:13), and both these gifts together in the sacrifice of Melchizedek (Gen 14:18). Similarly, as we have seen, the Christian
liturgy of the word is largely derived from that of the synagogue: the forms
of the community prayer and psalm singing, ritual proclamation and
preaching are all modeled there. The relationship between the synagogue's
"eighteen benedictions," a petition in eighteen strophes *(shemoneh ezreh)* at
the end of the synagogue worship service and the petitions of the Christian
congregation (see Justin) is unmistakable, at least in their basic features.

Moreover, the symbols of the other sacraments were also present in
the milieu of Jesus and the apostles, especially baths (for baptism), anointing, imposition of hands (as a ritual of blessing and reconciliation, but also
as a sign of induction into office for rabbis and official teachers in Israel).
In addition, the furnishings that later became customary in Christian
worship spaces, such as the presider's chair and the benches for the priestly
collegium, were familiar to Judaism. The early Christian group of Syrian-
Aramaic basilicas (4th–7th c.) stems from the structure of the synagogues
in the hinterland of Antioch on the Orontes, with the elevated *bema* or
reader's podium in the center of the nave and the concealment of the altar
behind curtains (following the model of the curtain before the shrine
holding the scrolls of the Torah).

Also Jewish is the seven-day week, even though very quickly the first
day of the week, as the day of Christ's resurrection, replaced the sabbath in
importance. Nevertheless, the principle of division of time remained. Easter
was for a long time celebrated on the same day as the Jewish Passover;
longer in the east (among the so-called *Quartodecimans,* who at first retained the Jewish 14th of Nisan) than in the west, where the date of Easter
was deliberately tied to a Sunday, thus documenting the new interpretation
of the Passover. Pentecost was also native to Judaism, as the "Feast of
Weeks" (= seven weeks: Deut 16:9) and as the "fiftieth day" ("Pentecost" =
50; cf. Tob 2:1; 2 Macc 12:32), and had a fixed relationship to the Passover
festival (Lev 23:15-16).

Another Jewish heritage was obligatory prayer: morning, evening,
and at the third, sixth, and ninth hour, surviving even today in lauds and
vespers, terce, sext, and none in the liturgy of the hours. Many prayer formulae are Jewish in origin, including invitations to prayer ("Let us pray,"
"Let us thank the Lord, our God") and conclusions to prayers (with the
so-called "eternity formulae"), as well as acclamations and shouts ("Amen" =
so it is, so let it be; *Hosanna* = help!; *Alleluia* = sing praise of YHWH), and
the response "and with your spirit." Finally, the style of the official priestly
prayers ("paradigm schema"), in which God is addressed, God's previous

saving deeds are named, and trust is expressed in the fulfillment of the petition now raised through Christ, our Lord—this, too, is derived from Jewish models.

The cult of the martyrs that was later to achieve such importance in the Church, especially in connection with the Mass and the altar, was already known in Judaism. The Pharisees decorated the graves of the prophets and righteous who had been killed for the sake of the truth (Matt 23:29-30; Luke 11:48). Whereas, under Roman law, graves were generally regarded as inviolable, the Jews had the custom of placing the dead first in a cave to decay, and then sealing the remains in small sarcophagi (ossuaries or *osteothekae*). The most recent archeological excavations around Jerusalem have revealed a great many of these "reliquaries." In connection with Jesus' burial it is said that he was placed in a "new" tomb "where no one had ever been laid" (Matt 27:60; Luke 23:53; John 19:41). Tombs could be used more than once.

The collecting and preservation of the relics of the martyrs for future veneration is encountered first in the account of the martyrdom of Polycarp of Smyrna (d. 156): "[After his body was burned] we later took up his bones, more precious than costly stones and more valuable than gold, and laid them away in a suitable place. There the Lord will permit us, so far as possible, to gather together in joy and gladness to celebrate the day of his martyrdom as a birthday, . . ."

Some of the early Jewish forms were later enriched with Hellenistic elements and sometimes reformulated as well. The Easter celebration almost totally eliminated the Jewish custom and its motifs, replacing them with a stronger emphasis on light symbolism, especially the breaking of dawn at the rising of the sun, which was probably suggested by the night-long celebration ending in the morning: Christ is celebrated as the light of the world (cf. Matt 4:16; Luke 2:32; John 1:5, 9; 8:12, and frequently). This rich symbolism had its effect on baptism: its administration at sunrise (especially in the Easter celebration) suggested the practice of speaking the rejection of the devil toward the west, and the acceptance of Christ to the east, where the sun was rising. The same sacrament also followed the model of secular bathing by adding a subsequent anointing, especially in the rituals transitional to confirmation—so much so that the anointing came to dominate the original confirmation gesture of imposition of hands (Acts 8:17). The acclamations already present in the Jewish prayer after meals were reshaped by use of the typically Hellenistic "*axios* acclamations" (*axios* = worthy, right) and constitute a dialogue before the eucharistic prayers or prefaces, even today.

Purely Hellenistic in origin, on the other hand, is the "arcane discipline" that was for a time dominant in antiquity, an obligation to secrecy like that practiced especially in the mystery religions. Especially in its language, the liturgy within the Roman empire shed the garb of Judaism (with the exception of a few acclamations: see above) and donned a Hellenistic robe, the essential lines of which are still apparent today in spite of all the changes in language: Eucharist and liturgy, hymn and anamnesis, mystery and epiclesis, epiphany and Pentecost, and so on.

2. Freedom and Order in the Formularies

When the Didache (10:6) permits the prophets to give thanks "in their own way," and Justin (First Apology 67.5) reports that the presider speaks the eucharistic prayer "to the best of his ability," the two remarks constitute something like a fundamental rule: In the early period, the presider had freedom to formulate the liturgical texts. It was part of the charism of the office of bishop or presbyter to be able to formulate and lead the community's prayer. In fact, the Latin word *orare* means both speaking and praying; the *oratio* was a "spoken prayer." In the early period the Pauline admonition, "do not quench the Spirit" (1 Thess 5:19) was the rule. We may suppose that there was a great variety of formulae in the beginning. Certainly there must very soon have been written texts, or those that had been received and learned by heart, but there were no prescribed and obligatory formulae.

This freedom was not license. Paul says explicitly, in 1 Cor 11:23, what he had "received from the Lord," what he "handed on" to the community, and apparently does not wish to see changed. We have already spoken of the normative intention of the synoptic accounts of the last supper. What is primarily important is the fidelity of the liturgical texts to the tradition of the common confession of faith: the "dogmatic correctness" of the texts, as later demanded, in the 5th century, by Pope Celestine I (422–432; *Indiculus* 8), according to the axiom of agreement between the *lex credendi* and the *lex supplicandi*. The desire for the unity of all who confess the name of Jesus combined from the beginning with traditional usage to form an important unitive force affecting liturgical custom. Thus, for example, Justin came from Palestine, was acquainted with practices in Asia Minor, and lived in Rome when he described the order of celebrating Mass; apparently it was quite similar everywhere. When Polycarp of Smyrna traveled to Pope Anicetus in Rome in 154, he accepted the invitation to preside at the Eucharist. The ritual from Asia Minor was thus scarcely different from that at Rome, at least not in the very similar basic structure of the liturgy of the word and the Eucharist.

This unity was highly useful in other ways: for example, the liturgy in the towns and principal cities of the individual Roman provinces (or later dioceses) of the empire stood as a model for that of the hinterlands. The principle of collegiality of bishops and their presbyters had a further leveling and smoothing effect. The bishops of the large cities maintained constant contact with one another. The later patriarchal constitution (see below) began to develop very early and found its model in Roman civil organization, which respected traditional historical districts and land divisions and their special traditions.

From the early third century, ca. 225, comes a valuable witness to the liturgy of the era of the martyrs, the *Apostolic Tradition,* which is especially interesting for this problem of freedom and obligation in the liturgy. This liturgical book comes from the Roman presbyter Hippolytus, who was very conservative in his views and little impressed by the apparently "more progressive" circles surrounding the later Pope Callistus (217–222), a freedman. Hippolytus was schismatic for a time, but was reconciled with the Roman Church in his martyrdom, and was later venerated as a saint. A productive and learned author, he wrote, among other things, a church order that he very deliberately entitled *Apostolic Tradition.* In it, he desired to stabilize the rites developed to date (not, of course, the rites of the "apostolic" period, as he pretended and surely believed they were). However, he attests the same liturgical usage we have already seen reported, for example, by Justin, some 60 to 70 years earlier. While Justin, in his "Apology" (see above), offers only a description of the rite, Hippolytus produces liturgical texts intended to serve as models: they did, in fact, come to serve that purpose, especially for baptism and the consecration of bishops. What is most interesting in this work is the canon, which quite recently (with variations) has been incorporated into the Roman Missal as Eucharistic Prayer 2. We present here the original text:

Bishop:	The Lord be with you.
All:	And with your spirit.
Bishop:	Up with your hearts.
All:	We have [them] with the Lord.
Bishop:	Let us give thanks to the Lord.
All:	It is fitting and right.
Bishop:	We render thanks to you, O God, through your beloved child Jesus Christ,

whom in the last times you sent to us as a savior and redeemer and angel of your will;

who is your inseparable Word, through whom you made all things, and in whom you were well pleased;

whom you sent from heaven into a virgin's womb;

and who, being conceived in the womb, was made flesh and was manifested as your Son, being born of the Holy Spirit and the Virgin;

who, fulfilling your will and gaining for you a holy people,

stretched out his hands when he should suffer, that he might release from suffering those who have believed in you;

who, when he was betrayed to voluntary suffering that he might destroy death, and break the bonds of the devil, and tread down hell, and shine upon the right-eous, and fix a term, and manifest the resurrection,

took bread and gave thanks to you, saying, "Take, eat; this is my body, which shall be broken for you;"

who also [took] the cup, saying, "This is my blood, which is shed for you; when you do this, you make my remembrance."

Remembering therefore his death and resurrection, we offer to you the bread and the cup, giving you thanks because you have held us worthy to stand before you and minister to you.

And we ask that you would send your Holy Spirit upon the offering of your holy Church; that, gathering her into one, you would grant to all who receive the holy things [to receive] for the fullness of the Holy Spirit for the strengthening of faith in truth; that we may praise and glorify you through your child Jesus Christ; through whom be glory and honor to you, to the Father and the Son, with the Holy Spirit, in your holy Church, both now and to the ages of ages.

All: Amen.[1]

This text is extremely important, inasmuch as it conveys the earliest of all eucharistic prayers, and testifies to the continuity of such prayers over almost two millennia. The starting point in Jewish table prayers (see above) is still clearly evident: The introductory dialogue, the praise of God for creation ("through your beloved child Jesus Christ . . . who is your inseparable Word, through whom you made all things") and for leading humanity to salvation, although here it is no longer the old covenant but God's action in Christ that is narrated and praised, specifically the incarnation, "gaining a holy people," redemptive suffering, death, resurrection, and the instructions at the last supper. The celebration of this memorial is, for Hippolytus, unmistakably the place of the Church's sacrifice, accomplished in the Holy Spirit (through the so-called *epiclesis*), who also brings about the saving effect of the communion. The conclusion (doxology) is almost the same as that used today, except that praise is given to the Father *and* the Son, rather than the Father *through* the Son. Characteristic of the style of this eucharistic prayer is the continuous flow of the language of the prayer, with relative clauses repeatedly taking up the initial address to God. In the translation, this style has been deliberately retained, although the clauses seem somewhat awkward compared to our customary usage. (In our new translations of the eucharistic and presidential prayers in the missal, the relative clauses have usually been rephrased as independent clauses beginning with a "you" form of address: "God, you have . . ."). In Hippolytus's text the character of praise appears clearly in the foreground. The Father himself is active, through his Son, in the Holy Spirit; it is the Father who effects salvation and therefore is deserving of praise.

For Hippolytus, such a form of eucharistic prayer is traditional, "apostolic," and therefore "canonical," and consequently worthy of imitation. We may suppose that other of God's saving deeds were also named; the text as a whole gives the impression of being a taut summary. According to B. Botte, O.S.B., the expression "stand before you and minister to you" is related to the concrete occasion of the consecration of a bishop that is being described here. It is also noteworthy that Hippolytus clearly says, at the end of his model text, that it is "not at all necessary" for the celebrant "to utter the same words that we said above, as though reciting them from memory," but later redactors erased the "not at all," with the result that it then appeared to be "necessary" to hold to the formulary as given.

Although its author was head of a schismatic Roman congregation, this text was felt to be entirely orthodox. It spread quickly throughout the whole Church; we have not only Latin but Egyptian (Sahidic, Bohairic, Arabic, Old Ethiopic) translations, so that the text was long transmitted as the "Egyptian Church Order," until in the present century its Roman origins were once again recognized (by Schwartz, Connolly, and Elfers). Hippolytus's "model" was also the basis for the (apparently) Antiochene liturgy in the so-called *Apostolic Constitutions* of the late fourth century. Evidently even then such a model text answered a widespread need. The time of the charismatics was coming to an end.

3. Turning to the East in Prayer

Orientation at prayer, that is, turning the body to face the east, appears of little importance to us today, but it acquired an essential influence on the early Church's liturgy, affecting particularly the orientation of church buildings from the third century onward, and later the place where the liturgist stood during the celebration of the Mass. Until very recent times, it seemed almost inescapable that our churches should face east (in other words, that the choir should be placed, or separately located, on the narrow part of the eastern side). Only important circumstances of city construction or the peculiarities of the site allowed deviation from this principle. For people in antiquity, it seemed highly important, even in daily life, that the course (from Cardo and Decumanus) of the principal streets of the city should be oriented to the axes of the four primary compass points: in this way, the order of the universe was reflected in the plan of the city; only then was everything "in order." Sacred edifices were still more bound by the necessities of such an orientation.

It is obvious enough that a person praying inside a temple turns toward the image of the god and the sanctuary, just as, when speaking with someone else, one turns one's body and face toward the other person. "Turning the face" and "lifting the hands to the holy place" is a frequent formula even in the Old Testament (cf. Ps 134:2, and frequently elsewhere). God, in turn, sends help "from the sanctuary" (Ps 20:2). Consequently, a believer, even when far distant from the sanctuary or dwelling in bitter exile or in the diaspora, turns toward the holy place not only with the heart's longing, but bodily as well. For example, when we were prisoners of war we knew very precisely the direction in which home lay.

We find the first record and explanation of this custom in Judaism in the post-exilic redaction of 1 Kgs 8:44-45, in Solomon's prayer at the dedication of the temple: "If your people go out to battle against their enemy, by whatever way you shall send them, and they pray to the Lord toward the city that you have chosen and the house that I have built for your name, then hear in heaven their prayer and their plea, and maintain their cause." Similarly (1 Kgs 8:48-49): "If they repent with all their heart and soul in the land of their enemies, who took them captive, and pray to you toward their land, which you gave to their ancestors, the city that you have chosen, and the house that I have built for your name; then hear in heaven your dwelling place their prayer and their plea, maintain their cause . . . ."

In fact, the ancient synagogues that have been excavated have a central orientation toward Jerusalem: in Dura Europos on the Euphrates toward the west, in Ostia near Rome or on the island of Delos toward the southeast, in Galilee toward the south, in Gaza toward the northeast, and so on. It is a question here of what is called a "central orientation," not a real "eastward-facing," which is actually the meaning of the word. We still use the expression "to orient oneself" in this sense, to mean "to get one's bearings," in order to "make a stand" or "get situated," sometimes meaning "to relate to some fact," "to inform oneself."

Originally, the doors or windows of the Jewish houses of prayer were oriented to Jerusalem, and were opened during prayer, so that nothing should obstruct the free flow of prayer toward the sanctuary. We find a reflection of this custom in Dan. 6:10[11]: "Although Daniel knew that the document had been signed, he continued to go to his house, which had windows in its upper room open toward Jerusalem, and to get down on his knees three times a day to pray to his God and praise him, just as he had done previously."

Later, from the second or third century C.E., it became customary to place on the wall of the synagogue facing Jerusalem a special holy shrine containing the Torah case (aron haqodesh) behind an obligatory curtain (parochet) with the seven-branched candelabra (menorah), and so on—features of the temple that were taken over by the synagogue. In this Torah sanctuary, where God dwelt in the divine word with God's people, one could feel oneself oriented toward the final end and the coming of the Messiah. Mishna and Talmud (b. Yebamoth 105b; b. Berakhot 4, 5, and frequently) presume this cultic orientation as a matter of course. Even today, a faithful Jew prays the daily prayers facing toward the temple, which, although it has been destroyed for a time, will be rebuilt in the days of the Messiah or (really or symbolically) will descend from heaven in those days. In this, we Christians are companions of the Jews in hope. For the messianic age, John also saw "the holy city Jerusalem coming down out of heaven from God, filled with the glory of God. It has the glory of God and a radiance like a very rare jewel, like jasper, clear as crystal" (Rev 21:10-11).

After the middle of the second century, at the latest since 200 C.E., when the last major Jewish revolts were crushed and Judaism had to bury its hopes for the central sanctuary, at least for a time, stance in prayer acquired an eminently messianic sense, but now for Christians and Jews that meaning differed to the point of becoming a point of confessional distinction: While a Jew naturally expected the *coming* Messiah in Jerusalem, Christians looked for the *returning* Lord in the east (Matt 24:27: as the lightning comes from the east and flashes as far as the west, "so will be the coming of the Son of Man;" cf. Rev 7:2). Hence, for Christians, prayer toward the east was always an eschatological confession of Jesus' divinity. If he or she, as a Jew, prayed in the direction of the old temple, it was a denial of Christ's divinity, as if Christ had not been the promised Messiah; but if a Christian prayed toward the east, she or he was expecting Christ as the Son of God, "who comes in glory."

Therefore it was a favorite practice for the sanctuary and, later, the apse of the churches to contain a cross in the east, painted or mosaic, as a precursor and "sign of the Son of Man" (Matt 24:30), who will come "on the clouds of heaven" to judge the world and perfect the reign of God. The one who prays toward the east, then, is praying in orthodox faith through Christ in the Holy Spirit to the Father. Not only the prayer, but even the individual's bodily attitude was thus a confession of faith. Nothing was more natural than that from the beginning the body of the church building should be conceived in such a way that it was easy, and even suggested by the spatial arrangements, to pray toward the east. The very oldest church space we know, in Dura Europos on the central Euphrates (from the mid-third century), is an east-facing room within a house. This cannot be accidental, because there were other available rooms with a different orientation. Most of the churches of the eastern parts of the empire had the apse on the east side from the start; Roman churches (Lateran, St. Peter in the Vatican, St. Paul on the road to Ostia, etc.) at first had western apses, but from 420 C.E. onward they also ordinarily placed the sanctuary on the east. In principle, however, the fundamental rule of an east-west orientation of the basilica was the same everywhere.

This principle of orientation had far-reaching consequences for the later periods. While there was not much application during the service of the word, up to the prayer of the day and the petitions, it was always important for the official eucharistic prayers. Thus very early the celebrant and people's facing each other in prayer changed so that they faced and prayed in the same direction, toward the east. In the long run that was important for the position of the liturgist at the altar: from now on this meant that he turned his back toward the people. Further, it caused the bishop's chair to be shifted from the vertex of the apse to one side of the sanctuary, and led to the movement of the altar from the center of the sanctuary to the back, where in time it became a kind of console on the wall. This eastward orientation has affected the axial placement and direction of our churches even in the present.

It is true that in the Middle Ages and in modern times the rule of orientation had long disappeared from Christian consciousness, but still people obeyed it, in the building of churches and placement of altars, faithful to tradition, but often without knowing why. Today, almost everywhere, people have drawn the conclusion that follows from a changed state of knowledge and replaced the altar in the center, between priest and people. Thus the "ideological" law of orientation, which certainly deformed and estranged the natural and original inclination of celebrant and people to one another, has been given up in favor of the older and, functionally speaking, undoubtedly more correct placement of priest and people facing. Still, even in the past the change in the position of the liturgist at the altar was never pursued with absolute consistency: For example, the so-called "papal altars" in the Roman basilicas retained, along with the papal Mass, traces of an older stage of tradition.

B. The Universal Church[2]

It was not just with the "Constantinian revolution," the official recognition of the Church by the state, which made it no longer dangerous, but even advantageous, to be a Christian, but throughout the whole of the third century that the Church moved from being "communities of sisters and brothers" to forming a broad "popular church" or "national church."

It is idle at present either to praise or lament this historical fact. If the Church was to remain faithful to the Lord's command: "Go therefore and make disciples of all nations, baptizing them in the name of the Father and of the Son and of the Holy Spirit, and teaching them to obey everything that I have commanded you" (Matt 28:19-20), it had to become a missionary Church, to grow in breadth, and necessarily to become all-inclusive. That was a logical consequence. Otherwise, it would have been necessary to accept without argument the idea that God's will to save human beings was not really universal, but aimed at a tiny church of the "elect" and "pure" (Greek *katharoi*, from which comes the German word for heretic, "Ketzer"). But that is not the Church's tradition. Certainly, a universal church presents itself differently from a tiny, persecuted community of believers. Just as, for example, a tree grows by adding ring after ring around its trunk, from the core to the outermost, thick cork under the bark, scarcely touched by the sap, so also a universal church had to transform the catechumenate, once sharply concentrated on the single moment of baptism for adults, into a lifelong process for those who were already baptized as children, if it was not to be corrupted by a "Christianity without a choice." Even today, the community around the altar is called, in all humility, to be the yeast that leavens the whole dough of the universal church (cf. Matt 13:33).

1. The Problem of Language

If we prescind, for the moment, from the very first Jewish Christian communities in Jerusalem and Judea, the language of earliest Christianity was Greek throughout. Diaspora Judaism also used Greek as its ordinary language. Accordingly, the Christians used a Greek translation of the Bible (the so-called Septuagint). The redaction of the New Testament writings took place, during the first century, in a form of Greek called *koiné*. Even the Christian groups in Rome spoke Greek, as did the middle and lower classes there generally. Only the African provinces continued to cling more tenuously to the use of Latin: the literature of African authors, such as Tertullian and Cyprian in the third century, was in Latin. However, in general the language barriers to internal Church communications were minimal: in fact, they were practically nonexistent.

Especially from the late third century onward we can observe in the Roman empire a process of disintegration, undoubtedly reinforced by a series of major political and military crises. The well-known "provincial reactions," centrifugal forces within the more or less unified imperial culture, altered the cultural landscape in fundamental ways: movements that were always active just beneath the surface, even though they were despised as barbaric, suddenly took on a new vitality. Often, as among the Egyptian *fellaheen* or in the Syrian hinterland beyond Antioch, they were enthusiastically supported by the Christians. In this period Christianity, in spite of its thoroughly cosmopolitan basic tendency, which rather aided cultural levelling than the reverse, was often the catalyst for reflection on older ethnic traditions and the development of new national cultures. The fact that, to this point, Christianity on the whole had missionized and acquired more influence among the lower classes of the population than within the groups representing the dominant culture was especially important in this regard: The provincial reactions tended to arise from the base rather than coming from above, from the apex of society.

We may regard it as axiomatic for the early period of the Church that the common language of everyday was always and unquestioningly used in community worship. For a long time, that language in most places was

Greek. Suddenly it was found that the situation had changed, and the problem of translation appeared—a problem all the more acute the farther one traveled from the Hellenistic Mediterranean coastlands and penetrated the hinterland. Thus, for example, Alexandria remained Hellenistic, but in the long stretch of oasis extending up the Nile the use of Coptic, Sahidic, or Bohairic became more and more prevalent. Something similar was true of Antioch on the Orontes, which, according to the well-known phrase of Victor Schultz, soon became "a Hellenistic island in an Aramaic sea."

Even in Rome, at the latest from the beginning of the fourth century, there was more and more use of the city's own Latin language. Hippolytus's Roman liturgy in the third century was, of course, Greek. But under Pope Damasus in the mid-4th century the problem of language, or rather of translation, had become acute. While Marius Victorinus still included Greek liturgical texts in his Latin commentary on Paul, written about 370, only some ten years later, in 380/390, the author known as Ambrosiaster (in an exegesis of the Pauline letters falsely ascribed by Erasmus to Ambrose) cited part of the Roman canon in Latin, but included a false translation that has never been corrected, namely that Melchizedek (Gen 14:18) was not *summus sacerdos*, "high priest," but *sacerdos summi Dei*, "priest of the most high god." We therefore have good reason to locate the beginnings of the official Latin liturgy in Rome around 380, under Pope Damasus. This inference is supported by the fact that at this same period Jerome was authorized by the same pope to make the Church's official Latin translation of the Bible, the "common translation" (Vulgate) of that era. It quickly replaced earlier, private translations.

The beginnings of the Roman Latin liturgy are relatively obscure. The oldest manuscripts come from the 7th–8th centuries and many of them are from Frankish scriptoria. Certainly, what they present is much older liturgical material, some of it—such as the canon—going back to the 4th century, or else stemming from (or claiming to stem from) popes like Leo (440–461), Gelasius (492–496) or Gregory (590–604). A great deal of philological, theological, and liturgical-historical energy has been expended on the analysis of sources, so that we can now perceive the process more clearly, although we do not possess complete certainty about everything.

What we encounter as the Latin liturgy, beginning with the 4th–5th centuries, is not simply a translation of Greek models, but a genuine rewriting in the new idiom. By no means were the older texts slavishly translated, word for word; the old liturgy did not simply don a linguistic gown dyed a different color. The whole liturgy was given a Latin form, a genuinely Latin garment. This is especially clear if one compares

Hippolytus's canon (see A. 2 above) with the Roman canon (see below, ch. 3, B. 2), or investigates the style of Latin prayers. While the canon of Hippolytus was characterized by the measured flow of the prayer, the repeated new beginnings of relative clauses with the substantive "God," who alone is active in creation and salvation history, the canon has now become a highly synthetic, but thoroughly artistic structure. It has its emphatic center in the words of consecration and the formula for the presentation of the gifts, with the insertions (grouped around them according to strict rules of symmetry) of the intentions for the sacrifice, the prayers of petition with the list of intercessors, and the (much obscured) consecratory and communion epicleses. Not only is the structure completely new and independent, but the style of the language also shows the unique usages of the jurists and rhetors of late antiquity, especially the doubling or tripling of adjectives and the overall impression (at least for us today) of a ceremonious manner of expression. The emphasis on the sacrificial character of the Mass has led to a structuring of the entire canon in light of that aspect. The elements of praise are now heard almost exclusively in the preface. Especially striking is the separation of the preface (which remains as the only variable element) from the sanctus, which, though originally it was certainly spoken by the celebrant alone, had very quickly become a kind of popular acclamation and, as a result of its being sung—very soon in artistic musical forms—overflowed its original limits.

Specifically Roman elements appear to be the various prayers or *orationes* by the presider, in their clear and catchy succinctness, their brief formulations and lapidary form. The prayers are often tiny artistic works of the highest literary quality, but also striking in their elegance. Probably even at that time they were too demanding, in their brevity and stylized character, for the simple faithful. But the Latin form of the liturgy deriving from the 4th–5th centuries has a paradigmatic significance for all time.

A liturgy can only be said to be fully implanted when it is not simply translated, but is reshaped in such a way that the concrete community at prayer senses its appropriateness, acknowledges it and finds its own expression in it. Such a form will scarcely ever be successful for all time; it requires repeated efforts to improve it and adapt it to the continually changing cultural environment. This is all the more true when it is performed and celebrated in a living popular, national language. Probably the liturgical order will also have to offer other possibilities for variation beyond the language itself, according to age, life situation, and the intellectual makeup of each community. Thus the period of transition from Greek to Latin is still quite suggestive and informative for us today.

2. Liturgical Centers

In the course of the 4th–6th centuries there developed within the great Church the so-called patriarchates, which were to be of great importance for liturgical development—so much so that "rite" became a characteristic designation and practically a synonym for "associated group of churches." As a religion of the cities, Christianity had from earliest times moved outward in its mission from the major cities of antiquity (including Antioch, Alexandria, and Rome, as well as Ephesus, Corinth, and Carthage) into the countryside. The bishop of the major city in each case, as presiding or archbishop, thus very early acquired precedence within the "diocese" or district created by naturally expanding relationships of dependency and association. When the founder of such an episcopal see was an apostle or the disciple of an apostle, the see in question was regarded as the protector of the authentic apostolic tradition. Antioch had an old Petrine tradition, Rome's tradition relied on both Peter and Paul, and Alexandria boasted of having been founded by Peter's disciple Mark. In this way, such bishops very quickly acquired a special privilege: they presided over regional Church assemblies and the ordination (or, when necessary, the deposition) of bishops in their region, they exercised judicial office when disputes arose, etc. This development was undoubtedly favored by the cultural and economic infrastructure of the empire as well: these cities were located at the hub of transportation routes, they were ports for the import and export of grain or oil, the seats of provincial government, possessors of cultural advantages, shining examples of urban construction, etc. Favorable location on transportation routes was also highly beneficial to ecclesial communications, as in the case of conferences and synods. Thus these structures of local association became the foundation on the one hand for the construction of larger groupings of Churches, but also of the early integration of these Churches to form a single ecclesial union.

The various imperial reforms in late antiquity, with the division of the empire into dioceses (administrative units), each with its metropolis (major city) at the head, brought certain changes in Church organization in post-Constantinian times; nevertheless, the older underlying ethnic and cultural structures were always respected. The rank of the ancient major cities, of course, continued undisturbed. The bishops of the metropolises, called "metropolitans," were gradually equated with, and acquired the rights of, the older "presiding bishops." Moreover, in many cases the offices were identical, as in Alexandria or Antioch. In other cases, however, the new metropolitan division proved in time to be superior to the old in terms of its future usefulness.

This was especially manifest in the positioning of Constantinople as the new Rome: Although in the beginning that see had to be separated from an older association, that of Heraklia in Thrace, and given a degree of ecclesial independence, even at the First Council of Constantinople (381, canon 6) the court bishop and metropolitan of the city ranked immediately after the bishop of old Rome, and his see was able, after assuming headship over the old province of Asia, to absorb the importance of the ancient apostolic seats such as Ephesus and the other very early foundations in Asia Minor, the "seven stars" of the Apocalypse (Rev 1:20).

In fact, over time, the new foundation at Constantinople also overshadowed the old sees and patriarchates of Alexandria and Antioch, which had been much weakened (especially by monophysitism); thus from the sixth century onward the metropolitan of Constantinople bore the title "ecumenical patriarch." Simultaneously with Constantinople, the bishop of Jerusalem, who was confirmed in his traditional place of honor by the Council of Nicaea (325, canon 7), ascended to the patriarchate.

In the West, on the other hand, the Roman bishop asserted his position as the sole western patriarch; there because of the stronger exercise of papal primacy, none of the archbishops or metropolitans was able to ascend to the rank of patriarch. The same was true of Carthage, which in the time of Cyprian was not inferior in importance to the eastern dioceses, but had lost much of its influence in the wake of the barbarian invasions: Under the Vandals, it was dominated by Arians; then, in the time of Justinian, it fell to Constantinople, and finally, in the 7th century, to the Arabs, at which point the formerly flourishing Christianity in the ancient province of Africa was almost extinguished.

In the course of the 5th-century christological struggles—with the Councils of Ephesus (431) and Chalcedon (452)—the Nestorian and Monophysite-Jacobite Churches went into schism and were lost to the empire after the Persian and Arab invasions of the 7th century. But even in these regions the patriarchal development continued in much the same way, however difficult it was made by persecutions. Thus in Edessa, in western Syria, as well as in eastern Syria and Persia, there arose major Church associations that even in the Middle Ages showed an astonishing degree of missionary activity toward the east, even reaching into China; then, after the attacks of the Tartars, they collapsed. Events in Armenia, which was the subject of strong contention, followed the same course.

These new patriarchal sees of the major Church associations, as we have already noted, also served quite naturally as primary liturgical locations, so that the association of episcopal sees belonging to them followed their lead closely. There arose whole liturgical families with only minor local divisions. Still, we should note that even before these divisions the general unity and comparability of all liturgies was quite significant, as we saw, for example, in the spread and use of the liturgy of Hippolytus in Rome and Italy as well as in Egypt and Antioch. Thus in all liturgies the fundamental basis is nearly identical; only in secondary rites are there acquired differences. Moreover, the influence of Jerusalem extended throughout all the liturgical provinces in antiquity; in A. Baumstark's well-known phrase, it was the "center of piety" for all liturgy.

An extensive listing and description of all these ancient Church liturgies would no doubt be highly interesting and also important at the present time from an ecumenical point of view, but it would exceed the limits of this explication of the Latin Mass. Therefore they will simply be named, in a very simplified and global fashion: the Markan liturgy of Alexandria, together with the Cyrillic-Basilian and Gregorian liturgies of the Copts and the apostolic anaphora of the Ethiopians; the Jamesian liturgy of Antioch, originally adopted from Jerusalem, but associated with other forms (such as the liturgy in the "Apostolic Constitutions," and the so-called "Clementine liturgy," which can ultimately be traced to Hippolytus), or— in the eastern hinterland—varying widely from it (as in the liturgy of west Syrian Edessa or the liturgy of the "apostles" Addai and Mari in eastern Syria). Most widely used, especially as a result of the later mission to the Slavs in the Balkans and in Russia, was the liturgy of Constantinople, which, with only a certain degree of justification, is named after John Chrysostom, a doctor of the Church from Antioch (354–ca. 407), who was patriarch of Constantinople from 398 to 404. This Chrysostom liturgy is of Antiochene and Cappadocian origin; it suppressed the Basilian liturgy that was in equally broad use at Constantinople to begin with and also influenced usage in Alexandria and Armenia. In the mind of the West generally, it is often regarded today as *the* liturgy of the "eastern Church."

The multiplicity of Latin liturgies in the West was greater in antiquity than is generally supposed. In fact, to a great degree that variety fell victim to the unification that followed the Council of Trent. The tension between commonality and local divisions is especially evident when, for example, we find the earliest attestation of some parts of the Roman canon not in Rome itself, but in the work *De sacramentis* of Ambrose, bishop of Milan, to whom, on the other hand, is attributed the local liturgy of Milan, which continues to this day (even though it was strongly Romanized in the Carolingian period).

Closely related to the Ambrosian liturgy was that of Aquileia, which was only abolished in 1594. In Benevento, in southern Italy, the liturgy also resisted greater uniformity, especially from the time of Gregory the Great, and maintained its unique character for a long time. The old Spanish liturgy flourished under the West Gothic bishops of the 7th century, survived the Arab conquest (711), and is thus popularly known as the "mozarabic liturgy" (from *mostarab* = "arabicized"). It was suppressed by Gregory VII (synod of Burgos, 1081), and remained in use after the missal of Pius V in 1570 only in a chapel of the cathedral in Toledo, where it is still used today.

The broad Gallic region in particular had its own liturgy in earlier times, the old Gallic (sometimes, but deceptively, called "Gallican"); it experienced strong eastern influence at a very early time. The particular liturgical usage of the Celtic-speaking peoples, especially in Ireland and the lands under its influence, was closely associated with the old Gallic and old Spanish liturgies, but gradually disappeared under Romanizing influence from the insular Anglo-Saxon Benedictines after the 7th century, vanishing in Brittany in the 9th century and in Ireland itself in the 12th century (Synod of Cashel, 1172). Even according to Trent, special traditions that were two hundred years old were not to be suppressed by the new missal and breviary. Nevertheless, this happened often enough, even as late as the 19th century. Surviving are the liturgies of Braga, Lyons, Milan, and (as mentioned above) Toledo, but there are individual ancient elements in the Latin special rites of the Carthusian, Cistercian, Praemonstratensian, Carmelite, and Dominican orders. It remains to be seen how far this special material will be retained in the future. In many cases this would be entirely desirable, with some appropriate reforms. In any case, out of all these developments we can discern more clearly today and give reasons for a degree of relativity in each familiar liturgical form and for the legitimate plurality that exists within the liturgy.

3. Collection and Codification

If one's own ability to frame a celebration independently is insufficient, one readily turns to borrowing from others—other periods, places, or persons: one collects. A popular church will most often do this, and the Church of the post-Constantinian period did so gladly. The greater and more acknowledged was the model quality of such collected forms, the more readily were people inclined to accept and appropriate them. However, what was appropriated was all the more respected according to the degree of authenticity it had or pretended to have. If necessary, the great names of the apostles, doctors of the Church or popes were borrowed. Many collections of texts, originally private, achieved wide circulation in the history of the liturgy because they circulated under borrowed names. Thus in the East, names like Mark, Chrysostom, Basil, or even that of the Roman bishop Clement, and in the West Ambrose, Leo, Gelasius, or Gregory were especially attractive and aided texts or whole liturgies to achieve very broad circulation.

Long-familiar things or those named for great people very easily acquire, especially in worship, the character of something eternally valid, and thereafter people are reluctant to change them. Modern sociology and psychology of cultic worship have discovered laws that we cannot and should not lightly ignore, even today. However, in some circumstances "codification" occurs much earlier from the bottom up than through the conscious effort of a lawgiver. A number of phenomena in the most recent round of liturgical reform have made us vividly aware of this.

Hippolytus is a highly significant example of this kind of regularity. He collected traditional texts, gave them titles—without the slightest hint of a bad conscience—that assured them respect as "apostolic tradition," and thus could immediately count on acceptance because what he presented really was something that had long been in use. The success of his collection was remarkable: it was as significant for the future in the uplands of Italy and in Rome as in Egypt and Antioch and (extending from there) in Constantinople. The fact that the acceptance followed so readily shows that the collection responded to an obvious need on the part of liturgists, whose creative power had slackened; it also showed that people were happy to make use of formulae which were thought to be "correct."

The earliest collections of presiders' prayers were not official Church documents, but private in nature: A liturgist wrote them in notebooks (so-called *libelli*) and incorporated everything he thought useful; they were then passed on to a successor or lent to a fellow cleric, who in turn entered other new material. Since the parish boundaries within a bishopric were not yet clearly defined at the outset, and the members of the bishop's presbytery were conscious of constituting a collegium, we must assume in general that the bishop's celebrations were taken as a model and that they were adapted to more modest circumstances. Given the relatively great fundamental similarity of liturgies among individual provinces, it was easy for well-tried texts to migrate to other regions. Pilgrimages, especially to the Holy Land and the tomb of Peter, the "bearer of the keys of the kingdom of heaven," in Rome, were of immense importance for the exchange of liturgical materials throughout the whole Church.

For the prayers of the later Roman missal, great importance attached to the so-called "sacramentaries," i. e., collections of prayers for the liturgical presider, the oldest of which may go back to the 5th century, but which are preserved for us only in much later, mainly Frankish manuscripts. Characteristic of them is that they were transmitted under the names of popes, who, however, had relatively little to do with them: Leo the Great (440–461), Gelasius (492–496) and Gregory the Great (590–604), of whom we of course know that they were all very interested in the promotion of the liturgy. It is also not to be excluded, in fact it is probable, that formulations of prayer texts by these popes, preserved in archives, may actually have been incorporated into these collections.

Thus, for example, one very old sacramentary, the *Sacramentarium Leonianum* (today usually called *Sacramentarium Veronense* for Verona, the place where it is preserved) pretends to be traceable to Pope Leo. It contains presider's prayers arranged according to the monthly schedule of saints' feasts, and it preserves purely Roman prayer material, although it was not collected by a Roman or for Rome. This sacramentary, therefore, did not achieve as much importance for a defined liturgical region as the extensive and many-faceted group of the *Sacramentarium Gelasianum*, of which we have two versions, one older and one newer. The first compiler and the place of compilation of the older type of sacramentary are in dispute. However, Pope Gelasius (492–496) was certainly not the author. The *Gelasianum* may have been compiled in Rome in the 6th century, but Campagna is also a possibility. It is arranged precisely according to the Church year, and contains formularies for Sundays and feast days, then for saints' feasts and numerous votive Masses for special occasions.

This collection quickly acquired great importance in Rome, but not for long; it lasted only a few decades. Instead, in the 7th–8th centuries it migrated—as a whole or in copied selections *(libelli)*—to France, mixing on the way thither with non-Roman (including Milanese) texts, as is especially evident in the formularies for the saints who were revered within particular regions. In its new homeland it almost completely replaced the old Gallic liturgical material. Here, in 8th-century France, there arose the rich variety of the so-called "newer Gelasians," which, especially after the popes became more deeply dependent on Frankish power, incorporated new Roman, especially "Gregorian" impulses. We will speak of this in the next section.

In Rome, the Gelasian sacramentary, after a few decades of dominance, was replaced by the *Sacramentarium Gregorianum.* While Pope Gregory the Great (590–604) was neither the author nor even the redactor, many of its formulations could be traceable to him. In addition, the manuscripts of this group preserve a great quantity of liturgical material from preceding centuries. Because of the reverence accorded Gregory in all matters liturgical, everything named for him, whether it really came from him or not, was willingly accepted outside Rome as well, even in France, as we will see. It should be emphasized at this point that our present missal is very strongly obligated to the tradition of the sacramentaries, so that many prayers in the missal today have an honorable age of nearly 1500 years.

It is not only from Rome and its region that sacramentaries have come down to us. We also know some from the old Gallic liturgical area (e.g., the so-called *Missale Gothicum,* the *Missale Gallicanum vetus,* and the *Bobbio Missal*), as well as from the Mozarabic, Ambrosian (Milanese), and Celtic regions (Stowe Missal). Individual prayers from these extra-Roman sacramentaries were incorporated into the *Missale Romanum* after Vatican Council II.

Whereas the sacramentary was the handbook for the one who presided at worship, the lectionary or book of readings belonged to the reader, whether a lector, deacon, or priest. As in the synagogal worship service, in the beginning the reading was done directly from the biblical book in question, and then primarily from a gospel codex. This was all the easier as long as "continuous reading" *(lectio continua)* or "linear reading" (with omissions from the complete text, *lectio semicontinua*) was preferred; for that reason, until about 1970 it was still customary to begin the gospel reading with "*Sequentia sancti evangelii secundum. . .*" ("the continuation of the holy gospel according to . . ."). Alongside the complete gospel book, a collected codex was used for the preceding non-gospel reading; it contained primarily the letters of the apostle Paul and consequently was often called *Apostolus.* But because it could sometimes be difficult or awkward to locate the appropriate readings or pericopes, and because efforts at condensation made them shorter and shorter in length, more practical books of readings replaced the precious, handwritten and unnecessarily heavy complete codices.

The books of readings were arranged according to the order of readings customary in the locality *(capitulare);* for the non-gospel readings there was the epistolary (also called the lectionary, taken in a narrower sense), and for the gospel the evangeliary (in the liturgical sense, or also "evangelistary") containing the gospel pericopes. When the missal was created later, these books, together with the sung parts, were incorporated in the plenary missal or complete Mass book; still, they remained in use for diaconal offices and for the solemn episcopal Mass. Comparable with these books for biblical readings were the newer pericope books for preaching in the vernacular *(pronaus)* from our recent past. The present lectionaries, which because of the happy augmentation of the biblical readings have become indispensable, have taken a load from the altar missals. They revive the old tradition of "books for special roles" or "cast books" in the worship service.

The high reverence for the words of the Lord led, in antiquity and the Middle Ages, to great care in the writing of the books of readings, their ornamentation with colored initial letters or pictures, expensive bindings, and often costly containers. The evangeliary in particular was revered in the service of the word as is the Lord himself: In the procession it was accompanied by candles and incense, and it was kissed after the reading. The parallelization of signs of respect between word and sacrament, evangeliary and altar, is quite obvious.

To the degree that the acclamatory songs of the people became more artistic, it became necessary, over time, to introduce a specially trained group of singers *(schola)* with a principal singer *(cantor)*. However, this very greatly reduced the people's immediate participation in the celebration of the Mass. The schola itself now had its own song book, for which a variety of names was used: *cantatorium, antiphonarium, graduale,* and so on. The number of names is extraordinary and often reflects local traditions and usages. These cantatoria contained both solo parts for a cantor and the relevant musical parts for the Mass: processional songs like the introit, offertory, and communion, as well as the gradual, tract, alleluia and sequences, but also the ordinary pieces, the *Kyrie, Gloria, Credo,* and *Sanctus.* Some of them contain the earliest instances of notation, and they are of immense importance for the history of music. Our present hymnals are to a great degree the "cast book" for the congregation.

A separate book of rules, the so-called *Ordo,* was created for the hands of the master of ceremonies. It described the structure and process of a liturgical action. Special importance attached to the so-called *Ordines Romani* of the 7th to 14th centuries, books in which the rite, the ceremonies, and the beginnings *(incipits)* of the liturgical texts were written; these included not only the Mass, but the forms for celebrating the sacraments, the dedication of a church, the special ceremonies for Holy Week, etc. The oldest Roman liturgical books or sacramentaries contained nothing but texts; there were no or very few indications about

how to perform the liturgical celebration. As the originally simple ceremonies became richer and more complicated, but especially after the Anglo-
Saxons in the 7th century and the Franks in the Carolingian period
introduced the liturgy *modo Romano*—that is, when the liturgy was
transferred to a completely different and new socio-cultural environment—the codification of customs, heretofore a matter of oral tradition,
became necessary. In line with their function, these ceremonial books for
the most part contained no texts, but only directions for the ritual that
then later moved into the missals and were inserted, in red (hence
"rubrics," from *ruber* = red), among the now combined elements drawn
from the sacramentary, antiphonary, lectionary, and evangeliary. They
were even incorporated into the liturgy of the hours. These *ordines,*
originally very helpful, later contributed essentially to a rigidification of
the rites—the canonistic rubricism of unhappy memory. On the other
hand, especially in the 10th century, and particularly in Mainz, these
instructions were augmented with the texts themselves (instead of
merely their *initia*), and thus became the foundation for the Romano-
German pontifical (the bishops' liturgical book), which reached Rome
under the Ottonian emperors; in a certain sense it also became the basis
for the *Rituale* and the *Ceremoniale Episcoporum.*

The appearance of these rule books, the *ordines,* is characteristic of a
portentous development in the Roman liturgy: The relatively simple celebration of the early days (at the time of Justin Martyr, for example) had in
the mean time become a precisely regulated ceremonial, with semiofficial
and obligatory actions performed by many participants within the apse,
while the people in the nave were more or less silent onlookers. The lively
community between presider and congregation had changed, in the course
of time, into a super-objectivized cultic action on an elevated tribune before
the eyes of the faithful. The reasons for this transformation, however, were
by no means present within the Mass itself; they were introduced from
outside. They arose from a new, augmented, and genuinely official public
position of the pope. As a result of Church concordats, with the intimate
involvement of the bishops, especially the Roman bishop, in public government and judicial procedures, a different relationship came to exist
between the clerics and the people, and this in turn had its influence on the
liturgy.

The bishops acquired governmental privileges in the Constantinian
period: they became members of the highest senatorial order, had their
own judicial powers, corresponding official insignia and honorific rights,
the title of *excellentissimi,* etc. After the division of the empire at the end of

the 4th century, the papal position was still higher, because the western Roman empire soon vanished. To be fair we must say that this development, at the beginning, resulted not so much from Church grasping after power, but arose from the obligation felt by the pope to care for the Roman people, who were experiencing endless suffering from wars and barbarian invasions, plundering, and famine. Charity easily arouses gratitude and creates standing. Standing brings power, and power, while not evil in itself, quickly finds a corresponding expression. The later, forged "Donation of Constantine," according to which, when transferring his residence to the east, to Constantinople, Constantine had handed over Rome and the West to the pope, appears as the posterior juridical ratification and consolidation of a situation that already existed in fact.

Thus it was not surprising that elements of court ceremony entered into the solemn Mass of the Roman bishop, and that many of its details were modeled on those of the imperial court in Constantinople: special clothing, including shoes and episcopal headgear (the *phrygium*, the Phrygian pointed hat, the origin of both the mitre and the tiara), symbols on the robe denoting rank in the hierarchy and a canon of colors, accompanying persons with candles and incense, the right to an elevated throne and a baldachino, the ceremonial supporting of the bishop by acolytes and greeting with entrance songs, kissing the objects to be handed to the bishop and receiving them with covered hands, bowing and genuflecting, systems of titles and court offices, and so on. This development appears in complete form around 700 in the so-called *Ordo Romanus I,* but in this ordo it has already been strongly spiritualized and adapted to the cult, so that the symbols of privilege noted above could appear to the faithful as appropriate to a patriarch of the West.

In the 9th–10th centuries a redactor at the Ottonian court (or a synod) inserted into the *Ordo Romanus II* the remark: "The bishops who preside over their dioceses should do everything as the pope does." What here appears as a requirement had already, at that time, been long in practice: From the time of Charlemagne, around 800, the Roman liturgy was the unified liturgy for France. The bishop's Mass was completely conformed to the papal Mass with its special court-ceremonial features. This appropriation seemed completely justified by the governmental situation in France, if only because already in the Carolingian period the clergy of the imperial chapel were preferred for promotion to bishoprics, and from the time of Otto the bishops had been elevated to the status of imperial prince-bishops; from the high Middle Ages to the baroque era they in fact acted as secular governors over territorial regions.

It is idle today either to endorse or condemn this development as Church "triumphalism" in general, or in particular with reference to the pontifical liturgy up to the most recent period. We are dealing with unalterable facts of history. A new conception of the ecclesial representative significance of the bishop's office appeared a long time ago. In regions where the Church is persecuted, it is certainly not a matter for discussion. The present practice of a bishop's concelebrating with his priests, varying in its solemnity according to the given situation in a chapel or cathedral, certainly corresponds better to the episcopal office than do many other historical phenomena. Pope Paul VI, in June 1968, significantly simplified the pontificals without falling into the opposite extreme of grey-toned puritanical severity. It appears that the Church has not yet acquired a sense of security about appropriate style for the kind of representation and solemnity fitting our own times. This is just as true, however, in the secular realm of democratic official ceremony.

Unfortunately, not one presbyter's ordo, such as might have been used in a Roman parish or titular church in the time of Gregory the Great, has been transmitted to us. If we had one, it would surely be closer to the liturgical procedure in Justin or Hippolytus than to a papal Mass. It would certainly be solemn and dignified, but not inflated with court rituals and alienated, as we find the *ordo* of the papal Mass for late antiquity to be.

C. The Mass of the Franks (8th–10th Centuries)

1. Frankish Appropriation of the Roman Liturgy

In about 500 the Franks, who had penetrated Gaul under Clovis, accepted Christianity—and, in contrast to other Germanic tribes, most of whom were Arians, they adopted Christianity in its Catholic form. This had far-reaching historical consequences, because it meant that the beliefs of the invaders and the conquered were the same, so that ethnic conflicts were not supplemented by Church differences. It was primarily because of this barrier of Church conflict that the Ostrogoths, Lombards, and Vandals did not take root in the lands they occupied and ultimately disappeared. For the Franks, their chances of becoming indigenous to Gaul were improved from the outset.

The Franks accepted Christianity—something that is not often realized—almost a century before the important liturgical activity of Pope Gregory the Great (590–604). At that time the old Gallic liturgy (sometimes wrongly called "Gallican"), which was relatively independent of

Rome, was at its height. It is true that the ritual language, like everyday speech, was a decadent form of Latin, but the liturgy was by no means Roman or Latin; it was a unique west Roman-occidental form that, among other things, had incorporated numerous elements from the eastern Church, because the ancient connection of Lyons and Marseilles with the Orient by way of the Mediterranean—the most convenient travel route of the time—was still active and not yet obstructed by Islam, as it was after the 7th century. Even Rome in the 6th–7th centuries, after the fall of the western Roman empire, was more or less politically oriented toward Byzantium/Constantinople as the guardian power against the Arian Ostrogoths and the Lombards, who at least at the beginning were highly intransigent. For example, even in 500 Pope Gelasius, a native of Sicily to whom the Roman liturgy owed a great deal, from whom, in fact, a whole group of sacramentaries took its name, certainly felt himself as much a Byzantine as a Roman.

The missionizing of the Franks was accomplished gradually by the native Gallic clergy after the baptism of the Frankish king Clovis and his chieftains (Christmas 498–499) by Bishop Remigius of Rheims (ca. 436–533). His famous words at the baptism: "Humbly bend your neck, Sigamber; adore what you have burned, and burn what you have adored," was a fixed formula, but certainly as a "short formula of faith" it was very short indeed! In fact, the next two and a half centuries were not a sparkling period of Gallico-Frankish Christianity: Scarcely any of the Frankish rulers died a natural death, confusion reigned almost everywhere, the Church was largely drawn into the general barbarity of morals and customs, and the construction of a Frankish Church was tedious and exhausting. Outstanding churchmen like Venantius Fortunatus or Saint Radegunde were isolated high points.

Itinerant monks from Celtic Ireland and Scotland aided in mission and pastoral service. Of course, they brought their own native customs, many of them monastic, and these also took root. Especially important for the future was their penitential discipline, sharply different from that of the ancient Church: Absolution was given not after public church penance had been carried out, but immediately after confession, when the one confessing undertook an obligation to subsequent "satisfaction."

In the beginning, strong connections between the Gallic liturgy and the more fixed Roman liturgy were more the exception than the rule, but such connections were occasioned by numerous pilgrims who had visited Rome. Rome, as the place of martyrdom and burial of the leading apostles, exercised a fascinating influence. The more time passed, the more did

Rome appear as the starting point for a possible consolidation of the Frankish Church, especially since, after 600, even the insular realm of the Anglo-Saxons had adopted the Roman liturgy as *the* model, and after the middle of the 7th century that Church sent increasing numbers of missionaries to the continent; these gradually replaced the Irish and Scottish missionaries who were more strongly attached to their own Church usages. Utrecht was the base for the Anglo-Saxon strategy of mission and reform, and it is no accident that many Anglo-Saxon missionaries, before beginning their work, first went to Rome to be consecrated as missionary bishops and took Roman names: Winfried became Boniface, Willibrord became Clement, and so on.

Also characteristic of their activity is their close cooperation with the Frankish kings, or their stewards, especially with Pippin, the son of Charles Martel and father of Charlemagne. Pippin went to the aid of Pope Stephen II against the Lombards, as a result of which he was anointed by the Pope in St. Denis in 754 as king and "patrician" or "patron," the protector of Rome. As a result of these developments not only the political, but also the ecclesial and liturgical orientation of France toward Rome was increased. Roman liturgical material began streaming into France again, and there arose a liturgical mixture between the "newer Gelasian sacramentaries" mentioned above, which combined old and new material, but failed to overcome the fragmentation of Old Gallic and Roman liturgy because of the lack of scriptoria which might have made possible a swift unification according to the Roman models, as the royal central authority desired.

Especially influential in this period was Bishop Chrodegang of Metz (742–766), who went to Rome in 753 to study the liturgy in order to introduce pure Roman usage among the Franks. Charlemagne continued his father's efforts with consistency: In the year 785 he received a Gregorian sacramentary from Pope Hadrian I (772–795), the so-called *Sacramentarium Hadrianum,* which he decreed as the *liber authenticus* ("Aachener Urexemplar," "Original copy of Aix"), which in future should serve as the single obligatory model. Unfortunately, while in its externals this codex was a valuable gift, it was internally incomplete, for it contained only the liturgy for the days on which the pope celebrated.

Thus the codex had to be expanded by a so-called "appendix" written by Abbot Benedict of Aniane (ca. 750–821). In doing so, he drew primarily on the newer Gelasians and added the feasts and rituals that had been customary in France. The originally separate appendix was soon worked into the authentic Roman model, to make it more easily useful, and the result was a mixed sacramentary containing essentially Roman, "Gregorian" liturgical material. While with this the liturgical fragmentation was largely overcome, the old Gallic usage was suppressed. This unified liturgy, or- dained by the political central authority as well as the bishops, became in future the basis for almost the entirety of western liturgical usage. Variety of liturgies, with all its unmistakable disadvantages, had come to an end, but it was replaced by a unity that very quickly became an obstacle to any kind of creative production of new forms or to any development. Anything that thereafter appeared as new was considered merely paraliturgical; it was eagerly welcomed by the people but, as we shall see, it escaped any shaping by the spirit of the ancient liturgy.

2. Enrichment of the Roman Liturgy in France

The Roman liturgy was not only adopted in France, but was also carefully tended and studied. This is attested especially by the writings of Amalar, Walafried, Alcuin, and many others. Attention was also paid to the task of rooting it among the people: In particular lyrical, but also dramatic and hymnic elements were introduced into the stricter Roman forms and were performed by the people in lively fashion.

From our present perspective we can only lament that at that time the linguistic barrier of Latin had not yet been overcome; had it been so, the Franks, and later the other Germanic tribes, could have identified with their worship in much greater numbers. But in that era the idea was still foreign: Tribal dialects were not considered suitable for liturgy, and as a result it seemed preferable to translate the old popular usages into Latin than to change the Latin liturgy into a universally intelligible vernacular. By the time when a German literary language had developed, the Latin liturgy had come to be regarded as untranslatable: It had become a complex of ob- jective, sacred rites that were thought to be sacrosanct: only thus and in no other way was the sacred preserved and administered. Liturgy was simply a mystery above human meddling; it was seen as having been willed by the Church, or even by God, in this form forever.

In the early Carolingian period the faithful, thanks to capable intro- duction and instruction, still for the most part experienced the liturgy emotionally and participated with active piety. In particular, sacred seasons like Holy Week and Easter, which were more susceptible to being filled out by the imagination, enjoyed great popularity. Thus came the palm procession with singing of hymns, the washing of feet on Maundy Thurs- day, and the veneration of the cross on Good Friday with the *improperia,* acclamations, and unveiling of the cross, the Easter liturgy with its inten-sively participatory rites of blessing of fire, introduction of the *lumen Christi* ("the light of Christ") into the dark church, the exciting *Exultet* hymn, the blessing of the paschal candle and the baptismal water, and the Easter celebration itself with its drama, giving rise then—somewhat later—to Easter plays with the singing of the apostles and holy women at the Holy Sepulchre, etc. Recent research has shown that these elements were not pre-Gregorian Roman usages that were incorporated, but were new Carolingian elements, not, of course, free from influence by the liturgy of Jerusalem.

Another characteristic of this period is a preference for solemn hym-nody, something different from the more measured, calm, and rational Rome of late antiquity. There the reserve toward ecstatic verve and charis-matic enthusiasm was considerable in all periods. Latin cultic hymns gen-erally encountered resistance there, if they could not be demonstrated to be "Ambrosian," or unless they developed within special groups, such as the Benedictine monasteries. The *Gloria* of the Mass, for example, was at first reserved to the pope alone; only in the Franco-German realm did it become part of the liturgy for Sundays and feasts. We should generally pic-ture the Carolingian liturgy as very festive and fond of singing.

The Old Testament attained great importance as an early foreshadow-ing of what would be perfected in the New. It was not merely that the menorah found its place in many churches; the many anointings—of the priest, the king, the church itself—were introduced at this time. We cannot fail to notice that the archaic Old Testament rituals were easily assimilated by these new peoples: The symbol, as a powerful sign, was more congenial to them than a strongly verbalized and rationally shaped worship service.

At this period, an important step was made toward the independent development of differentiated liturgical books. While the old sacramen-taries contained not only the texts for the Mass but also the models for administration of most of the other sacraments, in places like Mainz in the 10th century a number of practical books were prepared for the celebra-tion of the sacraments, the sacramentals, consecrations, and blessings. The individual formularies were separated from the old collections, enriched, and provided with appropriate notation, each in turn separately designated for the hand of the bishop or the priest in pastoral service. Thus were cre-ated at this time the bases for the later *Rituale* and Pontifical. Their origins can be traced to this period. The enriched formularies later returned to Rome and were important for the entire Church.

3. Return of the Altered Frankish Liturgy to Rome

The development just described was focused in the region between the Maas and the Rhine, especially in Mainz, which was the metropolitan see of the largest early medieval diocese. But many other places, such as Metz, were also of great importance.

In Rome itself the ninth century, and still more the tenth, the *saeculum obscurum*, were more than unfavorable to liturgical development. Under the tyranny of the Roman city patricians the papacy descended to its most humiliating depth. No wonder that the clergy celebrated the worship services carelessly and that the people's participation was negligible. There were no longer even any liturgical books being written. Thus, in contrast to the North, there arose a complete vacuum waiting to be filled. The Saxon Ottonian emperors in particular made efforts at reform, both in ecclesial politics and in the liturgy. They encouraged the acceptance of northern customs in Rome. It is significant that the emperor St. Henry II, during his coronation by Pope Benedict VIII in Rome in 1014, interrupted the Mass and categorically demanded that the Credo used in the north be inserted at the end of the liturgy of the word; ultimately, he succeeded in having it introduced into the Mass everywhere.

Special credit for the renewal of the Roman liturgy according to the Franco-German model was due to the monks of Cluny in Burgundy. This very region in the southern part of the Rhine-Maas belt achieved special importance, both for culture and Church, in the Middle Ages. In Huizinga's well-known phrase, it was the "melting-pot of western culture." The Benedictine Cluniacs refounded numerous monasteries in central Italy (such as Farfa) and in Rome (including St. Paul Outside the Walls), and thus became the transmitters of the liturgy from north of the Alps, which was now willingly and even enthusiastically received. The greatest influence was exercised by the Cluniac reform under Pope Gregory VII (1073–1085), who had become a monk of Cluny in 1047 and went to Rome in 1049 with Leo IX. In 1059 he became archdeacon of the Roman churches and finally, in 1073, was elected pope. In the spirit of reform, he set himself to a furious cleansing of the Church from everything undignified and worked to free it from civil control. The basic centralizing tendency of his activity was especially evident in the liturgy: Beginning with his time the improved Old Roman usage was that of the Latin Church everywhere. Nevertheless, even his active intervention could not prevent the liturgical collapse of the Middle Ages; the spirit of a new era imposed itself irresistibly and, blind to the structural principles of the Roman liturgy, turned toward medieval subjectivism.

On the whole, however, we can agree with Theodor Klauser concerning the epoch of the 9th–10th centuries: ". . . during a critical period, the Franco-German Church succeeded in saving the Roman liturgy not only for Rome itself but for the entire Christian world of the Middle Ages."[3]

D. The Subjective Shift

1. The Collapse of the Experiential Liturgical Community

In his *Short History of the Western Liturgy,* Theodor Klauser describes the period of the early and high Middle Ages, the half-millennium between Gregory VII and the Council of Trent in the 16th century, as the period of "dissolution, elaboration, reinterpretation and misinterpretation."[4] The reason for this negative development was ultimately that the consciousness of community in liturgical celebrations had gradually disappeared. The Mass, in the course of time—not only because of the language barrier, but primarily as a result of it—had become purely the priest's Mass. The people were silent spectators, by no means lacking in devotion, but unliturgical. They did not pray the Mass; they prayed during the Mass. The event at the altar was, theologically speaking, just as much the medium of salvation as ever, and it was piously taken as such, but as cult it was over-objectified, in its language and ceremonies scarcely comprehensible, if at all, and as a result it was no longer the action of the whole people of God. The living community between presider and people was interrupted, at least as regards the external signs that related the sacraments to the liturgical actions. It had been replaced by a simple simultaneous presence, and that in turn was interrupted only by occasional bell signals—at the consecration, for example—which were meant to call the attention of those present to especially important parts of the Mass liturgy.

There were many reasons for this simple juxtaposition of those present. In particular, the activities of the people had been completely reduced or suppressed. The offertory procession, for example, when the gifts were prepared, once an important spiritual and caritative self-expression of the congregation, had disappeared, and more especially because, from Carolingian times on, the ordinary daily bread was no longer the matter of the Mass, but had been replaced by unfamiliar, unleavened, "altogether different" bread. In addition, the spiritual countermovement, the procession to Communion, had almost completely disappeared, because ordinarily people no longer received the body of the Lord at Mass.

The Lateran Council of 1215 therefore found it necessary to insist sharply on the obligation to receive Communion at least during the Easter season as something required by commandment. Communion in the cup, occasionally still practiced into the 11th–12th centuries, had completely disappeared and then, in the late Middle Ages, it was strictly forbidden, although the movements of the Hussites, Wycliffe's followers, and others strongly protested against this. Even the acclamations, those short actions that were easily carried out even in congregations with little liturgical practice, were taken over by the ministers or altar servers. In general, the community sense of the territorial congregations was confused by a plurality of structures, feudal (including feudal governance of churches), corporative (for example, guilds and similar organizations), and devotional and social-critical (including the numerous brotherhoods).

In the cathedrals, chapters and foundations with their own clerical worship services increasingly divided the clerical liturgy from that of the people, so that the stone screen in front of the choir strikingly documented the actual situation: the two groups did not wish to disturb one another. It is true that there was usually a people's altar in front of this barrier, often called the altar of the cross, but it was only one among the many altars of the brotherhoods or Mass donations in side chapels or on the pillars of the churches, some of which were much roomier than necessary. The activity of the newer orders, especially the mendicants, was certainly a pastoral stimulation and an advance, but it was injurious to the established parish system. In addition, this parochial system suffered much from the problem of benefices and sinecures. The pastors, appointed from above, drew the income from their offices, often from many parishes at the same time, but they frequently left the actual work to an assisting clergy, often men of little theological education, who in many cases celebrated the liturgy negligently. To be fair, we should say that there were certainly some deeply religious men among the clergy in this period, genuinely committed pastors and "people's priests," but the liturgy and its rational celebration remained a pure "mediation of grace," unintegrated with their piety. These darker aspects of the Middle Ages are sufficiently familiar that they need not be more fully described here.

One significant destructive factor was that the liturgy was scarcely understood theologically and in its true nature any longer. It was reinterpreted, in line with what was primarily a juridical way of thinking, as the sum of a multitude of officially regulated rituals, in which humans desired and were obligated to pay to God the "honor that was due," and which in turn conveyed the "grace of God" in a manner that was often conceived in very material and quantitative terms. But ultimately the ritual and language were something incomprehensible; they were not intelligible in themselves, and stood, as an objective quantity, somehow above and beyond daily life. In order somehow to create access for the faithful to the liturgy in spite of this, pastors grasped at so-called "symbolism," an allegorical explanation of each and every detail in the worship service—an explanation not, of course, according to the real biblical and historical roots, but lumped together out of liturgically inappropriate and haphazard interpretations and misinterpretations. In the process, incidentals often became essentials.

For example, if, in the cruciform shape of a church—because of peculiarities of the ground or other factors—the axis of the choir deviated somewhat from that of the rest of the church, this bending of the axis was seen as a reflection of the head of Christ bowed in death. Because the altar represented Christ, the lector or subdeacon had to proclaim the Old Testament reading, which was generally regarded as referring to Christ, while turned toward the altar, not toward the people—and of course in Latin. The course of the Mass itself was seen as a scenic depiction of salvation history from Paradise to the last judgment; Calderon's famous dramatic presentation in the "Mysteries of the Holy Mass" was only a baroque echo of this idea. This symbolic and allegorizing literature began around the year 1000 and expanded in the 12th century, with Honorius of Autun (*Gemma animae, Speculum ecclesiae*), Rupert of Deutz (*De divinis officiis*) and Johannes Beleth (*Rationale*), and in the 13th century with Sicardus of Cremona (*Mitrale*) and especially in the *Rationale divinorum officiorum* of the bishop and canonist William Durandus the elder.

We may regard the skillful compilation of all the earlier writings by Durandus as constituting a *summa* of this kind of liturgical literature. Its numerous manuscripts made it a feature of all medieval libraries, and consequently it had great influence on people's understanding and celebration of the liturgy. This work is of the greatest historical interest. It characterizes as does no other the state of the decayed medieval liturgy: highly respected, but in its symbolic character uncomprehended and misinterpreted.

Medieval liturgy had, for the most part, lost its power to exercise influence on popular, private devotion. It had become frozen into a block of prescribed prayer formulae, and in the minds of the faithful it was enormously important, but ultimately an objective, salvation-bringing ritual that was no longer carried out by the community: it could be experienced only as reflected in the allegorization that misinterpreted almost as much as it construed. The human agents of the liturgy, the community in the New Testament sense, were involved in other social substructures as well.

Left to itself, popular devotion had to turn to what was most easily accessible: from among the facts of salvation history this was primarily the earthly life of Jesus with his birth, miraculous healings, passion and cross, resurrection, and ascension. This most readily expanded the imagination, and here pious or even mystical absorption was possible.

One of the loveliest testimonies to late medieval piety, the *Imitation of Christ* by Thomas à Kempis (1379–1471) reveals the endearing features of an introduction to meditation, but also its sacramental weakness: one is primarily (morally) close to Christ in emotion and subjective feeling, and one attempts to follow his example, but sacramentally one can almost dispense with him. There is here already an echo of a later churchless and a-liturgical pietism. That homage to Mary and veneration of the saints would, in light of these circumstances, acquire great importance is easy to understand; it is equally easy to see why this kind of piety threatened to expand beyond all limits in excessive veneration of relics and what appeared to be a quantitative works righteousness of processions and pilgrimages. The late medieval altar is highly revealing: The food elements of bread and wine still rest upon it, of course, but they are adored more than they are consumed. Above the altar, in beautiful and pious altar pieces *(retablos)* glowed an imaginary, heavenly world that spoke to the people at prayer, uninvolved in the events of the worship service itself, because it expressed the things that were important to the people themselves.

2. The "Private Mass"

In the early days of the Church, besides the principal community Masses, there were also celebrations of the Mass in smaller groups. They were distinguished from the Sunday celebration primarily by the fact that they could be held on any day of the week, especially for small groups and individual needs; they could be celebrated in a simpler form, without a great deal of clerical assistance and also in various spaces (dwellings, votive chapels, etc.). The so-called "votive Masses" (from *votum* = vow, concern, wish), at least in their origins, are derived from Masses celebrated in small groups. They are fully legitimate liturgical celebrations, because at no time in the history of the liturgy has what is private been completely obliterated by what is universal, which in that case could be misunderstood as being simply collective. Living community thrives naturally on the basis of active groups and individuals. Distinct from these Masses in small groups was another type: namely, the private Mass of a cleric, appearing around the end of the first millennium and arising for completely different reasons and out of quite other motives: the priest celebrated the Mass without a congregation, with a single person assisting. Even today, we cannot dispute the legitimacy of such Masses, although we may place a different value on them than at the time when they were at their height.

Private Masses most probably arose in the monasteries. These were, at first, purely lay communities having an idealistic democratic rule under the headship of their elected abbot as spiritual father. For example, Benedict permitted only tested monks to be ordained by the responsible bishop as priests for his monasteries, and then only as there was spiritual need; apart from the worship service they had no more rights than the other brothers (*Rule of Benedict* 64). When the monasteries began to be selected as bases for the missionizing of pagan lands (for example, as early as Gregory the Great for the conversion of the Anglo-Saxons), the situation changed: the number of monastic priests necessarily increased very quickly because only priests could carry out missionary and pastoral functions in foreign territory. For example, while the Scottish monastery of Melrose had only four monastic priests in 650, by about 784—in the period of the extensive Carolingian missionary effort—there were in St. Peter in Salzburg 22 priests among a total of 97 monks, which is roughly one quarter of the whole. In the tenth century there were monasteries with over 100 monastic priests, although some of them were doing pastoral duty in the surrounding country parishes. Nevertheless, the number of priests far surpassed the needs of the monasteries. Even if they had taken turns in presiding over their monastic community's liturgy, they could have celebrated only two or three times a year. On the basis of subjective and private piety, and particularly because of the newly developed theological teaching about the "fruits of the sacrifice of the Mass," the natural consequence was a desire to celebrate frequently, every day if possible, and this rapidly became the rule.

The secular priests soon followed this trend, especially since the desire of the faithful for the application of the fruits of the sacrifice of the Mass on behalf of the individual salvation of the living and the dead was especially congenial to this practice. This is the origin of so-called Mass stipends, gifts of natural products or money to the clerics; it is also the origin of the dedication of Masses and altars extending beyond the death of the giver: the one giving the stipend asked that the special fruits of certain Masses be applied to him- or herself, relatives or friends. What was at issue, however, was not primarily or at all the Church as a whole, within whose communion the individual stood and in which he or she was sustained in a community of salvation; it was a matter of the individual salvation of a particular person or of a group or smaller community. The turn toward medieval subjectivism is as evident here as is the vanishing of the New Testament awareness of a community of Jesus Christ that celebrates the Eucharist in the presence of God.

With the numerous priests in monasteries, all eager to celebrate individually, and further numbers of priests in the city congregations with their brotherhoods, large numbers of special groups and "endowed Masses," the result was a series of far-reaching changes in the ceremony of the Mass as it existed thus far. Of course, as little as possible of the sacred ritual was to be sacrificed because the form was regarded as sacrosanct, once and for all, and therefore as unchangeable. Nevertheless, when celebrated by an individual priest, the form of the Mass necessarily became attenuated. The shrinking of space necessitated by the erection of many altars side by side—for at the beginning the traditional principle that an altar could be used only once a day was maintained, and considered "rational" as well—and consideration for other Masses being celebrated within the same church (at the same time) compelled reductions that would have great consequence for the future: The singing of the choir had to be eliminated and was simply recited by the priest as a text for reading; there was neither space nor appropriate personnel to provide for numerous assistants with special duties; the movements that previously took place within the spacious sanctuary were reduced, and all actions, even the readings previously proclaimed at the ambo, were now carried out at the altar, where the only indication of the former movements remained the "marking" of the epistle and gospel sides. There was no longer need for a presider's chair, because the priest stood at the altar throughout the Mass. The sermon had long since disappeared; the offertory procession vanished, because the private stipend had replaced it; nevertheless the washing of hands—which in the mean time had lost its function—remained a requirement, even though the priest no longer touched any gifts of natural produce.

The audible acclamations, which would now be a disturbance, were spoken quietly by the server. In fact, silence was the most prominent characteristic of this new form, which was therefore quite rightly called a "silent" or "read Mass." The priest not only read his part silently or very quietly, he also took over the duties of the other "functionaries." The people stood silently near the altar, but separated from it by a "communion rail," although this last was seldom used for that purpose. Communication between the priest in quiet prayer and the silent attendees at the Mass was interrupted, and "active participation" was an illusion. Thus the believers prayed privately "during the Mass," or "at Mass." They did not participate in its living execution, even if they did not simply absent themselves, unequal to the demands of such a multiplicity of Masses on weekdays. Thus it occasionally happened that the celebrant, lacking a "server," had to greet himself with *Dominus vobiscum*, and answer himself *Et cum spiritu tuo.*

The form of the private Mass quickly began to exercise influence on the Sunday worship service as well; after the 13th century it constituted the universal norm. Even the bishop's private celebration of Mass, and, beyond that, the Pope's Mass in the chapel Sancta sanctorum in the Lateran was shaped from that period onward by the priest's private Mass. Only the solemn pontifical Mass for special occasions and the occasional festive high Mass of the parish community—in its levitical form a faint shadow of the old glory—were retained. But even here the ritual of the private Mass revealed its influence: The celebrant had to recite privately all the parts that formerly had been taken by others, including the words of the choral antiphons and the readings chanted by the deacon and subdeacon. The absolute priestly Mass had triumphed. Even concelebration, except in ordination Masses, had vanished. If a priest undertook the office of a deacon or subdeacon, he did not communicate at that Mass, but celebrated privately beforehand. It was required that the convent Mass of cloistered communities or the pontifical Mass in the cathedrals should always be preceded by the private Masses of the monks or canons.

It is not clear when the codification of the rites for these private Masses occurred. A rule of usage seems to have developed from the 10th century onward, perhaps first in Mainz or St. Gallen. In the year 1243, a chapter of the Franciscans in Bologna spoke of a fixed *ordo,* that is, a description of the rite, beginning with the words *Indutus planeta* ("Wearing the chasuble . . ."). It was presented by the General of the order, Haimo of Faversham. The *ordo* of Johannes Burckhard of Strasbourg, the papal master of ceremonies beginning in 1483, was first published in 1502, but it rapidly became the standard everywhere; it was adopted by the post-Tridentine missal of 1570 and remained valid until after Vatican Council II.

3. The Priest's Missal

The beginning of the missal (Mass book) was intimately connected—at least in its fundamental tendency and quite possibly also as regards its origin—with the beginning of private Masses. While previously, when Mass was celebrated, many officiants had cooperated, each with a single task to perform, in the private Mass the individual celebrant necessarily took all those duties on himself. Accordingly, we find in the missal all the texts that formerly had been distributed over many books collected in one: the priestly prayers from the old Gregorian-Hadrianite sacramentary meant for the hands of the one presiding at Mass; then the readings from the lectionary, formerly belonging to the deacon and subdeacon; the sung parts from the old antiphonaries or graduales of the schola or choir; and finally—written in red and therefore called "rubrics"—the old *ordo* or rule book of the master of ceremonies, who took care that the individual officiants did their parts at the right time and that the whole ceremony followed its well-regulated pattern. The missal was the ideal instrument for the needs of the private Mass. It is, in its unique character, a document of the clerical liturgy.

From as early as about 700 we have the Bobbio missal, and the Stowe missal dates from about 800. These were traveling missals in small format for itinerant monks, but they were put together only for special needs. After a number of changes and intermediate stages, the development of the so-called plenary missals reached a certain conclusive stage near the end of the 10th century. The full missals appeared almost everywhere, beginning with the 12th century, in place of the older specialized liturgical books, and from the 13th century onward they were regarded as obligatory, because even in the *missa cantata*, meanwhile, the celebrant was required to speak all the texts, even those spoken or sung by others.

At the beginning, ecclesial centers (including Milan, Mainz, Cologne, Lyons, Braga, Toledo, and others) and orders (the Cluniacs after 1080, the Cistercians after 1134, but also the Carthusians and Dominicans) had their own special missals. It would come to be of great importance that Francis of Assisi in 1223 adopted the missal of the Roman curia for his order and prescribed it as obligatory. This *missale secundum usum Romanae curiae*, later simply called the *Missale Romanum*, spread rapidly throughout the entire Western world. In 1277 it was required by Pope Nicholas II for use in all Roman parishes, and afterward it was adopted in many other places. Because of its widespread use—the *editio princeps* was printed in Milan as early as 1474—it later became the basis for the post-tridentine missal of 1570.

4. The Private Prayer of the Priest in the Mass

Since from the outset the missal was solely the priest's book, private prayers very quickly made their appearance there. From a purely external point of view, they are distinguished in their presentation from the priestly *orationes* primarily by the fact that, in reciting them, the priest did not extend his hands, but folded them; he did not pray them in the name of the community, and the congregation did not conclude them with the acclamation "amen." The priest said them for his own intentions. They served his personal need for recollection or attuning his thoughts, and they had (and have) their place before the reading of the pericopes, before communion, and so on. These prayers served not least to enhance the feeling of subjective unworthiness, especially at the beginning of Mass, but also throughout its course. For a time, especially in the 11th century, these confessions of sins or "apologies" grew like wildfire and were distributed throughout the entire Mass.

Elements of thanksgiving also emerged. It is characteristic of the new conception and evaluation of the liturgy that dominated at this period that even within the great thanksgiving of the Eucharist, small private thanksgivings appeared necessary: The Mass was a prescribed ritual to which one sought access—with difficulty within one's own subjectivity, or even in scrupulosity. But it was no longer in and of itself an adequate self-expression of the one celebrating. Often these private prayers were transformed ancient *orationes*—of course revised into the first person singular—sometimes originating in the older Gelasian sacramentary, adapted from other rites; sometimes they were new compositions.

Added to these were private prayers that interpreted the liturgical action, often in the sense of medieval symbolism. They explained actions that originally had no words connected with them: for example, the preparation of bread and wine at the offertory, the mixing of wine and water, the washing of hands, etc. The fact that, in this connection, formal prayers of offering *(Suscipe, Offerimus)* and an epiclesis of the Spirit *(Veni sanctificator)* were included, anticipating a kind of "little canon" at the preparation of the gifts or sacrificial offerings, is a clear indication of the inadequate conception at work. This kind of explanatory private prayer (meant to be helpful) was apparently necessary to the degree that the form of the action and the expressive character of the gestures were no longer understood in and of themselves. This is especially evident in the prayers for incensing the altar or the gifts. But the more these prayers became part of the ritual and, with daily repetition, became stereotypical, the more they fell short of their aim: They were simply recited and scarcely served any longer as impulses for thought or aids to recollection.

In a certain sense the weight of private petitions in relation to the canon also belongs in this context. It was precisely the personal concerns that were sensed in everyday life that had led to the multiplication of private Masses and brought about the system of stipends. Unquestionably, petition has always had its place within the larger context of the Eucharist. Petition is not simply the opposite of thanksgiving; on the contrary: In making a petition I acknowledge the power of the one who can respond to it. No one prays to someone who is powerless. But the new position given to the petitions shows clearly what a change had taken place: Whereas, in the beginning, the individual was quite naturally included and lifted up, as part of the Church and the community of salvation, in the petitions at the end of the liturgy of the word, especially in the times of silent reflection and prayer that stimulated personal petitions, now personal petition sought its own special place and in this fashion very quickly overspread the canon itself. It was pushed as close as possible to the consecration, which was interpreted as the high point of the mystery.

Even when I was an associate pastor, immediately after the war, I had daily experience of this: from Easter to autumn the "prayer for the growth of the products of the field," and in the winter months from autumn to Easter the "prayer for the first communicants" (who would receive Communion on the first Sunday after Easter) had to be recited—usually by one of the students in the higher classes. I sought unsuccessfully, at the monthly "corporate Communion" of my good sons in the Kolping society to shift the "prayer for the canonization of Adolf Kolping" (the canonization was finally pronounced in Rome by Pope John Paul II on 27 October 1991) from its obligatory place immediately after the elevation of the chalice and before the doxology of the canon, and to give it a more appropriate location. At that time I yielded to the express wish of the community, because otherwise I would merely have hurt them and—in the absence of a long prior process of liturgical education—would have destroyed more in their practice of piety than I would have improved.

The whole set of questions addressed here teaches us this: If no place is left for private intentions and needs in the Mass, they will find substitute expression, in a less appropriate way, somewhere else. When, quite early, the major petitions were replaced by the *Kyrie* litany, and the latter was then reduced simply to the *Kyrie* itself, private intentions overloaded the canon and even concealed it, or else they were transferred completely out of the Mass, so that, for example, pilgrimages often became the occasions of more popular and intensely experienced petition and thanksgiving than the Mass itself, which, although it was celebrated at the place of pilgrimage, was there completely overshadowed in its devotional character by the intention of the pilgrim. The privacy of prayer must never be suppressed by the liturgy; it must remain within it, in a way that is ecclesially appropriate, in order to give it life.

5. The Saving Gaze

The question much discussed in the Middle Ages—exactly when in the canon the change of the forms of bread and wine into the body and blood of Christ occurred—had originally a more practical than a theological purpose: What should be done if, for some reason (such as the sudden death of the celebrant) the canon was interrupted? To what point could one simply remove the bread, and at what point was it consecrated? As we know, this question still divides the eastern and western Church: Does consecration take place through the epiclesis, as the East believes, or through the words of consecration, which are understood more strictly as declaratory than anamnetic? The Church has not given a dogmatic answer to this question, but the general opinion of the Latin theologians favors the latter. It achieved acceptance about 1200 with the assertion that the change in the bread took place immediately after the corresponding "words of institution," and thus before the words over the chalice.

Therefore it became an established custom for the celebrant, immediately after the consecration of the bread, to genuflect reverently, repeating the same action after the consecration of the wine. But because during the canon the priest's body concealed the sacred species from the people, the elevation of these consecrated species was a demand that the people in turn should offer them the same reverence, kneeling and gazing. The natural movement for showing them—in fact, the natural posture for the whole— would have been to turn to the people. But this did not seem possible because of the obligatory law of facing east during the entire canon, and thus a rather strange substitute was found: The priest lifted the species so high that, even though he was turned away from the people, they were visible above his head.

The elevation of the eucharistic species of bread and wine very quickly achieved great popularity, for it responded to the general interest in looking at things. Intellectual curiosity as a whole, as well as participation in the celebration of the mysteries had, in the course of time, been reduced almost to nothing, so that now the eyes and the emotions longed for some kind of satisfaction. The desire to see the body of the Lord heightened until the idea emerged of a *communio per oculos*, a saving contact with Christ alone through the mere act of seeing. The priest was entreated to hold the host aloft as long as possible, and eventually he received a better stipend for it, or was given assistants to stand at his sides and, if necessary, to support his arms when he became weary. In large city churches and cathedrals, with their guild and brotherhood altars numbering as many as forty, it was popular to arrange things so that the elevations of the sacred species in the individual Masses at different altars followed successively, one after another, and processions developed from elevation to elevation, in order that—at least according to common popular belief—the people could achieve, through the sum total, a richer enjoyment of the fruits of this most holy event. Of course, this kind of quantitative notion of grace was never a theological teaching, but it played an important role in the minds of the faithful, and had a corresponding effect.

This enjoyment of seeing had already emerged, somewhat earlier, in the veneration of the relics of the saints: These were no longer concealed in chests or reliquaries, to be occasionally touched for a closer contact; now they were made visible in crystal cylinders. These *ostensoria* invited the introduction of the same practice with the sacred host. In fact, the earliest eucharistic monstrances were so similar to *ostensoria* for relics that they could easily have substituted one for another. In them, the elevation at the consecration could, in fact, be perpetuated, and the sacred body of Christ could be "exposed" for long periods of adoration.

The visions of St. Juliane of Liège (1192–1258) led in 1256 to a special festival of the body of Christ: *Corpus Christi* (German: *Fronleichnam*, from *frôn* = "Lord," and *leichnam* = "living body"). This feast, now officially called the "solemnity of the body and blood of Christ," was introduced to the diocese of Liège by Bishop Robert, but as early as 1264 it was extended to the whole Church by Pope Urban IV (1261–1264), who had been archdeacon of Liège from 1242 to 1247. However, because of Urban's death soon afterward, it was not immediately adopted everywhere. North of the Alps in particular the feast was eagerly accepted. The first Corpus Christi procession in Cologne was in 1277, and it is explicitly attested for Benediktbeuern in 1286. The most holy sacrament was carried in the monstrance through the streets of the city, often under a portable "celestial" canopy or on a litter. Priests in vestments, carrying candles or relics or chalices, singers, instrumentalists, "angel choirs" of boys, and the whole congregation followed the procession, which found its models in other processions within the church and city (such as those on Palm Sunday, at the translation of relics, and solemn visits to the dying).

The general popularity of festivals and the decoration of the streets are evident in ancient titles for the occasion such as "Day of Resplendence" *(Prangtag)* or "Day of Garlands" *(Kränzeltag)*, and so on. Very soon, so-called "living tableaux," visual interpretations of Christ's passion, were carried along on wagons. The addition of explanatory dialogue to these resulted in the Corpus Christi plays. The guilds competed in the decoration of the wagons for the feast.

Last of all, in most cases, came the wagons of the millers and bakers who made the hosts. This feast is a vivid example of medieval piety, certainly taking its origin from the liturgy, but in the end no longer normed or formed by it. Consequences that can scarcely be defended any longer included belief in the apotropaic, exorcistic effects of the Corpus Christi procession: "The demons shall see it and tremble." Therefore the sacrament was carried through fields if they were threatened by bad weather, and the blessing for good weather was given with the most holy sacrament.

St. Clare of Assisi (1194–1253), according to legend, defended her monastery and her sisters from the attacking Saracens in 1240–41 with nothing but the monstrance in her hand: therefore in iconography the *ostensorium* is her symbol. It is true that excesses were occasionally abolished in the late Middle Ages, but in 1551 (at the 13th session, chapter 5: Denzinger-Schönmetzer 1644) the Council of Trent defended the popular feast against the reformers as an express and appropriate cult of veneration "of his death, victory, and triumph." "For it is fitting to let victorious truth triumph over falsehood and heresy, so that those who deny it, in the light of such brilliance and joy, will either sink down, weakened and broken, or, seized and confused by fear, will come to understand."

This very example of medieval piety reveals what—according to modern taste—represents a bad combination of a religious core (or at least occasion) from the popular church with a folksy spectacle. Custom and folklore, musical groups and stage shows tend, in our society, to be attached to another kind of peg. But at that period the Church was still the enzyme of society. Festivals were primarily Church festivals. The anniversary of the dedication of the church or *Kirmes* had both a religious and a popular aspect. It would be unhistorical simply to haul the past before the tribunal of an "enlightened" present. In the present "ecumenical climate" we should easily be able to give a new interpretation to the tridentine declaration (which is not a dogma).

The activity of processions and parades might possibly, even today, provide a necessary corrective to the practice of having the community celebrating the liturgy sit quietly for a long time. This often produces an obvious restlessness, not only among young people, that unmistakably calls for relief. Therefore it is our task today to find forms of divine service that are not merely suitable for intellectuals. Reform is not simply clearing away and elimination of elements without providing any substitute. It is a reorientation according to essential and responsible criteria.

E. After the Council of Trent: Uniformity Replaces Unity in Variety

The desolate situation of the liturgy at the end of the Middle Ages, on the eve of the Council of Trent (1545–1563), was caused essentially by the misperception of its true character. A multiplicity of wild liturgical growths and one-sided and often misused elements from popular piety concealed, to a great degree, the fundamentals of the liturgy. The ivy had covered up the walls, and the walls in turn were not very stable. This was only one of the many defects in the Church as a whole: the great schisms, antipopes, defective or inadequate education of the clergy, buying and selling of offices, and the overall neglect of morals, often because of wars, political special interests, social disruptions, etc. The call for "reform of head and members" was general and unmistakable. But no pope or bishop alone, however pious and devoted to the Church he might have been, could have avoided the disaster. In the foreground stood, first of all, the wounds of the Church as a whole; liturgical reform therefore became only an occasional topic of discussion at the Council of Trent, when it was (negatively) a question of abolishing obvious excesses, but also (positively) of concern for missals and vernacular explanations of the Mass, especially as regards singing and hymnody.

In many places there existed a certain theological uncertainty. The attacks of the reformers on the ecclesial and scholastic edifice of teaching were often occasioned by the celebration of the liturgy and the way the sacraments were administered. Here we cannot address the question of the extent to which Luther's concern was, in fact, justified: namely, that the saving significance of the unique, redeeming sacrifice of Christ on the cross had been relativized and concealed by the Church's many Masses, that God's word in scripture were not being preached, and that it was "chained up," that popular "works righteousness" had banished faith, that ritual was more an obstacle to spiritual life than an encouragement, that the assertion of clerics and those in office that they constituted a special class repressed the community's legitimate sense of itself as the priestly people of God.

These questions would far outstrip the bounds of our topic. Calvin's and Zwingli's denial of the real presence of Christ in the Eucharist and their evaluation of offices and sacraments were ultimately frontal attacks on the traditional style of liturgical celebration as such. The Council of Trent (1545–1563), assembled with great difficulty and then repeatedly interrupted, saw its first and principal task as the theological clarification of the controversies of the Reformation, although, of course, always with a view to the practical requirements of the Church. The suggestion of Bishop Tommaso Campeggio (who, in Hubert Jedin's judgment, was a representative of the conservative and curial tendency) that a unified missal be prescribed for the whole Church did not succeed at first, especially because of the concern of many participants in the Council for the rights of individual bishops. But as time went on it was more and more obvious that the Council, in light of the existing status of theological discussion, including liturgical thinking, was simply not in a position to introduce and carry through a fundamental reform of the liturgy.

Councils, too, are the children of their own times. Thus for the time being they could only concentrate on eliminating what was negative and destructive. Hence at their last session, in 1563, the Council fathers, apparently already restless because the synod had by this time lasted eighteen years, handed over to Pope Pius IV (1559–1565), with significant consequences for the future, the right to appoint commissions for the redaction of liturgical books. The appointment was quickly made and was confirmed by Pius V (1566–1572). The outstanding member, and quickly the leader of the congregation for reform, was Cardinal Guglielmo Sirleto (1514–1585), a highly qualified and learned man, a friend of St. Charles Borromeo of Milan, the nephew of Pius IV and a strong advocate of reform.

The reforming commission worked rapidly and thoroughly. By 1568, under Pius V, it produced the renewed Roman breviary, and the *Missale Romanum* followed in 1570. In 1588, under Sixtus V (1585–1590), the commission was established as the highest Roman authority, the "Congregation of Rites," responsible for all liturgical matters. In 1596, the *Pontificale Romanum* appeared, covering all the bishops' sacramental actions, and finally, in 1614—happily as a "model"—the *Rituale Romanum* for the use of priests in pastoral work.

It is significant that all these agendas contained the emphatic addition of *Romanum*. The rites were purified as much as possible—for that time—but that meant that they were also sharply centralized in being unified, and their wording was strictly prescribed. It is true that all liturgical diocesan customs were permitted to survive if they had existed for more than 200 years in the local books for the celebration of Mass and the liturgy of the hours. But not all the dioceses and orders in which these conditions were fulfilled made use of their rights. Quite obviously, at that time people were in general completely satisfied with the temporary success and happy to be relieved at last of the most tiresome of their liturgical miseries.

The *Missale Romanum* of Pope Pius V of 1570 was, in the first instance, a purified missal: that is, the worst misuses were eliminated, a greater simplicity and stylistic discipline of the liturgical texts was achieved, the unity of the Latin rite was restored, the rubrics (from the old ceremonial books) were clear and unmistakable, even though they were also too decidedly juridical, frequently improper, and, from the point of view of liturgical history, sometimes very problematical. However, it appears that the missal achieved, liturgically, all that could be attained at that moment. We should not, at the present time, be too one-sided in judging the centralism that ruled at that period, even though it by no means corresponded to the relative independence of the bishops of the ancient Church in relation to the Petrine office, or to the manifold nature of liturgical usage; in the 16th century it was a historical necessity.

A papacy now renewed and purified of the defects of the Renaissance period was certainly—purely from the point of view of ecclesiastical politics—an advantage in the era of national states with their state-church ambitions, as well as in an era of episcopal special interests that scarcely gave heed to the good of the Church as a whole. French Gallicanism is sufficient evidence of that. A weak papacy could, and can, at no time be a source of assistance to local Churches under pressure. The criteria according to which this central power must and should be exercised is a question not to be aired here.

The positive guideline of the reform commission was a return to what was older, to liturgical praxis *before* the period of the medieval proliferations, and so in practice to the time of Gregory VII in the late 11th century. The usage of "the good old days" in the city of Rome apparently seemed at that time to be the ideal. That it really was necessary to go farther back; that it is not any one point in the history of the Mass or a fixed time within its development that can be the criterion of reform with respect to the whole history, but only Christ's intention—all this was outside the horizon of thinking of the theologians of the time, which was fixated on theological controversy with the reforming adversaries of what was, after all, the usage of a recent times. Theologians, too, are children of their own times. It is only distance from bitter conflict that frees one's perspective for the broader scope of truth and justice.

The principal characteristic of the liturgical reform was therefore the mere reduction of the most annoying and chaotic excesses. First and primarily, a multitude of improper votive Masses was eliminated, as well as sequences and other hymnic elements that were too subjective; next to go were numerous prefaces that did not match the older style. In particular, the calendar of the saints, which extended throughout the year and occupied every day with a feast, was rigorously reduced. Klauser has established that, just in the period between 1200 and the Council of Trent, about 200 saints' feasts had been introduced into the liturgical calendar. Now at least half the year was left free from feasts, especially the period in March and April during the forty days of Lent. In the first place, the memorials of those saints who were already venerated in Rome during the first millennium were maintained. The local Roman culture appeared especially evident, also, in the inclusion of the listing of the churches for the Roman station Masses, which were of little value for the Church as a whole, even though they occasionally offered a basis or contributed illustrative hints about the selection of texts for the various formularies.

We would say today that what was not achieved by the missal of 1570 was the long overdue restructuring of the whole service of the Mass according to the needs of a gathering of the whole people of God for worship. The "private Mass" still remained the ideal, as indicated by the *Ritus servandus in celebratione Missae* placed at the beginning of the missal. The celebrating priest and his actions at the altar, where, practically speaking, the entire Mass including the service of the word was concentrated, was the sole object of primary interest. The community aspect of the action remained very minor. The offertory procession was not revived; all that remained was the gifts placed in the "collection plate." The acclamations continued to be made by a server, or in the best case the church choir, which in turn was responsible for making the solemn form of the Mass to a great degree more of an object of aesthetic and musical enjoyment than a shared celebration.

Thus the people's participation remained more pious than liturgical, as was quite obvious from the practice of singing hymns during Mass, meditations for Mass, or the recitation of the Rosary during the service. The old petitions at the conclusion of the service of the word were not revived, even though in some sense the frequent use of the "general prayer" of St. Peter Canisius replaced them. Variable petitions would, even then, have been a welcome relief for the canon, and could have given a liturgical stamp to private petitionary prayers, as well as indicating their place and value. Probably the accumulation of priestly prayers can be traced to this situation: as many as seven collects, silent prayers, and post-communions sometimes appeared.

The structural elements of the Mass, too, have their own individual character, but their contours remained blurred; for example, the introductory rite passed into the liturgy of the word without a break when the priest, after the collect of the day, immediately began the reading at the same part of the altar. The beginning of the celebration retained a group of heterogeneous remnants from older, more extensive liturgical actions and simply lumped them together: private prayers of preparation, processional song, remnant of the litany, and gloria—all these went first, and only then was there a greeting, *Dominus vobiscum.* Having the readings in a foreign language prevented any genuine proclamation, even though we should consider that, at least at this period, Latin appeared to be one of the supports sustaining the unity of the Church. However, when recited in Latin the scriptural reading was simply part of the ritual, and not a proclamation. It is true that preaching increased at times, but too often without any contact with sacred scripture. In particular, eucharistic piety remained static adoration, by no means participatory, especially since frequent Communion was rare, and very often it was unfortunately displaced outside the Mass itself, so that most people communicated before, or after, or totally apart from the Mass. The meaning of Communion as an integrating part of the Mass was, under these circumstances, obscured.

Characteristic of the baroque Mass, at least in its higher forms, was the emphasis on solemnity and elaborate presentation, a very deliberate expression in contrast to the reformers' rejection of the Mass as sacrifice. The Roman foundation churches of the Jesuits, the 16th-century Il Gesù and St. Ignazio, indicated the program for the future. Grandiosely fashioned altars with the tabernacle in the center filled the headwall of festive interior spaces conceived like imposing throne rooms. The medieval screens dividing the space were removed from almost all Catholic churches, so that a view of the high altar and tabernacle was made possible.

In the sanctuary, consciously or unconsciously modeled on the proscenium of an ancient theater, a kind of sacred drama could unfold, performed by the clerics in their rich, ornate brocades—over-stylized, in fact, and scarcely resembling garments at all. A multitude of candles, incense, and shining gold enhanced the celebration, which proceeded according to a strongly rubricized ceremonial order and was able to compete with any secular courtly and absolutist monarchical pomp. All the art forms—architecture, sculpture, painting, crafts, and music—vied with one another in shaping the magnificent display of this liturgy. Yet at the same time we must note that an over-objectifying of the events in the sanctuary again hindered active contact; the placement of the seating in the church, usually permanent, directed the view from every direction toward the altar, but it did not involve those attending in the sense of the liturgy; instead, it restricted their participation—especially in the normal cases of lesser solemnity and the limited possibilities of small parish churches—to subjective adoration and piety, which then almost necessarily led to greater activity than was possible at Mass, taking the form of processions and pilgrimages. Certainly it would be unjust to dismiss all these forms as nothing but "triumphalism."

There was a genuine effort to give them subjective content by means of devotional practice, especially the veneration of the hearts of Jesus and Mary. Yet all these forms of devotion lacked any genuine and deliberate reference to the "source and origin, center and summit" of Christian life, the living eucharistic celebration. That kind of centering was not part of the theological consciousness of the baroque period. It continued its own course undisturbed, and apparently at this period that was felt to be what was liturgically appropriate.

One alteration of great consequence in what had been achieved by the missal of Pius V, namely the reduction of some elements, was soon evident in the new growth in the number of saints' feasts. We may certainly see in this a sign of Catholic self-awareness. In this way, the Catholic Church manifested itself as the church of the proven saints. Between 1570 and 1914 (when the calendar reform of Pius X took place), 117 new feasts were introduced, most of them as higher (or so-called duplex) feasts, which soon heavily encrusted the year of the Lord. The feasts of doctors of the Church, the representatives of pure doctrine, increased especially fast. While in the middle of the 16th century there had been only four, by 1959 one could count thirty.

The excessive emphasis on liturgical law was of particular importance. From the 17th to the 20th century, legal formalism and liturgical casuistry increasingly dominated liturgical life and were especially favored by privately and officially published decrees and responses of the Congregation of Rites and the wild proliferation of commentaries on the rubrics. Theodor Klauser is not unjust when he calls the three centuries between the establishment of the Congregation of Rites and the pontificate of Pius X the era of "rigid unification."[5] Thus resulted the phenomenon (very strange from a theological perspective) that even in the normative liturgical handbooks of the early 20th century (J. J. Navatel, Phil. Oppenheim, and many others) nothing was called "liturgical" unless it was decreed in the official books. The fact of being decreed made an action liturgical. What had previously been achieved was set in concrete; all development took place only within the framework of what was juridically prescribed and given. Necessary reforms did not take place, or else fizzled immediately.

F. The Modern Liturgical Renewal

In the 20th century the nature of the liturgy—as the celebration of the Church and the Church's faith—has again received deeper theological recognition: The powerful, saving celebration, in community, of the New

Testament people of God, gathered in the name of Jesus and organized hierarchically, which together, but acting according to different, unique and noninterchangeable "roles," consciously and devotedly celebrates these mysteries. The breakthrough, prepared by the long-misunderstood liturgical movement, took place with worldwide impact after Vatican Council II, which carried forward the reform that was already called for even before the Council of Trent, but for which the time was not then ripe. This continuity should be clearly recognized: The most recent liturgical reform is not something purely new; it has existed within the tradition of the Church from the beginning. This is precisely what Pope Paul VI emphasized in the fifteen paragraphs of his promulgation of the *General Instruction* of the missal, thereby rejecting the complaints of extreme traditionalists. The present missal is the "witness to unaltered faith," does not break with tradition, and—in full fidelity to the nature of the liturgy and liturgical tradition—represents a necessary adaptation to the changed situation in which the Church lives and works in today's world.

Simplifying somewhat, we may say that the reform of the Council of Trent proceeded from above to below, and that of Vatican Council II from below to above: after Trent, new, purified texts and books were prescribed, and compliance with them at the grass roots was strictly and judicially regulated and even compelled, although increasingly the means—namely order—became the end, and finally throttled all spontaneity. The reform of Vatican Council II, in contrast, proceeded more strongly from life at the grass roots level, was primarily if not solely pastoral in its principles, at first had to struggle against all kinds of resistance and suspicion, but as a result was forced to ongoing self-criticism and new reflection on its own positions before, finally, it became official within the framework of a newly considered teaching of the Church.

While the first reform was naturally threatened by legalism, the second is just as naturally subject, at times, to an annoying proliferation and short-sighted caprice. The swing of the pendulum from one to the other is easy to understand in historical and psychological terms, but need not be applauded. The long-needed reform was stored up like water behind a dam that threatened to burst and sometimes made it difficult to hold the flow within channels. The means of repair can certainly not be a new legalism or rubricism, but only the well-considered balance of freedom and obligation, spontaneity and order, care and consideration for the given and irreplaceable structures of the liturgy. Only in this way can, on the one hand, the traditions from the times of the Fathers be maintained, and, on the other hand, justice be done to the needs of every age. The reform is by no means complete, and never will be: Only the preservation of the fundamental structures that are valid for all time within the constant changing of their socio-cultural expression fitting a particular age can keep our celebration of the liturgy alive and make it an adequate sacramental sign of salvation.

1. The Liturgical Movement

The present liturgical movement, for which the Council opened the gates, is not something created by decree, but has grown slowly over a long period of time. It may in some sense be understood as the increasing expression of dissatisfaction and desire for reform in face of the immobility of the posttridentine forms of worship. That many of the present changes appear relatively serious is very naturally explained by the backlog of need for small, necessary steps toward reform that had been accumulating for a long time.

The sources of the desire for reform that became more audible and cropped up in increasingly broad circles in the 20th century were manifold: historical, pastoral, and also and primarily, theological.

Historical studies and textual editions gave access to a much greater wealth of liturgy than was previously known, both as regards the extent of the prayer resources and the greater vitality of liturgical action. This historical work began as early as the 17th century, with the Benedictines Jean Mabillon (1632–1707) and his student, Edmond Martène (1654–1739) in France, and with Gerbert of St. Blasien (1720–1793) in Germany, to mention only a few noteworthy names. In particular, the historical interest of Romanticism in the 19th century expanded knowledge of the history of the liturgy quite remarkably. These researches grew, and continue to grow today, to furnish a broader and broader flow of editions and studies.

The historical study of the liturgy could certainly have constituted a helpful corrective against rubricism much earlier, but unfortunately it was absorbed by another movement, the legitimist and restorationist trend of that same Romanticism, and in the second half of the 19th century it was virtually paralyzed. Fortunately, in spite of this, some scholarly work went on, so that the rich treasures of the great tradition of worship in the Latin Church were brought to light and made more broadly known. The work of these liturgical historians can scarcely be given enough credit: The liturgical movement of the years to come was sometimes over-enthusiastic and given to fantasy, but they had laid a solid foundation and established exact criteria for a healthy development. One may say without exaggeration that none of the promoters of Vatican Council II's Constitution on the Liturgy could have acted in any effective way without knowing the monumental work of Josef Andreas Jungmann, S.J. (1889–1975), the *Missarum Sollemnia*.

Especially important for the performance, and not merely the study of the liturgy, was the revival of Gregorian chant for the Mass and the liturgy of the hours, emanating in the 19th century from the abbey of Solesmes in the Department of Sarthe in central France. The great energy behind this was Prosper Guéranger, abbot of Solesmes (1837–1875), who encouraged not only music but liturgical spirituality: The liturgy and the liturgical year became the expression of the life of all the monastic communities he founded, and these soon extended throughout western Europe.

Important for Germany was Beuron, refounded in 1863 by Brothers Maurus and Placidus Wolter, who were inspired by Solesmes; they were soon supported by the monastery of Maria Laach in the Eifel and its later abbot, Ildefons Herwegen (1874–1946; abbot from 1913). The abbeys of the Beuron congregation were gathering places for those interested in liturgy, especially intellectuals, but they also shed their rays on pastoral work in parishes, both through their liturgical work and, more especially, through their missals for the people (e. g., the missal of Anselm von Schott from Maria Laach issued in 1883, and in its 67th edition in 1964). In particular, the encouragement of the chant cultivated by Solesmes was taken up by Pius X in 1903: The *editio Vaticana* of the books of chant rested on preliminary work at the abbey of Solesmes. The use of chant, formerly practiced only by a monastic community or a schola within it, was a first step toward greater activity on the part of the congregation.

Pastoral efforts at reform in the field of liturgy originated, in part, in the period of the Enlightenment and at least as early as 1800. Recent investigations are now prepared to accord this period of Church history greater acknowledgment, especially because we now have sufficient distance from its obvious weaknesses and narrow attitudes. The present elevation of the office of bishop has shown itself to be a necessary and effective outlet, combating the particularist and episcopalistic tendencies of the period of the Enlightenment. The didactic tendency of the Enlightenment particularly encouraged frequency and improvement of preaching, even though its themes were often restricted to morality and good behavior; in addition, emphasis was laid on methodical catechesis in Church and school. Demands for use of the vernacular, especially in the liturgy of the word, were made even at that time, as a means to enable a conscious and "rational" participation in the celebration.

The Enlightenment, with good reason, opposed everything that was overloaded, one-sided and "unintelligible" in worship, a merely quantitative increase in Masses, an excessive emphasis on processions, pilgrimages, relics, and indulgences; instead, it encouraged parish worship designed for the people ("German high Mass," German vespers) and renewed rituals for the administration of the sacraments. It also gave attention to better education of the clergy through programs of study, pastoral conferences, and periodicals. Names like Johann Michael Sailer (1751–1832) and Ignaz Heinrich von Wessenberg (1774–1860) are representative of many others. These very fruitful initiatives were also misjudged by the restorationists of the 19th century, although more for reasons of Church politics than on pastoral grounds. To the people of that time, a tight centralism seemed the only barrier against revolution, democratization, and nationalism, which particularly threatened the secular power of the papacy. The general dominance of political considerations in the Church was stifling to the pastoral needs of the Church as a whole. Here, too, the distance of more than a century has balanced the issues more justly.

Pastoral liturgy enjoyed a new breakthrough as a result of the decree encouraging frequent communion from Pope Pius X (1903–1914). It also lowered the minimum age for reception of the Holy Eucharist. At the beginning its liturgical significance was not recognized, but this very decree was the starting point for the recovery of the complete form of the Mass as sacrifice and meal. In Pius X's *motu proprio* on church music *Tra le sollecitudini* (1903), we find for the first time the liberating words *participatio actuosa*, referring to the active participation of the faithful. They were taken up by the brilliant Benedictine Lambert Beauduin (1873–1960) in 1909 at the annual Catholic congress *(Katholikentag)* in Mecheln (referred to as the "Mecheln Event"), as he demanded that the people must have a part to play in the liturgy (*il faudrait démocratiser la liturgie*, "we must democratize the liturgy").

The breadth of impact was highly unusual, and we may with good reason speak of the year 1909 as the real beginning of the pastoral phase of the liturgical movement in the 20th century. This new program was willingly adopted by many Benedictine monasteries. The strongest energy behind the reforms came from charismatic individuals and pastors, many of them subject to misunderstanding and scorn as a result. The liturgical movement had its broadest impact in German-speaking countries after World War I. The tiny streams were flowing together, more and more, to form a mighty river.

In Austria it was especially Pius Parsch (1884–1954), canon of Klosterneuburg, who pressed forward with his liturgical ideas. As a military chaplain in Kiev, he had experienced the lifegiving power of the liturgy, especially in the Easter celebration of the Orthodox Church. After his return, he founded his little "liturgical community" in St. Gertrud, where he committed himself particularly to a "people's liturgy" (a tautology in itself, because "liturgy" is derived from the Greek word *laos*, meaning "people"), which envisioned the participation of the whole congregation. Parsch recognized anew that Bible and liturgy (also the title of a periodical he edited beginning in 1926) were the foundations of Christian life. In mystagogical catechesis, he revived the historically "developed" symbols and freed them of ritual encrustations by discovering their new *Sitz im Leben* (life-situation) in daily religious life. A clever organizer, he set up his own publishing house, the "Liturgical Apostolate," to produce millions of pamphlets and books that propagated his concerns everywhere in the German-speaking world.

At the same time, vital cells of the liturgical movement were growing everywhere, especially within the Catholic youth movement ("New Germany;" "Quickborn," with its citadel at Rothenfels on the Main and the pioneering work of Romano Guardini; the "Catholic Youth" under Ludwig Wolker, etc.) from which the younger clergy emerged, organized, and carried the work to the people of the Church. The Church emergency during the Nazi tyranny and World War II caused congregations to gather more reflectively around the altar, and demonstrated the rightness and necessity of reform. After 1940, the bishops themselves advocated it decisively and cleared away the more resistant polarizations. For developments outside Germany, the foundation of the Centre de Pastorale liturgique in Paris (1943) may be mentioned as representative of many others. Its activities quickly began to bear fruit.

In the field of dogma, the newly acknowledged teaching that the Church is the mystical body of Christ was an aid and clarification for the liturgical movement: Church is more than an organized society, more than a *societas perfecta;* that aspect is only the external sign of the "primal sacrament," the Church, which as *Christ Répandu* [= Christ poured out, or Christ universal] (Bossuet) represents both God's saving action in the world *and* the sacrifice of praise from all humanity to God. The Church is the enduring and continually active, incarnate Christ: "What was visible in Christ has passed into the mysteries of the Church" (Pope Leo I). This teaching about the mystical body of Christ gained the general attention of theologians and of the whole Church through Pope Pius XII's encyclical *Mystici Corporis* in 1943. The consequence was that the liturgy also achieved a new value in the life of the Church.

The encyclical *Mediator Dei* (1947) deliberately took up the liturgical reform of Pius X and clearly described the nature of the liturgy as the

Church's participation in the priesthood of Christ. In doing so it especially condemned a one-sided view of liturgy in terms merely of its "character as decreed": "Therefore they are far from the truth and from the right understanding of the Sacred Liturgy, who judge it to be merely the external part of divine worship, the part which is the object of the senses, or who think of it as a sort of decorative series of ceremonies. They are no nearer the truth, who consider it to be a mere summary of laws and precepts which the ecclesiastical hierarchy has appointed to be carried out in the sacred rites" (MD 35). Pope Pius XII, in this encyclical, expressly commends the "singular interest in liturgical studies . . . both from the work of private individuals and, more especially, from the zealous and diligent labor of certain monasteries of the great Benedictine order" since the turn of the century (MD 4).

The concerns of the liturgical movement were taken up increasingly in Rome. Mediator Dei became the Magna Carta of liturgical reform. A series of practical steps quickly followed: rituales with vernacular texts were approved, the psalms were newly translated from the original text, Holy Week and Easter were reformed, evening Masses were permitted, the laws of eucharistic fasting were revised in such a way that, as things now stood, they were no longer a hindrance to frequent reception of Communion.

In the instruction on church music, a greater participation of the congregation in worship was both made possible and encouraged. In 1956, at the Congress on Pastoral Liturgy in Assisi, Pius XII described the liturgical movement as a clear and perceptible "progression of the Holy Spirit through the Church." John XXIII, in a partial solution, simplified the rubrics in 1960, but ultimately, for better pastoral effect, left liturgical reform through biblical and patristic sources to the Council, from which he expected an aggiornamento of the Church, something that of course remains a goal, and has by no means been attained.

2. Vatican II and the Revised Missale Romanum of 1969

Vatican Council II brought the final breakthrough for liturgical reform. On December 3, 1963, the liturgical constitution Sacrosanctum Concilium, was voted as the first major document of this Church council. John XXIII had quite openly regarded the questions of liturgy as the complex of issues that would most fundamentally and paradigmatically evidence the dogmatic and pastoral goals of the Council. The success achieved confirmed that he was right: All the subsequent consultations and debates were, to a high degree, affected both theologically and pastorally by this constitution. Yet, on the other hand, we must realize that not everything could be expressed in this first constitution; other aspects had to be discussed, acknowledged, and written down later, in the course of production of the other constitutions and decrees. All those who are concerned with liturgy at the present time would do well always to keep in mind the full conciliar context of the Constitution on the Liturgy, especially the Constitution on the Church *(Lumen Gentium)* and the pastoral constitution *(Gaudium et spes)*.

In particular, the significance of the liturgy in the life of the Church appears most definitively in the Constitution on the Church: Liturgy is only *one* of the three basic functions (self-realizations) of the Church. It is united with proclamation *(kerygma)* and service to the world *(diakonia* or *caritas)*, even though the liturgy "is the summit toward which the activity of the Church is directed [and] at the same time . . . the fountain from which all her power flows" *(SC* 9, 10).

These *three* kinds of activity of the Church in the world are therefore always to be seen in the closest contact with each other if we are to keep the whole in view and not merely individual aspects. Therefore it is necessary to insert the liturgy fully into the mystery of the Church: The liturgy is the event that constitutes and expresses the Church in its sacramental—that is, salvific—dimension. Certainly, this is emphasized in the entire first chapter of the Constitution on the Liturgy: God's universal saving will (1 Tim 2:4) was shown to our ancestors (Heb 1:1), but fully revealed in Christ as the mediator between God and human beings (1 Tim 2:5); for "his humanity, united with the person of the Word, was the instrument of our salvation" *(SC* 5). This mission of Christ is extended, according to God's will, in preaching *(SC* 6) and in "exercise of the priestly office of Jesus Christ . . . by signs perceptible to the senses. . . . From this it follows that every liturgical celebration, because it is an action of Christ the priest *and* of his body the Church, is a sacred action surpassing all others. No other action of the Church can match its claim to efficacy, nor equal the degree of it" *(SC* 7; emphasis supplied).

This description of the liturgy as a saving action of the Father through Christ (to which should be added: in the Holy Spirit) *and* of the faith of the people of God through Christ (in the same Holy Spirit) liberates it from the narrow views and defective ideas of the past. It ties the liturgy—not merely through some corrections of ritual—back to the New Testament and apostolic sources and foundations. Consequently, within pastoral practice liturgy is not merely a preference on the part of some people, but is the essential characteristic of the Church in the mutual love and common action of God with humanity within the community of the Church. God and the people of God constituted by the Church are the partners in a dialogue, the "new covenant in the blood of Christ." The "churchliness" of the sacraments, their "ecclesial dimension," their strict inclusion within the mystery of the Church, but also that of the faithful in the Church as primal sacrament: all this is now presented anew to theological awareness.

From this perspective, the pastoral dimension also gains a new importance; indeed, it was the fundamental concern of the Council overall to bring the "Church for the people" into focus once again. Hence the second, "anthropological dimension" of the liturgy achieved basic significance. The powerful saving action of the Church in the name of Christ, available to experience in transparent signs and in the proclamatory word effective in and for the present, is directed toward human beings: They should be enabled, in faith, to express themselves also in liturgical action, and to recognize the liturgy as their own. Both of these, the sign and the pre-understanding, sacrament and faith, should be vitalized by the liturgy.

This concludes the complex of reflections in this first part of the book. We return to what was already presented at the beginning, in the Introduction, as the sound teaching of the Church in the form of a commentary on the first article on the *General Instruction of the Roman Missal.* These statements, which the Pope—refuting some excessively conservative opponents of reform—describes as in accordance with Jesus' institution, in harmony with the tradition of the Church, and responsible and appropriate to the pastoral demands of the present, must always be the starting point for the theology, form, and exercise of the Mass. It is therefore a matter of making sure that the hierarchically organized people of God participates actively, consciously, fully, fruitfully, and devoutly in a liturgy in which the Father, through the Son, in the Holy Spirit effects (dialogically) the salvation of human beings and the Church—in faith, hope, and love—in the Holy Spirit, through, with, and in Christ offers to the Father the sacrifice of praise and complete self-surrender.

The following second part of this book should now encourage its readers to make that kind of participation practicable, in accordance with the directions of the new missal. The presentation that follows is concerned to maintain the tension between order and freedom: an *order* that signifies, on the one hand, the vertical-temporal dimension of the tradition and, on the other hand, the horizontal dimension of mutuality "of the Church throughout the world" (Canon II)—that is, the fundamental identity between yesterday, today, and tomorrow and of here-and-elsewhere. Only in the field of tension between order and freedom can the Church's worship be celebrated as a living worship, true to the liturgy and to the community.

The missal itself shows what is meant by this. It offers a space for adaptation that promotes celebration "in a particular place" and "in community." It will be the special task of the priestly presider to adapt the celebration of the liturgy of the Mass—within the framework of the obligatory regulations—to each particular situation in such a way that in this liturgy, on the one hand, community and Church can be experienced, and on the other hand individuals will feel and know themselves to be addressed by the celebration and mutually responsible for it. Because the symbols prescribed for the liturgy are almost all "developed symbols," so that their meaning, and the way they are meant to be presented, are more easily explained from the tradition, this book accords considerable space to history as the proper background for understanding. In this way, the participants in the celebration are not only told *that* they should behave in such and such a way, but also *why* many preceding generations have done the same.

Notes

[1] The translation is taken from R.C.D. Jasper and G. J. Cuming, *Prayers of the Eucharist: Early and Reformed*, but adapted to reflect the author's emphasis on the structuring of the prayer as a series of relative clauses.

[2] Translator's note: the German term *Volkskirche* (literally "church of the people") has no simple English equivalent; it is significant that dictionaries studiously avoid trying to define it. According to usage, it may mean something like "established church" or "national church," and in modern times often denotes a church in which believers may be registered for taxation purposes, whether they are active members or not. It is difficult to convey the idea in America, since here church membership tends to be more than nominal, and there is no established church or church tax. The author's thinking here, however, focuses on the distinction between a "universal" church, that is, an all–inclusive church for the entire population, and a sectarian or "pure" church for an elite group.

[3] Quotations of Klauser's work are taken from: Theodor Klauser, *A Short History of the Western Liturgy. An Account and Some Reflections*. Translated from the German by John Halliburton (London: Oxford University Press, 1969), here at p. 77.

[4] Title of chapter 3, 94–116.

[5] In the title of chapter 4, 117–52.

Part Two

THE CELEBRATION
OF THE MASS
IN ITS CURRENT FORM

At least since the middle of the second century, according to the report of Justin Martyr, but probably even in late apostolic times, the Mass of the Christian community has had two principal parts: the liturgy of the word and the liturgy of the Eucharist. The outer framework of various introductory rites and a somewhat briefer conclusion are partly newer, but both functionally and psychologically they are necessary elements of the Mass: "The Mass is made up as it were of the liturgy of the word and the liturgy of the Eucharist, the two parts are so closely connected that they form but one single act of worship. For in the Mass the table of God's word and of Christ's body is laid for the people of God to receive from it instruction and food. There are also certain rites to open and conclude the celebration" (*GI* 8).

The result is the present basic framework, handed down for centuries, which shapes the celebration of the parish Eucharist:

   I. Introduction
   II. Liturgy of the Word
   III. Liturgy of the Eucharist
   IV. Dismissal

Of these, II and III are the principal parts, I and IV the frame.

The most recent reform of the rites for the Mass has made the structure of the celebration clearer and easier to recognize by placing obvious breaks between the individual parts. The liturgy of the word and of the Eucharist each have their own location and focus, at the ambo and the altar respectively. The introduction of the ambo in particular is extremely important in this: while previously the liturgy of the word was performed at the altar itself, it has now, by the establishment of a fixed place for proclamation, recovered its own importance. In the past, the transition from the opening rites to the liturgy of the word was scarcely perceptible because after the collect—the end of the introductory rite—the celebrant began the liturgy of the word in the same place, reading from the same book, in the same posture with his back turned to the congregation. Now the situation is much clearer: The presider and people are seated in their respective places, the presider's chair and the pews; the lector goes to the ambo and reads the first reading, so that priest and people are gathered together in obedience to the word of God. The caesura between liturgy of the word and Eucharist is equally visible because of the change of place from ambo to altar. This clearer structuring of the Mass is very beneficial to a meaningful celebration.

On the other hand, the connection between the liturgy of the word and the Eucharist is clearly evident from the close association of ambo and altar within the same sanctuary—much more so than in previous arrangements whereby the pulpit was far distant from the altar. The difference and connection between the two parts of the worship service are clearly evident. The context that encloses both individual parts is impressively emphasized, in many places, by the architectural and decorative shaping of a functionally correct worship space.

First of all, in order to give a general overview of the course of the Mass celebration, as well as the meaning and function of the individual parts, we will present the wording of the individual relevant articles of the *General Instruction of the Roman Missal* for the missal as an adequate explanation:

> I. The parts preceding the liturgy of the word, namely, the entrance song, greeting, penitential rite, *Kyrie, Gloria,* and opening prayer or collect, have the character of beginning, introduction, and preparation.
>
> The purpose of these rites is that the faithful coming together take on the form of a community and prepare themselves to listen to God's word and celebrate the eucharist properly (*GI* 24).
>
> II. Readings from Scripture and the chants between the readings form the main part of the liturgy of the word. The homily, profession of faith, and general intercessions or prayer of the faithful expand and complete this part of the Mass. In the readings, explained by the homily, God is speaking to his people, opening up to them the mystery of redemption and salvation, and nourishes their spirit; Christ is present to the faithful through his word. Through the chants the people make God's word their own and through the profession of faith affirm their adherence to it. Finally, having been fed by this word, they make their petitions in the general intercessions for the needs of the Church and for the salvation of the whole world (*GI* 33).
>
> III. At the last supper Christ instituted the sacrifice and paschal meal that make the sacrifice of the cross to be continuously present in the Church, when the priest, representing Christ the Lord, carries out what the Lord did and handed over to his disciples to do in his memory.

Christ took the bread and the cup and gave thanks; he broke the bread and gave to his disciples, saying, "Take and eat, this my body." Giving the cup, he said: "Take and drink, this is the cup of my blood. Do this in memory of me." Accordingly, the Church has planned the celebration of the eucharistic liturgy around the parts corresponding to these words and actions of Christ:

1. In the preparation of the gifts, the bread and the wine with water are brought to the altar, that is, the same elements that Christ used.

2. In the eucharistic prayer thanks is given to God for the whole work of salvation and the gifts of bread and wine become the body and blood of Christ.

3. Through the breaking of the one bread the unity of the faithful is expressed and through communion they receive the Lord's body and blood in the same way the apostles received them from Christ's own hands (*GI* 48).

IV. The concluding rite consists of:

a. the priest's greeting and blessing, which on certain days and occasions is expanded and expressed in the prayer over the people or other solemn formulary;

b. the dismissal of the assembly, which sends each member back to do good works, while praising and blessing the Lord (*GI* 57).

It is obvious that this *General Instruction* is meant to be more than the old "rubrics" of the previous missal: it is in itself a theologically and historically well founded explanation of the Mass aimed at praxis. Of course, there is the disadvantage of duplication and a good deal of overlapping, since chapter 2 ("Structure, Elements, and Parts of the Mass"), in articles 24–47, gives a general overview of the Mass, but chapter 4 ("Different Forms of Celebration"), in articles 82–126, again offers a description of the "common form" of a "Mass with a congregation." Finally, there are also brief directions for the rites (the *Ordo Missae*) in the missal itself. These are printed in red as "rubrics" (cited as "Rubr."), and represent a short extract of the other two descriptions of the ritual. In the following chapters I will take these last as the basis for my explanation, but will continually refer to the corresponding passages in the *General Instruction,* placing the number of each article in parentheses.

Chapter One

The Celebration Begins

The introductory rites belong to the newer, additional elements of the Mass. From the point of view of their origin their present form largely represents a set of reductions and relics of originally more extensive actions: processions, litanies, preparatory prayers and acts of contrition, hymns, and special forms of greeting. In the various editions of the missal between 1570 and 1962, this accumulation and fragmentariness was still more obvious, especially because the greeting *Dominus vobiscum* was only given after the *Gloria*. As a result of the reform, the accumulation of elements of various types has not been completely eliminated, but the structure as a whole is more logical and more easily executed, especially if one makes a proper use of the variety of choices that is offered.

One might well deduce from the report of Justin Martyr (First Apology 67) or the pre-1955 liturgy for Good Friday that the Roman Mass originally began with the readings. Still, according to the directions in the Didache (14:1), penitential rites—at least on certain days—as well as forms of greeting or setting the tone must always have seemed opportune as well as functionally necessary. From the point of view of the psychology of prayer, some kind of preparation is simply a matter of course: As is the beginning, in its spiritual and physical attitudes, so will the whole usually be! The ancient Church liked to place an atrium at the front of the basilicas, which made possible a preparation of the whole person before entering the church. There, one could lay aside the hectic mood and the noise of the everyday world and collect one's thoughts for encounter with God. The appropriate architectural forms were brought to bear for this purpose. This task now falls to the "introductory rites" in the Mass. It is striking that the General Instruction also chooses this designation instead of the old phrase, "entrance rites," because the *introit* was and is only part of the whole. At present, the focus is on constituting a worshiping community and enabling it to listen and celebrate properly (*GI* 24b).

1. Entrance and Opening Song

The "assembly," the "gathering of the community" mainly takes place haphazardly today: in an age when everyone has a watch it is easy for people to gather at a fixed time and on short notice. This was not so in the past: a good deal of time might pass before all were present. The recitation of psalms, the office of Terce before the episcopal Mass in the medieval cathedral, the Rosary before high Mass on Sunday, and so on—all these were often exercises that passed the time and put the participants in the right frame of mind. To prevent disturbance, each went quietly to his or her place. This silent entrance into the church is still the rule today. But it would not be a bad thing for the members of the community to greet one another in an appropriate way. The congregation could also develop particular ministries, such as aiding disabled persons and helping them to their places. Other types of contacts would be possible, and all these would serve to remove or alleviate anonymity.

As a rule, the priest walks from the sacristy to the altar with those who perform a special ministry: lector, cantor, altar servers or acolytes. The servers may carry the cross, candles and thurifer, the lector or deacon the gospel book (cf. Rubr.).

The route from sacristy to sanctuary can be the shortest one possible, but, depending on the arrangement of the church or the solemnity of the day, a longer route can be chosen, and the procession can then move down the length of the church through the center aisle. In the ancient church, the sacristies or similar service areas were usually placed at the entrance to the church; in the Middle Ages they were shifted to a location near the sanctuary in the apse. This occurred first in the cathedrals and monastic churches, so that those obligated to choral prayer could more easily don their liturgical robes and travel only a short distance to the "choir" (which, from that time, became the true and, in fact, after that the only accurate designation for the space around the altar). The parish churches followed soon after. This led to a decline in the original procession, which had been the rule especially in episcopal and papal Masses of antiquity. We cannot fail to observe that this kind of entrance can have great value in setting the tone. For that reason, it is rightly being revived today in many places.

The objects carried in the procession, and the cross, are set down in the sanctuary: the candles on the altar or beside it, or on a table at the side; the gospel book on the altar; the processional cross ideally in a stand on the floor or in some similar arrangement behind the altar, on the central axis of the church, so that it stands before the community during the celebration, unless the priest's chair is located there. In that case, a placement at the side is preferable. If there is already a fixed, standing, or hanging cross in the sanctuary of the church, or a painting or mosaic of the cross on the wall behind the altar, it should not be duplicated by the processional cross. There is no prescription requiring use of a cross with corpus; that form occurs only since the Middle Ages. There is a much longer tradition of the *crux gemmata,* with precious stones or enamel medallions, and from the point of view of symbolism it better unites the cross and resurrection.

"After the people have assembled, the entrance song begins as the priest and the ministers come in" (Rubr.; cf. *GI* 25 and 83). This song has a number of purposes. First, it marks the beginning (cf. *GI* 25). All types of didactic experience suggest the usefulness of beginning a celebration with congregational singing: It makes obvious that this is the beginning of something special; the participants, by the very necessity of breathing deeply when singing, are put in a spiritual and physical disposition for celebration; there is less distraction; and concentration on text and melody prepare for what is to come. The *General Instruction* declares that "Song is the sign of the heart's joy (see Acts 2:46). Thus St. Augustine says rightly: 'To sing belongs to lovers' [Sermon 336, 1]. There is also the ancient proverb: 'One who sings well prays twice'" (*GI* 19).

We should keep in mind that processional songs—including also those at the preparation of the gifts and the distribution of Communion—have a very practical purpose, one derived from experience: namely, they prevent any kind of restlessness by internalizing physical movement. Processional actions by their very nature can easily disturb devotion and cause restlessness, not only for children. Singing, as an organizing and harmonizing force, can diminish or prevent undesirable distraction better than a prayer, which can easily pass unnoticed. On the other hand, occasional elements of movement in the worship service are very helpful to prevent stagnation, which also is not only something that happens to children. We should recall that, after all, people "go" to a feast! In liturgical tradition, a prayer usually ends the procession. To that extent the entrance procession and collect are closely connected, whatever other introductory rites there may be.

Singing promotes a feeling of community, and in ritual it is, in itself, a communal action. In the singing, the actions of coming and being together acquire a new emotional dimension. The content and form of the song should correspond to the mystery of the liturgical season or day, and the degree of solemnity. Thematically, too, the songs are always in some way related to the celebration. When the *General Instruction* (§25) gives as the purpose of the entrance song "to open the celebration, intensify the unity of the gathered people, lead their thoughts to the mystery of the season or feast, and accompany the procession . . . ," it is hinting at a historical recollection. In the time of Constantine the primary purpose of the song was to give honor to the bishop who was entering, as was the practice with other high or consular officials. The entrance song was a part of the "monarchical ceremonial," and a sign of respect for the bishop. For good reason, this aspect was quickly suppressed in the Church in favor of more pastoral ideas. However, even today the anthem *Ecce sacerdos magnus* is designated for the bishop when he visits a church, or on other occasions, and the well-known cry *Evviva il papa*, when the pope enters the church derives from the same intention to give honor and greeting.

There are many possible types of entrance song; especially desirable is a responsorial anthem for schola (and/or cantor) and congregation. This form is preferable to all others because it best expresses the community of action by all those present. The traditional *introit* anthem was sung, from earliest times, in alternation between a choir, which usually sang the verses of a psalm, and the people, who repeated the responsorial antiphon after each verse or pair of verses. Thus, in a reductive form of the ancient custom, the old missal still structured the *introit* with antiphon, verse, *Gloria Patri,* and antiphon. The abbreviation of the psalm to a single verse as given there is explained by the disappearance of the earlier procession, which took more time.

The antiphon of the day chosen for the entrance is always a short, pithy, easily memorable and musically simple verse that can be entrusted to the congregation without a great deal of rehearsal. It is often taken from the psalm that is sung, or it may suggest the choice of the psalm from which it is taken. However, the opening verse could and can be drawn from other biblical writings. Occasionally it is a new combination, but it is preferable that it adhere to the idea of the feast. Earlier, as attested, *inter alia,* by the dating of documents, the beginning of the antiphon assigned to a given day often gave the Sunday or feast in question its name (cf. the Sundays in Lent: *Invocabo, Reminiscere, Oculi, Laetare,* etc.). The antiphons in the revised missal were chosen with great care. Especially when they are not sung and could easily be overlooked, they are well adapted to form the starting point or theme for a brief introduction, which might follow the exchange of greetings between priest and congregation.

In Germany strophic hymns frequently replace an alternating chant involving schola and congregation. These hymns are preferred because they are generally familiar and do not require much practice. Still, care should be taken that they are not universal hymns; they should be well adapted to the particular day. Often only a single verse of a hymn is appropriate.

A choral song, such as a motet or similar composition, should be the exception, because it leaves the congregation uninvolved, and the desired formation of community and commonality is less likely to be achieved, even though the power of the music itself should not be underestimated. Even so, the reception of something given is always less involving than personal activity. The same may be said of organ music, perhaps as a variation on a hymn that is appropriate to the beginning of a particular Mass. In that case, it would be a simple matter to sing a verse of that hymn after the organ prelude.

The so-called *Kyrieleis* hymns have a long tradition in German-speaking countries. If one of these is chosen as an entrance hymn, the *Kyrie* itself can be omitted, and the entrance rites will be more "streamlined."

The rubrics of the missal for the dioceses in German-speaking regions offer the alternative that the priest may approach the altar in silence. This can most often be recommended in small congregations on weekdays, but less for the community's Sunday service. A religiously motivated silence demands certain preconditions that are not always present in every congregation, and especially not at the very beginning of a worship service.

2. Reverencing the Altar

When the priest and those accompanying him have reached the altar, they reverence it. The altar represents Christ; in greeting the altar, the one who presides over the community salutes the master of the house of God and of the community assembled there.

The *General Instruction*, §84, describes this rite of reverencing more precisely: the sign of veneration is a low bow or genuflection, if the Eucharist is reserved in a tabernacle on the altar; the priest kisses the altar and sometimes incenses it.

The low bow, unlike a simple bow of the head (cf. *GI* 234) is cultically older than genuflection, and has been preferred in the east from ancient times. It is noteworthy that, for example in the description of the Roman papal Mass (in *Ordo* I, ca. 700) the pope, on entering, greets the *sancta* (that is, the remains of the Eucharist from a preceding Mass, which are then later placed in the chalice before communion) with a low bow, whereas otherwise genuflections are made to the pope himself: these, in turn, stem from court ceremonial. Thus in its origins, a low bow is no less respectful than bending the knee, although nowadays we frequently understand it differently. Consequently, genuflection is accorded only to the eucharistic elements; it has come to be viewed as the more profound sign of respect. If the tabernacle is on the altar (which, according to *GI 276*, should be the exception) or near it, a genuflection is called for. This may also be the case if the procession passes by the sacrament (*GI 233*).

After the bow or genuflection, the priest (and concelebrants, if any) approaches the altar and kisses it (*GI 85*), spreading his arms slightly and placing them on the altar, bowing and touching the top of the altar with his lips. The kiss, like the bow or genuflection, is for the altar and, in the altar, Christ himself. In itself, a kiss is an impressive physical gesture, the symbol of a unity desired or obtained, and is almost always combined with an embrace. This form of kiss has the most ancient tradition behind it. It is still common today in the Orient, for friends and especially for guests, and very frequent in countries of Romance heritage as the so-called "accolade," also familiar to us as an ostentatious sign of friendship among socialist politicians and functionaries. This gesture of embracing and kissing is frequently accompanied by words and expressions of peaceful intent: *salaam, shalom, pax tibi*. Even in pagan rituals, a kiss was given not only to persons, but also to sacred objects: idols, the threshold of the temple, the curtains of the entry, etc. Popular piety in many religions is familiar with it, even though it differs in frequency from time to time and from region to region.

However, the kiss probably entered our liturgy by way of court ceremonial. It was customary to kiss whatever was to be handed to the ruler; in turn, gifts were received from the ruler's hand with hands covered by a cloth. These devotional forms of the kiss were much more common in the previous missal than they are now: Thus, during the preparation of the gifts, the celebrant kissed the paten; in solemn Masses the deacon kissed the foot of the chalice and the cruets containing the wine and water; during the vesting in the sacristy, the vestments were kissed before they were donned. In order to make these gestures of respect transparent to their true meaning, a small cross was engraved on chalice and paten, and frequently was embroidered or appliquéd on the vestments (amice, stole, maniple, etc.). There were also more kisses given to the altar: before every *Dominus vobiscum*, during the canon, etc. The reduction in their frequency makes the kissing of the altar at the beginning of the celebration (and before leaving the altar, but then only by the principal celebrant: *GI 208*) more impressively significant and solemn.

As we have said, the kiss is for the altar as such and as symbol of Christ. Previously, it was interpreted as given also to the relics in the altar, the remains of the bodies of martyrs and confessors. That was suggested especially by the prayer spoken by the priest while ascending the altar steps, after the so-called "prayers at the foot of the altar": "We beseech thee, O Lord, by the merits of thy saints (kisses the altar) whose relics are here, and of all the saints, that thou wouldst vouchsafe to forgive me all my sins. Amen." This prayer has been eliminated from the present missal; moreover, the relics are no longer obligatory, except for the solemnly consecrated high altar (*GI* 266). Formerly, in altars that were not specially dedicated, they had always to be kept in the so-called altar stone beneath the altar cloth. The renewed liturgy no longer refers to the so-called sepulchre for relics in the altar. The interpretation of the kiss as belonging to the altar alone is therefore probable, and it is correct.

The incensing of the altar is optional: "the priest *may* also incense the altar" (*GI* 27, emphasis supplied). "*If* incense is used, he incenses the altar while circling it" (*GI* 85). However, incense can be used in *any* form of Mass (*GI* 235). Therefore it is also an option for a Mass celebrated in a small group, but it is not prescribed even for solemn celebrations. The priest places the incense in the thurifer and blesses it with the sign of the cross, but without any accompanying words (*GI* 236); it is sensible for this to be done in the sacristy, before entrance into the church and sanctuary.

After kissing the altar, the priest walks around it with the thurifer; according to the *General Instruction* it should be the exception rather than the norm for the altar to be attached to the wall, in which case it is impossible to walk around it. In such cases, the right side should be incensed, then the left. "If there is a cross on or beside the altar, he incenses it before he incenses the altar. If the cross is behind the altar, the priest incenses it when he passes in front of it" (*GI* 236). This emphasis on the incensing of the cross, which is a still more impressive and comprehensible symbol of Christ than the altar, again highlights the christological aspect of incensing the altar.

The incensing of the altar is subject to discretion: certainly not that of the principal celebrant alone, but also with reference to what is customary in a particular place and congregation. For a time it appeared that incense would disappear entirely from worship, but it seems to be enjoying a resurgence in popularity. I want to speak in favor of incense, for ecumenical reasons among others, because the eastern Church is extraordinarily fond of it and has been from ancient times. Certainly, it remains a matter of debate whether it was already mentioned by Ephraim the Syrian in the 17th

Nisibenian poem (ca. 363), or whether the reference is only symbolic; the same is true of Ambrose ("Commentary on Luke" I, 28). In the Roman west, incense was not used for a long time; it is possible that there was a lingering memory of the Decian persecution (ca. 250), when offering incense to the gods and emblems of the state represented apostasy from the faith. As a consequence, those who had apostasized were simply called *thurificati,* that is, "those who offered incense (thus, *thuris*)."

At any rate, from a literary standpoint such a memory was entirely possible. In the west, it appears that incense probably entered liturgical usage by way of court ceremonial. In antiquity, for very practical reasons, the nobility could have a servant precede them through the unlighted streets, carrying a torch that, if extinguished by wind or rain, could be rekindled from a swinging charcoal brazier carried by another servant. This custom was then stylized in the context of the court for use in closed spaces, even in throne rooms or consular offices. Candles replaced torches, and the thurifer took the place of the brazier. In this way, candle and thurifer became tokens of honor to which the aristocrats of society were entitled.

This makes it easy to explain why, according to the *Ordo Romanus* I (ca. 700), to which we have frequently alluded, the incense carried in the procession, and the seven candle-bearers accompanying the pope, were at first intended to honor the pope at his entrance, but that honor was quickly transferred to the altar and the book of the gospels, both of which represent Christ. In any case, incense only became customary in the west in post-Carolingian and early medieval times. Its use may have increased as a result of intensified contact with the east during the Crusades. According to early editions of the *Missale Romanum,* incense was prescribed for solemn celebrations, and was only permitted at such times.

From a religious-historical point of view, incense appears in paganism as an apotropaic means, that is, for keeping away spirits, especially at burials and exorcisms; it was also used for cleansing and purifying (of the chalice, for example, in the Ethiopian liturgy). In addition, it was a sensible sign of sacrifice, especially in the Old Testament: In Malachi 1:11, frequently taken as a prediction of the New Testament sacrifice, "incense" is mentioned together with the "pure offering" (cf. also Exod 30:34; Lev 2:1, where the food offering is associated with incense). Incense also, quite obviously, participates in the symbolism of the cloud: The glory of the Lord appears in the cloud (Exod 16:10, and frequently); the cloud is God's dwelling, God's *shekinah* (1 Kgs 8:10, and frequently). In paintings from the Ottonian period, the cloud, or a hand emerging from the cloud, is simply a symbol for God.

After reverencing the altar, the priest and those accompanying him go to their places (Rubr.; cf. *GI* 86). The priest's chair is something new in the furniture of the sanctuary, and is still not well understood, even though it is not simply an innovation: it really represents a return to the earliest Church practice. The chair for the celebrating priest is by no means derived from the so-called *sedilia,* which were formerly common: small chairs on which the priest and assistants took their places, for example during extended choral singing (e.g., of the *Gloria* and *Credo*) at solemn Masses. These *sedilia* were simply concessions to the weariness of liturgists, and a matter of thoughtfulness to them. The priestly chair, in contrast, is placed in sight of and facing the congregation, and is an expression of the hierarchical organization of the people of God: In the officiant, the Lord himself presides over the worship service (cf. *SC* 7). The chief celebrant is his representative. The official chair had been preserved only in episcopal Masses and cathedrals (which took their name from the *cathedra,* the bishop's chair). With the rise of private Masses, in which the liturgist always stood at the altar during the whole celebration, a special seat for the priest disappeared altogether.

Even the bishop's chair had changed its location over the centuries because of the rule of facing eastward during prayer (as described above). From the curve of the apse or the wall behind the altar, it shifted to the side of the sanctuary. Even in antiquity, and in the synagogue, it was the right of the teacher to sit on a special stool or chair. The head of the synagogue, on the "seat of Moses" (Matt 23:2), sat facing the congregation. This place represented a special dignity and showed that the one who occupied it was an ordained rabbi in Israel. Thus the stereotypical expression in rabbinic literature reads: "Rabbi NN sat down, opened his mouth and taught" (cf. Jesus' procedure at the beginning of the Sermon on the Mount: Matt 5:1-2).

Again today, the priest's chair is the normal place for the presider when the sacred liturgy is celebrated. The celebrant sits there when not exercising some function—for example, when a lector is reading at the ambo during the liturgy of the word. However, the priest can also exercise certain functions from the chair, as during the opening and closing rites. Thus the priest's chair fulfills, for the community liturgy, the same function as the episcopal chair at a pontifical celebration. It is therefore by no means simply a practical piece of furniture; it has a theologically based significance. The construction of the priest's chair should be practical and appropriate; it should not be showy, but neither should it be modestly placed in some inconspicuous spot, because the office it represents belongs to the community.

3. The Cross and Sign of the Cross

"After the entrance song, the priest and the whole assembly make the sign of the cross. Then through his greeting the priest declares to the assembled community that the Lord is present." The people answer: "Amen." (Rubr.; cf. *GI* 28. In *GI* 86 the "amen" is again explicitly said to be the response of the people.)

In the previous missal the sign of the cross already served as the beginning of the "prayers at the foot of the altar," and thus opened the celebration of the Mass. As a general introduction to prayer, the sign of the cross has its own ancient tradition as a crossing of oneself, a blessing of oneself before prayer. A sign of the cross correctly and reverently made, from the forehead (as the seat of understanding) to the breast (as the place of the heart and emotions), and from one shoulder to the other (as the roots of the arms and hands with which we work and act) is certainly an expressive and disclosive gesture of prayer, faith, and devotion.

This gesture also appears in the liturgy as a sanctifying crossing of other persons and objects, especially in connection with the administration of the sacraments and sacramentals. The formula of blessing is taken from the baptismal commandment in Matt 28:19b. Unfortunately, the connection between sign of the cross and baptism scarcely exists any more in the popular imagination; however, it should and can be revived. "Crossing" or "sealing" (Greek *sphragizein*) was for a long time in the ancient Church the word for "baptizing." Our sign of the cross derives from a mysticism of the cross, attested since the time of the Fathers of the Church, and theologically well founded: All salvation comes to us through the cross of Christ (John Chrysostom, *Hom. in Mt.* 54,4; Tertullian, *Adv. Marc.* 3, 22); from the wound in the side of the Lord dying on the cross (John 19:34) flow the sacraments of the Church.

4. Exchange of Greetings

From his chair—not from the ambo—the priest turns to the congregation and greets them with gesture and words, namely with extended arms and a formula of blessing. Both the expressive sign and the words that expand on it correspond, in general, with the way we are ordinarily accustomed to greet one another. In the liturgy, extending the arms (except for the very different *orans* gesture during the presider's prayers) can have two meanings: invitation, in which case the palms are turned slightly upward, or in reduced form as a collective embrace of greeting, when the palms are held more vertical and facing one another. The *Sitz im Leben* (setting in life) of both variants is readily discernible even today, especially if they are not done in a cramped, ritualistic manner, but in a human, friendly and natural way as a genuine expression of feeling. The sacramental structure of ecclesial actions (made up of sign and word, "matter and form") is also retained in this greeting: The gesture is determined and clearly named by the blessing. As in everyday life, so also in the liturgy, a greeting can become nothing but a dried-up convention. That can be prevented by a heartfelt tone and by using alternative formulae or expanding on those given. This is exactly what the missal anticipates; on the one hand, in explicating the theological meaning of the greeting through the accompanying words, and on the other hand by providing a number of different formulae of greeting.

A liturgical greeting is more than the expression of personal good will and comradely feeling: "This greeting and the people's response express the mystery of the gathered Church" (GI 28). Indeed, one purpose of these rites is "that the faithful coming together take on the form of a community" (GI 24). The German missal provides a total of eight formulae of greeting; most of them are taken from the conclusions of Pauline letters (2 Cor 13:13) or their beginnings (Rom 1:7; cf. the constant pairing of "grace and peace;" 1 Cor 1:3; 2 Cor 1:2; Gal 1:3; Eph 1:2, and others; cf. Rev 1:4). (The American missal has three.) Within the framework of these biblically influenced formulae, it is also possible to emphasize the festal character of the celebration, but unobtrusively.

Fundamentally, the formulae offered in the missal are only extensions of the old, familiar Dominus vobiscum ["The Lord be with you"] (or the episcopal Pax vobis ["Peace be with you"]), which also appears in the German missal as the first option. The wording of this brief greeting and extension of peace is biblical in its background (Luke 24:36; John 20:19, 21, and frequently). It is the Easter greeting of the Risen One to the disciples. Peace is more than freedom from war or strife; it is the essence of eschatological salvation, the expression of the reign of God itself (Rom 14:17), the fruit of the Spirit (Gal 5:22). Christ is identical with this peace: "For he is our peace" (Eph 2:14). Thus the episcopal and priestly greeting are ultimately the same in their intention and are differentiated only by old habit.

The congregation's response [in Germany] is "And with your spirit." From a purely philological point of view, this expression is simply a Semitic version of "and also with you." For that reason, translations frequently suggest this simpler form [and that is the form now in use in America]. However, such a translation is an impoverishment of the meaning of the greeting. Just as the presider's greeting is not simply about his personal good wishes and openness to communication, but is a proclamation of salvation in the name of Jesus Christ, so the congregation does not simply answer the priest in personal terms, but greets in the presider the office of those who are "servants of Christ and stewards of God's mysteries" (1 Cor 4:1). The exchange of greetings is designed to create human community, but that is only the precondition for a faith-filled declaration of "the mystery of the gathered Church" (GI 28). Therefore a recourse to secular forms of greeting is quite out of place. For ecumenical reasons as well, it is wise to retain the expanded greeting, with its happy effect of alienating those present from everyday banality: "The Lord be with you. And with your spirit."

In earlier times, this exchange of greetings, together with the kissing of the altar, was often regarded as the introduction to the priest's official prayers, before the collect or the concluding prayer, and comparable to the more extended call to prayer before the preface. That is wrong, but it remains true for Oremus ["Let us pray"]. More prominent and a better guide is the comparable structure of the greeting at the beginning and dismissal: In both cases, the exchange of greetings is coupled with a longer blessing, especially if the expanded forms of blessing are used to correspond to the expanded formulae of greeting. In both cases also, the words are combined with a communicative gesture and a reference to the Trinity. The fact that Paul formulated the beginnings and endings of his letters in similar fashion gives a foundation for the liturgical tradition.

5. Introduction to the Celebration

"He [the priest] or some other qualified minister may give the faithful a very brief introduction to the Mass of the day" (GI 86). In a certain sense, this introduction continues the entrance and greeting, to the extent that it is designed to promote the communal character of the celebration. It should always be spoken freely, be very short, and, if possible, should be mystagogical in nature. This introduction should not repeat the words of greeting; that would empty and debase the solemn liturgical opening of contact between presider and people. Still, there is always the possibility of a personal expansion of the official greeting, or of offering a special welcome to someone if this affects the whole community and is not simply done to honor some individual. This might happen especially if a sacrament (such as baptism or marriage) is to be administered as part of the celebration.

The one who gives the greeting is usually the one who presides at the Mass. It is a constitutive part of the presider's task. It remains an exception when, as the rubrics foresee, someone represents the presider in this matter. Nevertheless, it may occasionally be possible, given the character of the introduction, which is to be freely and briefly formulated as mystagogy—that is, introduction to the mysteries of salvation. One could also imagine that the pastor would extend the greeting when the bishop presides over the community's liturgical celebration (as at confirmation, the dedication of the church, etc.).

This introduction is not, as yet, a part of the liturgy of the word. Therefore it would be a mistake to speak of the biblical readings at this point, unless the order of the lectionary suggests a particular theme for the service. More appropriate to consider in the introduction, in most cases, is the introductory verse of the Mass, either because it has already been sung and there is a spiritual advantage to be had from expanding on it, or because it has been replaced by a hymn or something else, and would otherwise be easily overlooked. These verses, as we have already said, have been chosen with great care for the present missal, and experience shows that they are almost always suitable for a thoughtful commentary.

The introduction should be brief (Rubr.) At the present time there is widespread fear and criticism of an over-rationalizing and verbalizing of the liturgy. Therefore the introduction should by no means expand into an initial sermon. The better this introduction is prepared, the briefer and more succinct it can be. When the faithful are asked to sit down because of its length, this element of the introductory rite, so laudable in itself, has already failed in its real purpose. In addition, it should not be misused as an alibi for prohibited "lay preaching" at Mass.

6. General Penitential Rite and Act of Contrition

An act of contrition before Mass responds to the human condition—our condition—as sinners. The synagogue also had an occasional penitential liturgy before worship. The ancient Christian *Didache* (14:1) enjoins: "Confess your sins to one another."

In the earlier missal, a pentitential rite containing the so-called *Confiteor* was a fixed element at the beginning of every Mass. It was only in relatively recent times that this confession had been transferred from the sacristy to the steps of the altar ("prayers at the foot of the altar"). However, other penitential rites were also used, including the prostration on Good Friday, when the priest and ministers stretched themselves on the floor at the foot of the altar. This form of penitential action is also retained for that day in the present missal, and it is certainly very impressive.

However, we should note that originally (in the ceremonial of the Persian court) this ritual was more properly a rite of devotion and subjection than a confession of fault. Thus also the term *proskynesis* (a Greek word still occasionally used today), is derived from the Greek *kyon* (= dog), and thus certainly refers more to a humbling of oneself than to an acknowledgment of moral guilt. However, the two attitudes of guilt and subjection are not so very far removed from each other.

In the present missal, the penitential act is in some way an integrating feature of the opening rites, at least in most cases. This responds to an internal necessity. The new order provides a welcome opportunity for variation, in contrast to the older rite: Quite appropriate for penitential seasons is the first form found in the missal, with an appropriate time for examination of conscience and an explicit confession of sin like the old *Confiteor,* which, because of its stereotypical repetition in every Mass, even at major feasts like Easter, was scarcely appropriate by itself. A second form, with psalm verses, is perhaps most appropriate for Sundays and feast days, while the new *Kyrie* litany, as a third variant, combines penitential act and litany, which in themselves are independent. There is also the opportunity to replace either of the first forms with a penitential song.

The greeting and confession of sin are omitted if another liturgical action precedes the Mass, such as a Corpus Christi procession or the like, but also when candidates for baptism are brought in or at a wedding, each of which provides its own form for beginning the service. For example, when there is a baptism within the Mass, the renunciation of sin and confession of faith in God would duplicate the penitential act.

It is good that the old *Asperges* procession, a vivid reminder of our own baptism, and an element in the opening of the Sunday Mass that was very popular among the people for a long time, is being honored once again and may replace the penitential act: After all, baptism is penance, a change of attitude *(metanoia),* and repentance pure and simple. It is an important task of the liturgist to exploit to the full the rich range of choices, and thus to keep truly alive the sense of penance and confession of sin.

The ritual of confession of sin in the proper sense has, as we have said, three forms or variants, but each of them has the same four-part structure: Invitation, a short period of silence for reflection and examination of conscience, confession of guilt, and prayer for forgiveness. This division is logical and arises out of the very nature of the event.

In all three variants, the invitation to repentance, spoken by the priest, well reflects the liturgical sense: preparation for the mysteries to be celebrated and plea for God's mercy. In their content, the three formularies are almost identical: according to need, they can be varied somewhat. All three nuance the same intention.

The second element, a *short* period of silence, is psychologically indispensable if the penitential act is not to remain mere ritual. It should be long enough, but not too long. The old liturgical custom was to suggest the so-called "length of the Our Father," which in fact often led to the actual repetition of the Our Father at this point (previously at Compline, and similarly in the so-called *preces* of the liturgy of the hours; at the *Libera* after the requiem; and wherever there were, in fact, supposed to be pauses for reflection). Naturally, this misunderstanding led to a situation in which the pause for reflection, honestly offered, was not used; instead, it was taken up by the Our Father as a kind of "all purpose formula." This, happily, has been changed and reformed. However, experience has shown that this is a good length for the period of silence; it corresponds to spiritual tradition and could still furnish a rule for measuring the pause.

The confession of sins itself has three forms: a confession similar to the traditional *Confiteor*, a set of penitential versicles, and a *Kyrie* litany. The old *Confiteor*, probably adopted as a formula from the Orient in the 6th or 7th century, and generally used in the Frankish liturgy since the early Middle Ages, but at first often prayed privately by the priest in the sacristy as preparation for Mass, was in the course of the Middle Ages transferred to the beginning of Mass. We were long familiar with it, in the duplicated form of the individual confessions of priest and altar servers (representing the people), from the missal of Pius V of 1570. The *Confiteor* was constructed with strict symmetry: Confession before God, the saints, and those present (in the case of the priest); acknowledgment of guilt, with a threefold striking of the breast as a gesture of penance; request that the same saints and those present (or the priest, in the case of the altar server's prayer) would intercede with God. Undoubtedly, the theological and ecclesial dimension of penance was clearly expressed in this way—more clearly, in fact, than was often the case in private confession. The list of saints, both in the confession and prayer for intercession, occasionally varied; for example, until very recent times the old Orders mentioned their founder.

The revised form of the *Confiteor* has eliminated the duplication of confession by priest and people: all together are, after all, touched by sin in the same way. The first person singular form of the confession, however, permits each to appear as personally guilty, but no longer only through sinful actions in thought, word, and deed; now guilt is acknowledged as a result of the omission of what is good, something that is often far more serious. In addition, the old, strongly symmetrical structure has been abandoned: Confession is made before God and the brothers and sisters in the community, the Church; the request for intercession now mentions only the blessed virgin Mary, all the angels and saints, and again the brothers and sisters. The fact that the priest is not separately mentioned as an intercessor is not serious, but it is a grave matter that *the* intercessor and mediator, Christ, is not named either in the old or in the new version of the *Confiteor*. The specific acknowledgment of sin at the center (with the threefold striking of the breast) remains unchanged. This first form of penitential act, with its extensive self-accusation, is felt in the mind of the majority to be especially vivid and urgent; it is therefore best suited to penitential seasons and days.

The second form of confession consists of a double pair of psalm versicles: in the German missal these are "Have mercy, O Lord our God, have mercy, for we have sinned against you. O Lord, show us your mercy, and grant us your salvation." [The American missal uses a shorter version: "Lord, we have sinned against you. Lord, show us your mercy and love."] The structure is not dissimilar to the *Confiteor*, both in its acknowledgment of guilt and in its plea for mercy. Experience has shown, however, that this form continues to feel strange to us; and yet it deserves to be at home in our communities. It is short and succinct and relieves the introductory rites from the piling up of elements that are sometimes quite disparate. This second form is therefore very well suited, for example, for use at Sunday Masses throughout the year, except during penitential seasons.

The third form of penitential act is a redefined *Kyrie* litany. We will still have to speak about the *Kyrie* itself and the liturgical form of a litany. The new form is, first of all, distinguished from the old *Kyrie eleison* by the fact that the prayer is not directed to the Father, as the *Kyrie* litanies in the Church of East and West originally were, but to Christ. The classical order of liturgical prayer was, however, at all times: to the Father, through Christ the mediator, in the Holy Spirit—thus representing the dialogical human countermovement to God's movement of redemption and revelation: from the Father, through the Son, in the Holy Spirit. However, there are many prayers to Christ in the Mass, especially in the acclamations. The litany form has also been altered: Instead of the usual statement of the content of the prayer with the congregation's plea for help following it, there is now a statement of praise (like the old "tropes") to Christ ("Christ-predication") combined with the cry of repentance. But originally the *Kyrie* was not a penitential cry ("have mercy *on us*"); it was, rather, a cry of homage and a plea ("have mercy," in the sense of "Lord, be gracious to us and hear us"). Still, it would be unreasonable to criticize this new, or reshaped form, for that reason alone: the historical productions of a particular time are not sacrosanct; they can be adapted to the needs of a different age.

Each of the three forms of acknowledgment of sin is followed by a prayer for forgiveness, modeled on a familiar formula *(Misereatur, Indulgentiam, Aufer a nobis)*. All the versions of the confession are deliberately written not in the indicative, but in the optative mood. This means that they are not formulae of absolution; they are *requests* for forgiveness, even though spoken by the priest. Although they are certainly not words of sacramental absolution for sins that must be confessed, their theological and sacramental significance for repentant sinners can scarcely be in doubt. As we have said, the penitential act can be replaced in all Sunday Masses, including the Saturday evening Mass, by the blessing and sprinkling of holy water. The custom of the old *Asperges* procession, so called from the first word of the antiphon that is sung at the beginning (Ps 51:9), has been very widespread and popular since the early Middle Ages.

The *Asperges*, as the whole rite was formerly known, is both a recollection of baptism and a penitential rite. However, it was customary only at "high Mass," the principal Mass on Sunday. Its extension to all Sunday Masses, including the Saturday vigil, responds to the situation of our own time. The rite proceeds in this way: immediately after greeting the congregation, the priest turns toward it and, facing the container of holy water, calls on the people to pray: "Dear friends, this water will be used to remind us of our baptism. Ask God to bless it, and to keep us faithful to the Spirit he has given us." After a period of silent prayer, he blesses the water with one of the three suggested *orationes*, the third of which makes special reference to the Easter mystery. The priest, according to local custom, can bless salt and silently mix it with the water. Then he first blesses himself with the holy water and sprinkles the ministers, the clergy and the congregation, either from his chair or while walking through the nave.

Meanwhile, the community sings one of the three anthems for the Sundays within or outside Easter time. They are all taken from scripture: the antiphons from Ps 51:9 (the old *asperges*, somewhat altered, which is placed on the lips of David after his sin with Bathsheba), from Ezek 36:25-26 (pouring forth of pure water as a promise of baptism), or a hymn based on 1 Pet 1:3-5 (which praises the Easter mystery of Sunday). During Easter time a version of the formerly customary *Vidi aquam* (following Ezek 47:1ff.), or a song in praise of God's election of the people as God's own nation of priests (1 Pet. 2:9), or of the fountain of water opened in the side of Christ on the cross (cf. John 19:34), the essence of Easter and sacramental salvation, may be used. At the end there is a deprecatory prayer for the forgiveness of sins: "May almighty God cleanse us of our sins, and through the Eucharist we celebrate make us worthy to sit at his table in his heavenly kingdom. Amen."

7. Kyrie eleison

Then the *Kyrie* begins, unless it has already been included as a part of the penitential rite. Since it is a song by which the faithful praise the Lord and implore his mercy, it is ordinarily prayed by all, that is, alternately by the congregation and the choir or cantor.

As a rule each of the acclamations is said twice, but, because of the idiom of different languages, the music, or other circumstances, it may be said more than twice or a short verse [trope] may be interpolated. If the *Kyrie* is not sung, it is to be recited (*GI* 30).

The acclamations of the *Kyrie eleison* are the remnants of a litany. A litany is constructed in such a way that the appeal, with reference to the intention of the prayer, is followed by a stereotypical response from the people. Such a form is very simple and practical, because it makes few demands on the congregation. These litany forms (called *ektenia* in the eastern Church) are very frequent in the Byzantine liturgy. For anyone who has participated in a Greek or Slavic liturgy, the polyphonic *Kyrie eleison (Gospodi pomilui)* is probably unforgettable. The origins of this litany are in the secular liturgy of imperial acclamations from late antiquity: praise to the ruler, sung by a cantor, was followed by popular assent in a cry of veneration and petition, often supported by the polyphony of a *hydraulis* or water organ. The transfer of such political or courtly forms to Christ, the *Kyrios*, or to God was a natural thing for the faithful from late antiquity onward: The form itself is both simple and magnificent. The disadvantage of such litanies is that they permit no interval for personal prayer and internalization of the petition between the call to prayer and the response, although one must say of the Byzantine liturgy that the *ektenia* are always offered in a most fervent atmosphere of prayer, something that is probably promoted especially by the singing.

The *Kyrie* litany has eastern origins. It was introduced into the Roman liturgy by Pope Gelasius (492–496), a Greek from Sicily, as a replacement for the older petitionary prayer at the end of the liturgy of the word (cf. Good Friday). A litany, by its very nature, can mention as many intentions as desired, five or nine or twenty, although established schemata of intentions and petitions developed very quickly when the litany became a fixed element in the liturgy of the Mass. The Gelasian *Kyrie* litany later fell victim to the well-known efforts of Gregory the Great (590–604) to shorten the liturgy. That pope eliminated the stating of each petition or intention, restricted the acclamations (all that remained of the litany) to a schema of 3 x 3 (a total of 9), and fixed the alternation of *Kyrie eleison* and *Christe eleison*. That laid the basis for a trinitarian interpretation of the acclamations: Three to the Father, three to the Son, three to the Holy Spirit.

It is difficult to determine who was originally and primarily addressed by the *Kyrios* acclamations. The Father, or God in general, seems most likely. In the Septuagint, the Jewish translation of the Old Testament into Greek, *Kyrios* is always the translation of "YHWH, God." The old liturgical rule of directing all prayers to the Father through Christ would also suggest this interpretation, and it has been retained in the Byzantine liturgy to the present time. But even in the New Testament, especially in the writings of Paul, Christ is regularly referred to as *Kyrios Jesus*, "the Lord Jesus." This title of *Kyrios* designates him as divine. Add to this that in the Arian controversies (because Arius, as we know, described Jesus as only similar to God, not equal to God) the western anti-Arians in particular, for obvious reasons, gave special prominence to prayers to Jesus. It is noteworthy as well that popular acclamations in the Mass were frequently addressed to Christ. Thus even in the canon, the style of which is entirely that of an address to the Father through Christ, after the priest's words, "Let us proclaim the mystery of faith," the people's response is an acclamation to Christ. The result, at least superficially, is a disruption in the style of the prayer.

The *Kyrie* acclamations were, as such, purely the people's part; the priest was not involved. However, praxis soon obscured this fact: from ancient times the priest and ministers (representing the people) alternated in giving the acclamations, and the three acclamations for two sets of people often presented difficulties. In the past, as ministers or altar servers we were frequently more concerned to begin our *Christe eleison* at the right point in the second exchange than to remember that we were calling on God for mercy.

Today, the rule is three pairs of acclamations, alternating between priest and people (better and more sensibly between cantor and people). However, sets of three involving cantor or priest, schola, and congregation is also possible. It is important that the number of acclamations is no longer fixed by rule. This corresponds to the old tradition of the litany. Following the same tradition, we may again insert texts (so-called "tropes") in the litany. The revised *Kyrie* litany as the third form of general confession of sin, discussed above, is an example of this.

The wording of the acclamation is either the untranslated *Kyrie/Christe eleison* or the English "Lord/Christ, have mercy." The Greek version, retained without translation in the Latin Mass, is also placed first in the present (German) missal. There are good ecclesial and ecumenical reasons for this. The simple clarity of the expression can be presumed everywhere, especially if the Greek and English words are alternated from time to time. There can be no confusion in such an alternation because the people are always following someone who intones the acclamation for their response.

In the German version, equal place is given to the options "Lord, have mercy" and "Lord, have mercy on us." [The American missal has only: "Lord, have mercy."] However, the difference in nuance is not minor: the acclamation without the pronominal phrase is more a veneration, that with the phrase more an appeal for mercy. These should be varied, depending on the season in the liturgical year and the solemnity of the day.

In any case, the people are to take part in the acclamations. An additional alternation with the schola would, of course, make sense, but to hand over this whole part of the Mass to the church choir (for example, when using a polyphonic Mass) can scarcely be justified, even though the choir may seem to be serving as the delegates of the congregation. Short acclamations like the *Kyrie* or Amen, or responses to the priest's greeting, should never be performed by representatives nowadays; they are to be expected from the persons who are immediately concerned. There can be no doubt that sung acclamations should always be preferred to those that are simply spoken.

To avoid repetition, the *Kyrie* is omitted if the penitential act has already taken the form of the litany (formula 3), or if a *Kyrieleis* hymn was sung at the beginning (e.g., the German hymns *Christ ist erstanden, Nun bitten wir den Heiligen Geist, Mitten in dem Leben,* etc.). The addition of *Kyrieleis* to early German hymns (which for that reason are called *Leisen*) was very popular and is practiced even in the present time.

8. Gloria—A Venerable Hymn

"This hymn is said or sung on Sundays outside Advent and Lent, on solemnities and feasts, and in solemn local celebrations" (Rubr.). "The *Gloria* is an ancient hymn in which the Church, assembled in the Spirit, praises and prays to the Father and the Lamb. It is sung by the congregation, by the people alternately with the choir, or by the choir alone. If not sung, it is to be recited by all together or in alternation" (*GI*, 31).

Historically and theologically, the *Kyrie* and *Gloria* are closely related, both in their structural form and in their character as acclamations. The form of the *Gloria*, as a hymn of praise, at the same time constitutes a kind of contrast to the *Kyrie*, especially as in the course of time the latter was shortened and hence understood less as a reverent acclamation (its original purpose) and more as a penitential acclamation and appeal for mercy. For that reason, it quickly came to seem necessary to give additional expression of joy in the *Gloria*, especially on feast days.

We do not know when the *Gloria* was introduced into the Roman liturgy. The *Apostolic Constitutions* (VII, 47–49), written in the region of Antioch around 400, offer a model of the hymn. On internal and form-critical grounds, however, it appears that the *Gloria* appeared only after Gregory and the Trinitarian interpretation of the *Kyrie* that stems from him; the *Gloria* should then be understood as a supplement to the *Kyrie*.

In the Gregorian sacramentary, the bishop introduces the hymn on Sundays and feast days, the priest only at Easter: In spite of the fact that it begins with the song of the angels (Luke 2:14), the *Gloria* thus by no means originated as a Christmas hymn, as is often supposed. Since the early Middle Ages, the priest has also prayed it on Sundays and major feasts except during Advent and Lent. This hymn, one of the few in the Latin *Ordo Missae*, has enjoyed great popularity since Carolingian times, even outside the Mass. When the emperor Charlemagne led Pope Leo III into the imperial parliament in Paderborn in 799, the people sang the *Gloria*.

Although the structure of the *Gloria* in the *Apostolic Constitutions* has three strophes and numerous biblical quotations, it appears to be incomplete in the Latin version that has come down to the present. The trinitarian schema is very obvious in the prior Greek form: "To you, O God, be the glory: to the Father through the Son in the Holy Spirit forever. Amen" (VII, 48, 3). A new composition of this hymn would certainly have presented some advantages, but evidently no one wanted to change the "ancient [and venerable Christian] hymn" (*GI* 31), perhaps out of respect for musical compositions from Gregorian chant to the time of Palestrina and the classical composers and into the present.

The first part of the *Gloria* is praise to God, beginning with the angelic song from Luke 2:14. Together with the threefold "holy" of Isa 6:3, these words were regarded as "authentic heavenly songs of praise." Their use at the beginning of this hymn, and in the liturgy generally, is therefore altogether sensible. In the introductory phrases, the two-part text, following the version in the Vulgate, has been chosen: "Glory to God in the highest, and peace to his people on earth [German: to those who enjoy God's favor]." The Greek text (*Ap. Const.* VII, 47, 1), in contrast, has three parts: "Glory to God in the highest, and peace on earth, grace to all people." The German text retains the customary subjunctive, "let there be [glory, peace]." One could also choose the indicative, because all forms of praise, beginning with Judaism, emphasize the fact that God's glory is praised in heaven and on earth, and not merely the desire that it be praised.

This (revealed) song of praise is followed (in the German version) by five acclamations from the Church and those praying (reduced to three in the American version):

> "We praise you,
> We bless you,
> We worship you,
> We glorify you,
> We give you thanks for your great glory."

Acclamations of praise of this type in the liturgy are very ancient. They were customary in the public cult of the emperors, and—in revised versions for the Church—in similar form in the Martyrdom of Polycarp of Smyrna (ca. 150) and in the early eastern liturgies.

These praises of God give way, then, to specific praise of each divine person: first the Father (in a three-part form in the original text: *Domine Deus, rex caelestis, Deus pater omnipotens*). The German translation has four acclamations, the English three:

> 1. "Lord God, heavenly King, almighty God and Father." [The German divides the last of the three into "God and Father, ruler of the universe." In the American version, these acclamations precede those given above.]

Then the hymn praises the unique Son, Jesus Christ:

> 2. "Lord Jesus Christ, only Son of the Father, Lord God, Lamb of God." [The German expands again: "Lord, the only-begotten Son, Jesus Christ, Lord God, Lamb of God, Son of the Father."]

We would expect praise of the Holy Spirit at this point, as in the Bangor antiphonary or a recension from Milan. But the introduction of the fact of salvation in the description of Jesus as "Lamb of God" (John 1:29, 36) apparently invited the unknown author to expand on Christ's redeeming activity in a three-part acclamation:

a) "You take away the sin of the world: have mercy on us;
b) "You take away the sin of the world: receive our prayer;
c) "You are seated at the right hand of the Father; have mercy on us."
[Reduced, in the American version, to two strophes by collapsing (b)
and (c): "You are seated at the right hand of the Father: receive our
prayer."]

These appeals then move effortlessly into a three-part doxology of Christ:

"For you alone are the Holy One,
you alone are the Lord,
you alone are the Most High, Jesus Christ"

and this leads immediately to the necessary and triumphant Trinitarian
conclusion:

"with the Holy Spirit
in [German: "to"] the glory of God the Father. Amen."

Thus the Holy Spirit is mentioned only in this concluding praise. There is
a certain similarity to the structure and thought pattern of the Apostles'
Creed: there also, the predications of the Father are relatively brief, those
of the Son very extended, and the Holy Spirit is only mentioned.

The concluding doxology of the *Gloria* also has a counterpart in the
canon of the Liturgy of St. John Chrysostom. At the elevation of the sacred
species the priest cries: "The holy things for the holy people!" The choir
responds: "One is holy, one is Lord, Jesus Christ, to the glory of God the
Father."

All the acclamations in the *Gloria* have their origin in the Bible: The
first comes from Lev 11:44, the others from 1 Cor 8:6 and Phil 2:11. We
find the same words of praise, also closely associated with "Glory to God
in the highest" at the same point in the Mass in the so-called "Clementine
liturgy" in the *Apostolic Constitutions* (VIII, 13, 13). The description of the
Gloria as an "ancient [Christian] hymn" in *GI* 31 is thus not mere verbal
embellishment: In the *Gloria* we are following and praying with the oldest
liturgical tradition.

It is therefore all the more important that this hymn have an appropriate place in the community's Mass. The rubric in the missal for German-
speaking countries prescribes that "the *Gloria* will be sung together *or*
alternating between the congregation and choir *or* by the latter alone." The
General Instruction (§87) also offers some choices for the beginning of the
hymn: "Either the priest or the cantors or even everyone together may

begin the *Gloria*." We should maintain the fundamental principle that the *Gloria* is a part belonging to the people. If the priest begins it, he of course functions legitimately as the leader of the assembly, but it would be better for him to leave the intonation to the cantor, as representative of the people, according to the axiom that each should do those and only those things that belong to him or her.

If there is no cantor, the intonation of the hymn easily falls to the priest himself. But if he speaks or sings only the first verse, as was formerly the practice in sung Masses or those with polyphonic music by the choir, he awkwardly breaks up the biblical song of the angels. Therefore it would be better for the one who intones to sing or speak the whole first part of the hymn and let the people begin with the acclamations. Moreover, the alternating between congregation and choir (or cantor) during the rest of the hymn, suggested as a possibility by the rubrics, should not be a mechanical alternation, verse by verse, as in the psalms. The structure of the acclamations is not in pairs, but in groups of three or five; this alone forbids such a verse-by-verse alternation, unless one wants simply to ignore the aesthetic and theological construction of the hymn. Thus, in the performance of this part of the liturgy, more care should be taken to consider formal structures than has usually been the case in the past. For this reason it could now and then be the more appropriate solution to leave this song entirely or primarily to the schola, if the congregation is simply not up to the demands.

Perhaps in that case one would soon find (musical) forms that provide for brief acclamations by the people. It is possible, according to the rubrics, for the congregation to *speak* the *Gloria* together, but it is not aesthetically pleasing and hence scarcely defensible spiritually, at least in the long run. Therefore the third rubric in the German missal in this case (and only here) suggests, as a kind of emergency solution (and with a tone of resignation) that "the *Gloria* may be replaced by a *Gloria*-hymn." The immediate dilemma is that we can scarcely point to any "suitable" *Gloria*-hymns in the new congregational hymnal [the German *Gotteslob*]. The songs that might be considered at all are much less rich in their content than their great model, and at best they present only one or another idea from that rich hymn of praise. It should therefore be recommended to composers, as a worthwhile task, that they create musical settings that are easy to sing and also materially and structurally appropriate. In their efforts, they should give attention to the sense, and not produce a mechanical alternation among cantor, schola, and people. Only then will the *Gloria*, with its rich content inviting to meditation, become native to our communities—something that, as the only hymn in the Mass, it certainly deserves.

9. Concluding Prayer of the Day (Collect)

The collect of the day concludes the opening part of the Mass. In general, it is one of the structural principles of liturgy that every liturgical celebration, or a relatively complete section within it, ends with an *oratio*. This is true of every part of the Mass, and also of the liturgy of the hours, independent liturgies of the word, etc. All spiritual experience, namely, indicates that we should first fill the imagination and spirit and awaken faith (at best with the word of God) before turning to God in prayer.

At the present time we can regard the collect simply as the conclusion to the whole of the opening rites, without any special liturgical-historical inquiry about exactly which part of the opening it concludes. But a purely mechanical listing of the forms of beginning the Mass, both the traditional ones and those suggested by the present missal, would not do justice to the praxis of opening the celebration; instead, the *General Instruction* and the rubrics intend that particular accents be placed within the introductory rites, according to the character of the day (degree of solemnity, season within the liturgical year, combination of Mass with administration of a sacrament or another liturgical action, etc.).

I would therefore recommend to every liturgist, in consideration of this necessary variation in the opening, always to begin by looking at the collect of the day, whether prescribed or specially chosen, and with that as a starting point to develop a deliberate composition of the entire opening of the Mass so that this *oratio* (which is not unjustly called the "collect," that is, the "prayer that gathers together") will really summarize and conclude the principal motif of the opening and the underlying atmosphere of the day. Thus, instead of a mere summary of all the elements in the opening section, the result will be an organic whole that can effect a specific attitude in the congregation, comparable to a musical overture. This is a general matter of experience (religious experience included): As is the beginning, so is the whole!—most often, at any rate. The objection repeatedly raised, namely that the many opening rites are too disparate and numerous, is only justified if no one has taken any pains over the shape of the ritual.

The "excess" of possible suggestions represents a great opportunity for the liturgist. There are openings for variety, accent, and nuance especially if one gives *sensible* attention to all the "rubrics," for they are not intended merely to establish negative boundaries, but to offer help.

The collect of the day, together with the prayer over the gifts and the concluding prayer, belongs to the group of *orationes* or "presider's prayers," the official prayers of the presiding priest, who must always speak or sing them personally; in this, the priest cannot be represented by another (lector, concelebrant, etc.). The word *oratio* comes from *orare*, which means "to speak," "to preach," "to proclaim," as well as "to pray." It would therefore be appropriate to translate *oratio* as "prayer speech." In the ancient church, the ability to carry out the service of the word in preaching *and* public prayer was one of the most important charisms of office and criteria for the priestly profession. Of course, as we have seen in the previous section, the body of formulated prayer material was soon collected and written down in *libelli* to serve as models, so that afterward such prayers were repeated word for word or used for suggestions in the formulation of newer prayers. Only over a long period of time did the presider's official prayers become fixed formulae.

The *orationes* are the most Roman texts in the missal. From the time of their first appearance (in writing since the 7th–8th centuries, but in oral form certainly much earlier, beginning with the 4th–5th centuries) they astonish us with their extraordinary richness and classical form: There is not a single superfluous word, and they are couched in the firm and artistic style of Roman orations and lofty forms of speech. The *orationes* are the creations of a long tradition of Latin rhetoric. Literary historians hold them in the highest esteem because of their perfected form, and for that reason they have been enthusiastically praised in every age.

The Roman *orationes* are tiny productions of literary artistry, clear, succinct, and memorable, examples of polished formulation and lapidary form. Their language is elevated above everyday speech and every type of banal folksiness. In many cases, such language presumes that those who pray these prayers are biblically and theologically sophisticated, and often ascetic and monastic as well. But, just as unmistakably, these great advantages bring with them many disadvantages: a certain reserve or lack of feeling, relative difficulty of interpretation, poverty of biblical imagery, and hence a great many problems of understanding for the simple people praying in our communities. We can scarcely criticize the petitions in the *orationes* for being very general, not especially concrete or detailed in expression; it has certainly enabled them to endure over a long period of time, for something that is directed very explicitly to *one* situation is often appropriate only once, and perhaps even then not for everyone. In contrast, a certain generality in formulation makes liturgical texts acceptable and applicable on many different occasions.

Unmistakably, the precise and molded Latin form of the *orationes* creates difficulties for translation. Consequently, modern translators have made an effort to enrich the *orationes* somewhat, without falling into the trap of wordiness, which would be contrary to the spirit and the tradition of the prayers.

The *orationes* have a fixed structure: invitation to prayer, silence, prayer with concluding Trinitarian formula, "amen" from the congregation. The invitation to prayer is the shortest possible: "Let us pray." This succinctness makes it suitable for every occasion, but gives no specific intention for the prayer, something one might expect when the prayer of the day is also called a "collect," a "summarizing prayer." Consequently, there have been many suggestions for expanding the invitation to prayer somewhat, as in the petitions on Good Friday. (The first of these, for example, reads: "Let us pray, dear friends, for the holy Church of God throughout the world, that God the almighty Father guide it and gather it together so that we may worship him in peace and tranquility.") That would introduce a particular intention for the pause that follows. Of course, the disadvantage is a certain duplication between the invitation to prayer and the prayer itself.

The purpose of the period of silence is given in the *General Instruction*, §32: ". . . together [priest and people] observe a brief silence so that they may realize they are in God's presence and may call their petitions to mind." Quiet silence is a part and a structural element of the liturgy. This was emphasized by the Constitution on the Liturgy (article 30), and it is repeated in the *General Instruction*, §23, which also makes a distinction regarding the purposes of silence: recollection at the penitential rite and after the invitation to pray, meditation after a reading or homily, and prayer and praise of God after Communion. Common prayer is only worship in spirit and truth (John 4:23) when it is sustained by and saturated with private prayer. The instruction *Musicam sacram* of 1967 (article 17) says: "The faithful are thereby [by pregnant silence] not made outsiders and silent spectators at the liturgical action; instead, they are absorbed more deeply into the mystery being celebrated through the inner preparation that comes from hearing the word of God, from singing and audible prayers, and from their spiritual communion with the priest, who pronounces the parts that belong to him."

One must take note that, according to the missal, the period of silent prayer is no longer something optional; it is required. Therefore it should never be omitted. Its length should be appropriate.

The collect of the day is spoken or sung by the chief celebrant. It summarizes the prayer of all participants. "[It] expresses the theme of the celebration" (*GI* 32): Sundays, feast days and fixed seasons, memorials of saints, remembrance of the dead, etc. Earlier, it was the custom (and sometimes even a requirement), for example in Masses accompanying another ritual such as a marriage, that the Church year and saint's day be commemorated, and certain obligatory *orationes*—up to seven—be added. But that is in the past. Today, a *single oratio* indicates the character of the celebration. One may, when there is good reason for it, include some "commemoration" in the "ad lib" introduction at the beginning of the Mass, or bring some special intentions forward in the petitionary prayers of the liturgy of the word.

The classic Latin *oratio* had a more or less fixed schema:

Address to God, often expanded with an adjective (sometimes two);
Praise of God in an appositional phrase or added relative clause (so-called "relative predication");
Petition for something, usually beginning with *praesta quaesumus, concede,* or something similar (so-called "supplication");
Conclusion of the prayer, differing in form according to whether the prayer is addressed to the Father or to the Son; and
Acclamation of the congregation: "Amen."

Thus, for example, the *oratio* for Palm Sunday reads:

Omnipotens sempiterne Deus,
qui humano generi, ad imitandum humilitatis exemplum, Salvatorem nostrum carnem sumere et crucem subire fecisti,
concede propitius,
ut et patientiae ipsius habere documenta et resurrectionis consortia mereamur.
Per Dominum nostrum Jesum Christum Filium tuum, qui tecum vivit et regnat in unitate Spiritus Sancti, Deus, per omnia saecula saeculorum.
Amen.

The early *orationes* were always addressed to the Father. As we have already noted, those addressed to Jesus appeared at a later time, often under the influence of an anti-Arian theology. The missal has attempted to reinstitute the old situation, to the extent possible. Hence the General Instruction, §32, says: ". . . the priest's words address a petition to God the Father through Christ in the Holy Spirit." In our language area an effort was made to apply this axiom more consistently than in the Latin model. *Orationes* addressed to the Holy Spirit, which of course would be theologically possible, were a rare exception even before (occurring only in a few formularies like that for the consecration of virgins); none has been retained in the present missal.

In making translations, it has proved advantageous or even necessary, both for stylistic reasons and for the sake of greater clarity and intelligibility, to dissolve the unified and artistically interwoven Latin model with its sets of three members (address to God with "predication," petitionary formula with "supplication," and trinitarian concluding formula) into three logically successive sentences. Thus, for example, the English version of the Roman collect for Palm Sunday, given above, reads:

> Almighty, ever-living God,
> you have given the human race Jesus Christ our Savior
> as a model of humility.
> He fulfilled your will by becoming man
> and giving his life on the cross.
> Help us to bear witness to you
> by following his example of suffering
> and make us worthy to share in his resurrection.
> We ask this through our Lord Jesus Christ, your Son,
> who lives and reigns with you and the Holy Spirit,
> one God, for ever and ever.

The theological and liturgical content of this *oratio* has been retained, as far as possible, in the translation; the demands of an elevated syntax have been met; in addition, the "predication" in the first sentence is designed to remain as close as possible, at least by association, to the text that lies behind it (Phil 2:8), and to give a more biblical flavor to the language of the Latin version, which tends to be more didactic and dogmatic.

The spiritual orientation of the *orationes* is very well considered. After the address to God, with mention of some characteristic that is usually prominent in or key to the particular celebration (omnipotence, eternity, love for humanity, fatherhood), a clause or apposition speaks of God's mighty deeds in creating and sustaining the world, revelation and redemption. In this, the *orationes* are akin to the piety of the psalms, which love to praise God's dealings with his people. For God is faithful: Whatever God has done, he will continue to do. Therefore human beings may pray with confidence for the fulfillment of God's promises (Matt 7:7-8; Luke 11:9-10), especially in the name of the one mediator, Jesus Christ (John 14:13-14; 15:16; 16:23, 26). That is why the *orationes* emphatically pray "*through* our Lord Jesus Christ."

"The people make the prayer their own and give their assent by the acclamation, *Amen*" (*GI* 32).

In conclusion, let me say a few words about physical posture during the *oratio:* The presider speaks the collect of the day, like all the presider's prayers, in the so-called *orans* posture, with somewhat open arms and hands held at an upward angle. The missal no longer contains a precise, rubricistic direction for this. The customs of a given cultural context can legitimately influence the *orans* stance.

From the point of view of religious history, the lifting of the hands corresponds to the earlier worldview and is an expressive gesture of prayer to the "gods above." On the other hand, the veneration of chthonic deities suggests bowing and praying with lowered arms. Religious history attests both elevated altars for the "gods of heaven" and deep caverns for the earth deities as places of sacrifice. General anthropology has also shown us that among all peoples, the offering and showing of the open palms, which therefore cannot hold weapons or anything dangerous, is a sign of peaceful intent. Waving or signaling with the open hand, which were also forms of greeting for the Fascists and Nazis, ultimately derived from this primitive human phenomenon. A prisoner of war knelt in ritual submission and held up both weaponless hands; he also made appeal, by presenting his unprotected breast, to the victor's magnanimity in not using his sword. Thus open hands uplifted are a universal human gesture of peace, confidence, and petition; in contrast, a clenched fist means threat and challenge to battle. In the Old Testament, lifting the hands to God (Exod 9:29, 33; Ps 28:2; 63:5; 88:10, and frequently), or toward the Temple (1 Kgs 8:38, and frequently) was a universal custom.

This Jewish gesture of prayer was apparently adopted by Christians for private as well as communal prayer. Tertullian refers to it (*De oratione* 14): The Jews, because of their feelings of guilt, do not dare to lift their hands to Christ. "But we not only lift them, but even extend them, imitating the Lord's passion, as we also confess Christ in prayer." The oldest depiction of the crucifixion of Christ (still very muted, because otherwise so scandalous to Romans), on the wooden portals of Santa Sabina on the Aventine in Rome (6th c.) shows the crucified Lord with slightly bent arms and open, nailed hands, but without an express depiction of the cross— almost as if he were standing in front of the framework of a house. This is precisely the form of the *orans* posture as Tertullian pictures it: In the Christians who are praying in this way, the Father also sees the dying Son on the cross. Naturally, this interpretation of the *orans* posture is secondary and allegorizing, but it is still interesting and revealing.

It is possible that the whole community in antiquity may have prayed in this way, at the Our Father, for example. Of course, this could easily have led to disturbances, so that in the end it was only the presider who did so. Such reductive developments are not uncommon in the liturgy. It may be that the gesture of crossing the arms on the breast also stems from the mystical thought world of Tertullian, mentioned above, or more generally from ancient attitudes: Among the Byzantines, this posture was a strict obligation, beginning with the 9th century; Pope Nicholas I expressly approved it in a letter to the Bulgarians (866), and it is still in use in the Romance-language area.

The placing of the palms together, as in the priest's private prayers during Mass, but also in other circumstances, such as when going to Communion, probably stems from feudalism and is a gesture of surrender and fidelity; at the ordination of priests it is still used in the same sense as part of a ritual promise of fidelity to the bishop. The clasping or folding of the hands with fingers interlaced, which is very often used today, is also quite ancient. Gregory the Great speaks of it (*Dial.* I, 1, 33) in connection with Benedict's sister Scholastica: "She placed her hands on the table, her fingers interlaced." All these gestures have a profound power of expression in the liturgy, both for body and spirit, and are worth considering (cf. *GI* 20 and 21). The one praying can make them devoutly; on the other hand, when they are done deliberately, they can make the one praying devout.

With the collect and the congregation's "Amen," the introductory rites are concluded. The *oratio* at the end collects everything that has gone before in words and signs; at the same time, it puts a seal on them, showing that the meaning of these preparatory actions has been fulfilled in the power of the Spirit to: "take on the form of a community and prepare themselves to listen to God's word and celebrate the eucharist properly" (*GI* 24).

Now all those assembled take their seats. The lector approaches the ambo. The whole community is united in the word of God. God comes to the people in the word.

Chapter Two

The Liturgy of the Word

1. The Spiritual Structure of the Liturgy of the Word

The introductory rites are a preparation for the entire Mass, made up of liturgy of the word and Eucharist. They prepare for the coming and activity of God in word and sacrament. However, they naturally and immediately introduce the celebration of the word of God. This celebration of the presence of the Lord in his word demands a high degree of readiness to listen. "In the readings, explained by the homily, God is speaking to his people, opening up to them the mystery of redemption and salvation, and nourishing their spirit; Christ is present to the faithful through his own word." (*GI* 33).

In saying this, the *General Instruction* is expounding the teaching of Vatican Council II: "[Christ] is present in His word, since it is He Himself who speaks when the holy Scriptures are read in the church" (*SC* 7). ". . . in the liturgy God speaks to His people and Christ is still proclaiming His gospel" (*SC* 33). These words are not mere allegory, but the real truth of faith.

The structure of the liturgy of the word corresponds to the faith-event itself: God alone can initiate human salvation; without God we can do nothing (John 15:5). ". . . faith comes from what is heard, and what is heard comes through the word of Christ" (Rom 10:17). The content of the message is the reconciliation of human beings with God, accomplished once for all in Christ. "All this is from God, who reconciled us to himself through Christ, and has given us the ministry of reconciliation; that is, in Christ God was reconciling the world to himself, not counting their trespasses against them, and entrusting the message of reconciliation to us. So we are ambassadors for Christ, since God is making his appeal through us; we entreat you on behalf of Christ, be reconciled to God" (2 Cor 5:18-20). Whoever accepts the message received in faith will be saved: "because if you confess with your lips that Jesus is Lord and believe in your heart that God raised him from the dead, you will be saved. For one believes with the heart and so is justified, and one confesses with the mouth and so is saved" (Rom 10:9-10). But ". . . no one can say 'Jesus is Lord' except by the Holy Spirit" (1 Cor 12:3).

The structure of the liturgy of the word follows this "logic of faith." "In the readings, explained by the homily, God is speaking to his people, opening up to them the mystery of redemption and salvation, and nourishing their spirit; Christ is present to the faithful through his own word. Through the chants the people make God's word their own and through the profession of faith affirm their adherence to it. Finally, having been fed by this word, they make their petitions in the general intercessions for the needs of the Church and for the salvation of the whole world" (*GI* 33). Or, to illustrate it once more with the lovely image from Isaiah already cited above (Isa 55:10-11), the word of God comes like rain on the earth in the proclamation of the readings; it penetrates and drenches, like rain on the earth, the hearts of the people as they reflect on what they have heard, and as it is opened for them and applied in the homily, "making it bring forth and sprout, giving seed to the sower and bread to the eater." The faithful respond in the confession of faith and in praying as representatives for all humanity and the whole world; then they receive "bread [for] the eater," as their nourishment.

It is true that the liturgy of the word has its own irreplaceable dignity and importance, but it also stands in the closest relationship to the Eucharist, although this does not mean that it should be taken lightly as simply the "preliminary part of the Mass." "In the Christian community itself, . . . the preaching of the word is needed for the very administration of the sacraments. For these are sacraments of faith, and faith is born of the word and nourished by it [cf. *SC* 35, 2]. Such is especially true of the Liturgy of the Word during the celebration of Mass. In this celebration, the proclamation of the death and resurrection of the Lord is inseparably joined to the response of the people who hear and to the very offering whereby Christ ratified the New Testament in His blood. The faithful share in this offering both by their prayers and by their recognition of the sacrament for what it is" ("Decree on the Ministry and Life of Priests," 4).

This relationship between word and sacrament is expressed in many of the documents of Vatican Council II, and also in the *General Instruction,* through the allegory of the two tables: "the table of the divine law and of the sacred altar" ("Decree on the Appropriate Renewal of the Religious Life," 6); "the twofold table" ("Decree on the Ministry and Life of Priests," 18), and frequently elsewhere. The phrase "table of the word" may seem somewhat odd at first glance, but its basis and presupposition is the contrasting biblical pair of bodily nourishment and nourishment with the word of God: "'One does not live by bread alone, but by every word that comes from the mouth of God'" (Matt 4:4; cf. Luke 4:4). This is a literal citation from Deut 8:3 or from the words of the prophet Amos (8:11): ". . . not a famine of bread, or a thirst for water, but of hearing the words of the Lord." Human beings live by and from the word of God: it is like food for them and gives them strength. The image of the twofold table is multiply attested in the Church's literature, from the time of the Fathers (Hilary) to Thomas à Kempis's *Imitation of Christ* (IV, 11).

2. The Readings and the Selection of Pericopes

In the foreground of the liturgy of the word stands God's own word. Christ is present in the readings (cf. *SC* 7). "The readings lay the table of God's word for the faithful and open up the riches of the Bible to them" (*GI* 34). This reflects an admonition of the Council: "The treasures of the Bible are to be opened up more lavishly, so that richer fare may be provided for the faithful at the table of God's Word. In this way a more representative portion of the Holy Scriptures will be read to the people over a set cycle of years" (*SC* 51).

As early as the year 150, Justin Martyr (First Apology, 67) speaks of a number of readings, the "memoirs of the apostles" and "readings from the prophets." Today, with the contents of the canon of biblical writings having been established, we would call these "parts of the New and Old Testaments." Undoubtedly this reflects the heritage of the synagogue, with its readings from "Moses and the prophets" (Luke 16:29).

Very early in the history of our Mass liturgy the selection of the readings was withdrawn from the independent choice of the presider at the service. This supported the Church's efforts to have the whole of the scriptures, containing all the truths of revelation, read in worship within a specified length of time, to the degree possible. We can suppose that, in the beginning, relatively long passages were read. People took time to listen, to *vacare Deo,* to be free for God. The reading was most easily done in the form of what is called "continuous reading" *(lectio continua),* beginning each time at the point where the reading had previously ceased. Very early the custom of mixing the books of sacred scripture from the Old and New Testaments in a particular order was established. For example, the Chaldeans still have the custom of four readings, two from the Old Testament (law and prophets) and two from the New Testament (an apostolic letter and the gospel). Constantinople and Milan had the same custom for a time. Rome, in the early period, had three readings, at least on Sundays and feast days: Old Testament, apostolic letter and gospel. At least, this is what has been suggested (among other possibilities) from analysis of the different structures of responsorial song; but it is not as certain as is often assumed.

The Syrians, on the other hand, often have up to six readings, and the Copts have four from the New Testament alone. It was by no means the absolute ideal that the portions read should represent a strict thematic agreement. The idea was not to present thematic ideas, but simply to listen to the word of God, celebrating the mystery of God's speaking to human beings. We find, at an early period, obligatory readings for the liturgical year and its feasts.

In the west they were often called *comes,* meaning "guides" or "companions." The *comes* of Würzburg, often mentioned, was written in England in the 8th century. It reflects 7th century Roman custom, which had been adopted in the island. The lectionary of Luxeuil reflects Gallic custom. The assignment of readings to the different seasons and feasts of the liturgical year reveals particular catechetical ideas and interests. The attempt to relate the two readings (epistle and gospel) to each other is especially obvious in the Lenten season, but the harmonizing of the pericopes was often frustrated by later abbreviations because the sentence or verse that was key to the whole thing was eliminated.

For the Sundays after Pentecost, too, there seems to have been a certain arrangement at the outset, but it was lost, perhaps as early as the 7th century, because of a rearrangement of the gospels, with the result that the epistle was always one Sunday too early. Still, what has been said shows that there were occasional efforts at a "thematic order," even though it was not considered absolutely necessary.

The 1570 *Missale Romanum* contains only an impoverished, meagerly trimmed selection of readings. In this reduction, important truths of revelation were entirely omitted. There was not even an order of readings for weekdays any longer. Either the pericopes from the previous Sunday were repeated on the days of the week on which no feast occurred, or the same parts of the so-called common Masses, the common formularies for particular groups of saints, were read over and over again on the saints' feast days, which had gradually overspread the entire year of the Lord. I still remember, with vivid discomfort, the year of my residence in Rome, where, in the local calendar for the city of Rome, all the memorials of the saintly popes were feast days, with the result that the same pericopes were read on more than half the days of the year.

Still worse was the abuse in many parish churches, where all the "Masses requested for those who have died" were celebrated from the common "Mass for the Dead." The reform of the order of pericopes was thus more than overdue. The first edition of this reformed order was published in 1969, the second in 1981. It presents what is close to an optimum of possibilities: first of all, in the purely quantitative increase in the number of pericopes. In a cycle of three years, the readings for every Sunday are based on a selection from the synoptic gospels (Matthew, Mark, and Luke), augmented by selections from the gospel of John, especially during the Easter season. In addition, every Sunday and major feast now has three readings instead of the previous two.

For weekdays *(feria)*, there is a two-year cycle, in which the gospels remain the same (because of the limited length of these four books), but the readings from Old and New Testament change: Cycle I is used in the odd-numbered years, and Cycle II in the even-numbered years. In addition, the selection of pericopes for the saints' feasts and memorials, and for Masses for various occasions, has been increased. Often there are several choices. Moreover, the range of choices for special pastoral purposes has been expanded a great deal, so that those in pastoral ministry have a rich selection to choose from. Certainly, this kind of freedom is more time-consuming than a strict order! Every individual Mass formulary calls for some effort *before* the celebration, in order that pure laziness will not cause us to fall back into a spiritless monotony, or to choose the first reading that comes to hand every time.

The basic rules for the choice of the present order of pericopes are given in articles 318–320 of the *General Instruction,* as an extract from the *Ordo lectionum Missae* of 25 May 1969. Especially helpful is the expanded *Pastoral Introduction to the Mass Lectionary according to the Second Authentic Edition of the Ordo lectionum Missae* (1981), appearing as volume 43 in the series *Acta Apostolicae Sedes.*

On Sundays and feast days there should be three readings: "prophet," "apostle," and "gospel," that is, an Old Testament reading, another usually from the apostolic letters, and one from the gospels. The inclusion of Old Testament readings is meant to bring "the Christian people to the knowledge of the continuity of the work of salvation" (cf. *GI* 318). In the apostolic constitution *Missale Romanum* of 3 April (Maundy Thursday) 1969, with which Pope Paul VI introduced the new edition of the missal, this successor of St. Peter placed special emphasis on this: It is to "accentuate the dynamism of the mystery of salvation, shown in the words of divine revelation." This is evident on the individual Sundays, especially because the Old Testament reading is related as closely as possible to the gospel, often as foreshadowing and fulfillment, the theme and the full concerto. This schema is interrupted only in the Easter season: following ancient precedent, the first reading during these fifty days is taken from the Acts of the Apostles.

The plan of three readings on Sundays has been criticized by many, including the post-conciliar Synod of Bishops in 1967. Some think that three readings are an excessive demand on the listeners, especially when there is no direct thematic connection among the three readings and preachers see themselves confronted with the alternative either of choosing to concentrate on one reading or of treating all three. This last must and need not always occur. Nevertheless, the final admonition of the *General Instruction* (§318) should be taken to heart: "It is expected that there will be three readings, but for pastoral reasons and by decree of the conference of bishops the use of only two readings is allowed in some places. In such a case, the choice between the first two readings should be based on the norms in the Lectionary and on the intention to lead the people to a deeper knowledge of Scripture; there should never be any thought of choosing a text because it is shorter or easier." There is no doubt that a special degree of responsibility is required in dealing with this particular chapter concerning the reform of the pericopes.

On weekdays, special readings are provided for every day of the year within the two-year cycle. These pericopes should, as a rule, be read on the days appointed for them, unless a major or minor feast suppresses them. It is usually advisable, on the days of saints' memorials, to give preference to the order of readings for the weekday, unless there are serious pastoral reasons for acting otherwise. In such cases, the readings for the week, or at least the most important passages, can be taken together on the remaining weekdays.

At Masses for special groups (school classes, family associations, etc.) there is also the opportunity to choose other readings that seem more suitable. Thus, for example, it is surely advisable when celebrating a Mass with school children to replace the story of the rescue of the chaste Susanna with something more appropriate—even though this story plays a very important role for the Fathers, and in catacomb iconography, as an "image of salvation." However, *GI* 316, guarding against too much exercise of subjective whim, recommends that:

> If he celebrates with a congregation, the priest should first consider the spiritual good of the faithful and avoid imposing his own personal preferences. In particular, he should not omit the readings assigned for each day in the weekday lectionary too frequently or without sufficient reason, since the Church desires that a richer portion of God's word be provided for the people [cf. *SC* 51].
> For similar reasons he should use Masses for the dead sparingly. Every Mass is offered for both the living and the dead and there is a remembrance of the dead in each eucharistic prayer.

Special readings are provided for Masses accompanying the administration of sacraments (or sacramentals); they make appropriate preaching on such occasions easier and lead to a deeper understanding of the event itself. Here, the readings also serve mystagogical purposes. In such cases, it is generally preferable to interrupt the weekday cycle and choose the special readings, a large selection of which is offered for these occasions. More generally, one could argue about how the accents are placed in Masses accompanying the administration of sacraments (baptism, confirmation, marriage, even the anointing of the sick). Is the sacrament integrated into the liturgy of the word? Or does this integrated administration of the sacrament somehow replace the "normal" service of the word? This is a theoretical consideration, but its consequences are eminently practical in nature.

3. The Order of the Liturgy of the Word

(a) The reading

After the conclusion of the introductory rites—that is, after the collect—the lector goes to the ambo for the (first) reading (*GI* 89). A reading from the altar can only be the exception, for example in the narrow confines of very small chapels. The *General Instruction* (§80b) presumes that the lectionary is already lying on the ambo. On the other hand, *GI* 82c suggests that the gospel book can be carried by the lector in the entrance procession and laid on the altar after the altar is reverenced (*GI* 84). The lectionaries used in German-speaking areas contain both the readings and the gospels; however, there are also special gospel books, some of them richly decorated. All this means that the questions here raised about appropriate arrangements can be solved.

The congregation is seated while listening to the reading. Sitting is, generally speaking, the most relaxing and relaxed posture for listeners and best enables them to understand. It should be a matter of course that the congregation are all in the same posture; if necessary, the presider can invite them to be seated, but there should be no suggestion of military parade-ground discipline. "The uniformity in standing, kneeling, or sitting to be observed by all taking part is a sign of the community and the unity of the assembly; it both expresses and fosters the spiritual attitude of those taking part" (GI 20).

When it is customary for the community to make a response after the reading, the lector ends the reading with the spoken or sung words, "The Word of the Lord," to which the congregation answers: "Thanks be to God." This custom is not in use everywhere, and need not be, because the real response to the reading is not so much an acclamation as the subsequent meditation, by which the people internalize the text. Still, the acclamation can clearly mark the caesura before the responsorial psalm, especially in cases when there is no psalmist or cantor, and the lector must read the psalm from the ambo.

(b) The responsorial psalm

"The cantor [or psalmist] sings or recites the psalm, and the people respond" (Rubr.) "The responsorial psalm or gradual comes after the first reading. The psalm is an integral part of the liturgy of the word and is ordinarily taken from the lectionary, since these texts are directly related to and depend upon the respective readings. To make the people's response easier, however, some texts of psalms and responses have also been selected for the several seasons of the year or for the different groups of saints. These may be used, whenever the psalm is sung, instead of the text corresponding to the reading" (GI 36). The responsorial psalm is—together with the acclamation just mentioned—the congregation's response to the word of God. It has a meditative character and assists the people's spiritual appropriation of what they have heard. Because of its relationship to the reading, the responsorial psalm is quite different from the processional chants (including those at the entrance, the presentation of the gifts, or during Communion): it promotes reflection on God's saving deeds for the people, and is thus within the tradition of synagogue chants. The use of a psalm that is intended for use throughout an extended period of the church year and focuses on narrower community considerations is, of course, less suitable and somewhat farther from the ideal.

"The psalmist or cantor of the psalm sings the verses of the psalm at the lectern or other suitable place. The people remain seated and listen, but also as a rule take part by singing the response, except where the psalm is sung straight through without the response" (*GI* 36). According to this, the response is not to be assigned to a schola or other group: it belongs to the congregation. The psalm should also be sung unpretentiously and without long, decorative *melismata,* so that it can be easily understood and thus readily fulfill its spiritual purpose. It would not make sense to have it prayed in alternating verses by the congregation. If the assembly takes part, it should be by reciting or singing the acclamatory response.

Other possibilities for (Latin) chants after the reading are the gradual (from the *Ordo cantus missae* or Roman Gradual) or the responsorial or *alleluia (Hallel)* psalms from the Simple Gradual (Rubr.; cf. *GI* 36c). The old graduals are melismatic, artistic melodies and must therefore be assigned to a schola. Their disadvantage is the greater difficulty of understanding them and the textual abbreviation of the psalms; their advantage lies in the rich spiritual treasures of Gregorian chant.

The missal for German-speaking dioceses makes it possible (as a less than ideal solution) for some other suitable hymn to be substituted for the responsorial psalm. However, that should really be a last resort, because, to tell the truth, there are no hymns that are truly suitable for this purpose! Even the strophic psalms available are not real substitutes. Having the organ play, without any reading or singing of a psalm, is not suggested as an alternative, but in some cases it might at least be considered, because it could easily offer a space for meditation on what has been heard. Still more demanding would be a pregnant silence, but that is certainly possible only in smaller groups. Experience shows that there is need for some guidance if silence is to be understood as a response to the reading.

If a second reading follows, it is also read by a lector at the ambo and is concluded in the same way as the first pericope.

(c) The anthem before the gospel

"The *alleluia* or other chant follows [the second reading]" (Rubr.; cf. *GI* 37). This second chant is related, structurally speaking, to the gospel, which follows. It has a less meditative and more acclamatory character, and is directed to the Lord present in the word. Hence the verse is usually taken from the gospel; the acclamation of the assembly is always *alleluia,* except during Lent. According to the introduction to the *Ordo lectionum Missae* of 1969 (art. 9), an alternative to the alleluia for the Lenten season is "Praise to you, O Christ, king of endless glory," or something similar.

Because the chant before the gospel prepares for its proclamation, and thus belongs within the context of the gospel, the congregation should be standing for this chant (or acclamation), as *GI* 21b intends. With appropriate preparation, this is easily done; moreover, it is altogether sensible.

The *alleluia* and gospel verse are important especially (although not solely) when there are two readings before the gospel. The possibility of full realization is closely related to the question whether the chants between the pericopes are those "officially" provided in the *Ordo Missae* or not.

On weekdays, or on Sundays when there is only one reading, the range of choices is quite broad: there may be a responsorial psalm *or* an *alleluia* with verse, or *both* together, or *only* the responsorial psalm; during Lent the choice is only between the responsorial psalm and the gospel verse (Rubr.). However, the first choice is always the responsorial psalm. Because of its meditative character and the elements related to the reading, it naturally takes the highest place; it best corresponds to the structure of the liturgy of the word. This also explains why *GI* 39 demands that the responsorial psalm should be spoken whenever it cannot be sung, whereas in such a case the alleluia and verse before the gospel may be omitted.

A sequence is prescribed only for Easter and Pentecost; it is permitted on other days (*Lauda Sion* for Corpus Christi and *Stabat Mater* for Our Lady of Sorrows). The *Dies irae* from the requiem survives only as part of the liturgy of the hours. The sequence *Victimae paschali laudes* is strongly recommended for festive Masses during the octave of Easter. The same is true of Pentecost (*Veni Sancte Spiritus*) and the other two days that have a sequence. Structurally, the sequences are closely related to the verse and alleluia; like them, they point toward the gospel and originated from the melismata or subordinated tropes in the alleluia melodies.

(d) The gospel

The gospel is the high point of the celebration of the word of God. Since the 4th century it has been proclaimed at least by a deacon, and is either sung or read. "The liturgy itself inculcates the great reverence to be shown toward the reading of the gospel, setting it off from the other readings by special marks of honor. A special minister is appointed to proclaim it and prepares himself by a blessing or prayer. The people, who by their acclamations acknowledge and confess Christ present and speaking to them, stand as they listen to it. Marks of reverence are given to the Book of Gospels itself" (*GI* 35).

From earliest times, the exaltation of the gospels above all other biblical books derives from the fact that they speak directly of Christ's words and deeds; they are regarded as the "good news" (the *eu-angelion*) itself. The authority of St. Jerome in matters biblical led to their identification with the "four living creatures" (Rev 4:6-9; 5:6, 8; esp. 4:7), by reference to the beginning of each gospel: Matthew, the creature with a human face (iconographically most often an anthropomorphic angel) because of the genealogy of Jesus' human descent (Matt 1:1-17); Mark, the lion, because of John's "crying in the wilderness" (Mark 1:3); Luke, the ox, because of Zechariah's sacrifice (Luke 1:5); finally, John, the eagle in flight, because of the spiritual "flight" of his prologue (John 1:1-17).

The book of the gospels enjoyed the highest respect. It was given an expensive binding from an early date (and thus, according to *Ordo Romanus I,* was sealed up in a casket after the Mass); it was adorned with gems and ivory plates. The text was given decorative miniatures and initials. Oaths were often sworn on the book of the gospels, both in ecclesial and secular law; the one swearing laid a hand on the book while reciting the formula of the oath: "By the help of God and his holy gospel, which I touch with my hand." It was especially popular to lay the hand on the hymnic beginning of the gospel of John. Many ancient manuscripts reveal clear evidence of wear at that point.

The gospel represents Christ himself, present in his community through the word. The honors paid to the gospel book correspond to those given to the altar: kiss, bow, incense, procession with candles and acolytes, etc. (see the remarks on the veneration of the altar, above). If incense is used, the priest or bishop places it in the thurifer, silently, during the alleluia. The song before the gospel is an acclamatory element and, as we have seen, its content is already part of the proclamation of the gospel. The priest, if he is to read the gospel, bows before the altar and prays the preparatory prayer for purification of heart and lips. Thematically, this prayer refers to the purification of the lips of Isaiah by a seraph bearing a hot coal (Isa 6:6-7) before the prophet, having seen a vision of God, is sent to proclaim his mission. The present version of this prayer is somewhat shorter than its predecessor, and the explicit reference to Isaiah is no longer in it.

If a deacon proclaims the gospel, he asks in a low voice for the blessing of the bishop or priest, and receives it. The formula of blessing is a deprecative version of the prayer of preparation. The deacon (or priest) takes the gospel book from the altar and goes to the ambo. Ministers may accompany him with candles and incense (Rur.; cf. *GI* 94). "At the lectern the priest opens the book and says: **The Lord be with you.** Then he says: **A reading from . . .**, making the sign of the cross with his thumb on the book and on his forehead, mouth, and breast. If incense is used, he then incenses the book. After the acclamation of the people, he proclaims the gospel and at the end kisses the book, saying inaudibly: **May the words of the gospel wipe away our sins.** After the reading the people make the acclamation customary to the region" (*GI* 95).

The procession with the gospel book has been a custom in almost all the liturgies of east and west from ancient times; it is especially solemn in the Liturgy of St. John Chrysostom, but also in the papal liturgy of *Ordo Romanus I*. The carrying of candles and incense in such processions has an old tradition behind it, ultimately deriving, as we have said, from court ceremonial. While otherwise, since the Middle Ages, the rule with regard to cathedral liturgies and solemn parish Masses was one of sharp reduction, this procession always remained relatively important. Even in private Masses that were simply read, the missal, which in the mean time had incorporated the gospel book, was carried by the altar server from the "epistle side" to the "gospel side." This designation of the sides of the altar retained an ancient reminiscence, that the right side (as seen from the bishop's chair in the apse) was the more dignified. The former practice of placing the book and lector with a slight inclination to the north also retained a memory of the greater nobility of assisting the bishop on the right side; a medieval allegorical interpretation of this inclination to the north (the north being the home of darkness, and the gospel the light of the world, cf. John 1:5) is secondary.

The exchange of greetings ("The Lord be with you") before the beginning of the proclamation further accentuates what follows. While there used to be a great number of these exchanges during Mass, the few that remain have been given greater significance by the reduction in their number. They are now found only at the beginning of Mass (where the greeting is often paraphrased) and before the final blessing, at the beginning of the gospel proclamation, and at the beginning of the eucharistic prayer. The parallelism of honor given to word and sacrament is again evident in this feature.

The subjunctive usage ("The Lord *be* with you"—note that Latin lacks an auxiliary verb, as do the Greek and Hebrew that preceded it) could equally well be indicative: "The Lord *is* with you," for the Lord is present in the word. The subsequent announcement of the section of the gospel to be read would then exemplify the presence of Christ in this specific pericope of the good news. The older *Sequentia sancti Evangelii . . .* has been abandoned, because that formula ("the continuation of the gospel according to . . .")

really presumes a strictly continuous reading. The adjective "holy" before "gospel" is optional in the German missal: At present we are somewhat more reserved in our religious language with regard to the accumulation of adjectives about "holiness." The other suggestion, "A reading from the gospel of Jesus Christ . . ." is worthy of respect, although the word "gospel" in itself already describes what follows. The choice is left open. The greeting and announcement can be sung, even if the gospel is spoken.

The sign of the cross on the book, and then on the forehead, lips, and breast, a signing of the object and the self, participates in the theology and mysticism of the cross to which we already referred when speaking of the introductory rites. It is not prescribed that the congregation should also cross itself as is customary in many places; however, it is an appropriate gesture. The meaning of the crossing of forehead, lips, and breast (heart) is revealing: thoughts, words, and works—the whole person and his or her actions are dedicated to Christ.

If incense is used, the deacon (or priest) incenses only the book. Originally, the thurifer was merely carried in the procession; beginning with the Middle Ages the gospel book was incensed, as was the altar itself. We already spoke of the meaning of incensing in relation to the veneration of the altar at the beginning of Mass. The gesture of honor to altar and gospel book is intended for the Lord himself. The use of incense is optional and is governed by local preference; however, it is entirely appropriate and is comprehensible for the faithful even today, to say nothing of the ecumenical aspect.

The congregation stands while listening to the gospel (*GI* 35). The significance of standing, as a sign of greater readiness in contrast to sitting, is easily grasped. Even Neh 8:5 reports: "Ezra opened the book in the sight of all the people, for he was standing above all the people; and when he opened it, all the people stood up."

Kissing the book at the end of the reading is a gesture of honor and devotion. Its meaning corresponds to the kissing of the altar (see above). According to the old *Ordo Romanus I*, after the proclamation of the gospel one of the assisting subdeacons took the gospel book, and holding it with covered hands against his breast, went to all the clergy in the sanctuary in turn, so that they could kiss the book. In solemn high Masses in the very recent past, the subdeacon carried the book to the celebrating priest (or bishop), and even in Masses that were read *(Missa lecta)* the celebrant kissed it; the only exception was the requiem Mass. Under the present regulations, only the one who proclaims the gospel kisses the book, but this is true for all Masses.

In many places a ceremonial conclusion is customary: the deacon (or priest) follows the gospel with the sung [or spoken] acclamation: "The gospel of the Word," to which the congregation responds: "Praise to you, Lord Jesus Christ." This acclamation was previously given only by the ministers or altar servers, but in the 20s and 30s it was adopted by the whole congregation in so-called community Masses. The present missal in our language area translates the rhyming optative formula spoken quietly by the one proclaiming the gospel (*Per evangelica dicta deleantur nostra delicta*) into an indicative petition: "Lord, through your gospel take away our sins." (The ICEL version retains the optative mood: "May the words of the gospel wipe away our sins.")

The power of the word of God to forgive sins is attested by sacred scripture: "Very truly, I tell you, anyone who hears my word and believes the one who sent me has eternal life, and does not come under judgment, but has passed from death to life" (John 5:24). "If you abide in me, and my words abide in you, ask for whatever you wish, and it will be done for you" (John 15:7).

(e) The homily

The homily has been an integrating part of the Christian liturgy of the word from the most ancient times. It actualizes the message in concrete terms for today. The quantitative increase in scriptural readings and their translation into the vernacular demands, even more today than before that there be a commentary and actualization of what is heard. In the New Testament community there is no more room for a magical conception of the words than there is for such a treatment of the signs. Faith comes from hearing with understanding. The word of God, given millennia ago in a different socio-cultural context, must be able to be received by the hearer as something living, contemporary, and illuminating for today. "By the . . . word of Scripture the ministry of the word . . . takes wholesome nourishment and yields fruits of holiness. This ministry includes pastoral preaching, catechetics, and all other Christian instruction, among which the liturgical homily should have an exceptional place" (Dogmatic Constitution on Divine Revelation [*Dei Verbum*] 24).

> The homily is an integral part of the liturgy and is strongly recommended: it is necessary for the nurturing of the Christian life. It should develop some point of the readings or of another text from the Ordinary or from the Proper of the Mass of the day, and take

into account the mystery being celebrated and the needs proper to the listeners.

There must be a homily on Sundays and holydays of obligation at all Masses that are celebrated with a congregation. . . . It is recommended on other days, especially on the weekdays of Advent, Lent and the Easter season, as well as on other feasts and occasions when the people come to church in large numbers.

The homily should ordinarily be given by the priest celebrant" (*GI* 41 and 42).

Thus the homily is part of the liturgy. A Mass with a congregation that has no homily, or at least a brief word of interpretation, should be regarded as far from ideal. Article 25 of *Dei Verbum* urges that all should "hold fast to the sacred scriptures through diligent sacred reading and careful study, . . . lest any of [those active in the ministry of the word] become 'an empty preacher of the word of God outwardly, who is not a listener to it inwardly' [Augustine, *Sermons* 179, 1] since they must share the abundant wealth of the divine word with the faithful committed to them, especially in the sacred liturgy." Above all, "at those Masses which are celebrated with the assistance of the people on Sundays and feasts of obligation, [the homily] should not be omitted except for a serious reason" (*SC* 52).

The readings should be interpreted in relation to "the mystery being celebrated" (*GI* 41). It will therefore be necessary to keep in mind also the individual texts of the Mass of the day, the so-called "proper." The most recent reform has made an effort to relate these texts to the readings, but only to a certain degree and insofar as possible, because the two series of pericopes extend over two and three years respectively. Here the "ordinary," the part of the Mass that remains the same, should by no means be forgotten.

As a rule, the one who presides over the service should give the homily. Naturally, in some cases one of the concelebrants or the deacon could preach. There has been much discussion of preaching by lay persons, but it is forbidden for them to give the homily at Mass, when it is part of the liturgy itself (cf. *CIC* 1983, canon 767). In principle, the whole structure of the liturgy of the word makes the address to the people at Mass the right of the celebrating priest.

The head of the synagogue in Pisidian Antioch, for example, asked Paul and Barnabas: "Brothers, if you have any word of exhortation for the people, give it" (Acts 13:15). In the ancient Church, the charismatics who were not part of the clergy but had special gifts for the building up of the community preached, and their right to do so was unassailable. Preaching by the laity was forbidden for the first time in the 13th century, in reaction to heretical movements. It can no longer be said today that preaching by lay persons is totally forbidden. "Lay persons can be admitted to preach in a church or oratory if it is necessary in certain circumstances or if it is useful in particular cases . . ." (*CIC* 1983, canon 766). At the same time, the homily at the celebration of holy Mass is reserved to the priest or deacon (see above).

There can be good reasons for "dialogue homilies." They were formerly a matter of course in worship services with children, and they are often used at the present time as well. What is possible and sensible with children can certainly be equally so with adults from time to time, provided that not only those persons speak who like to hear the sound of their own voices. This is a question of the spiritual discipline of the community. An appropriate service to the word of God remains subject to the whole body of the Church's faith, but it must be inventive in its forms if preaching is to be more than the threshing of worthless straw. Of course, the homily cannot undertake to cover all forms of Christian education; there must be an established place in the community for catechesis, sermon cycles, colloquies, adult religious education, etc. Here is a special place for the work of the laity. Within all this, the homily is a spiritual word in a special and very specific sense.

(f) The confession of faith

The *Credo*, as it is now placed within the liturgy of the word, has the character of an acknowledgment by the people of what has been heard "in the readings and through the homily" (*GI* 43). The essential truths of faith are called to mind before the eucharistic part of the Mass begins.

The *Credo* was originally an element in the baptismal service, not the Mass. In its formulation, it is an expansion of the Jerusalem baptismal creed: The one asking for baptism had to learn it by heart and repeat it to the bishop as a kind of test (the so-called *redditio symboli*). As a personal acknowledgment, therefore, it is couched in the first person singular, which in itself indicates that it was not originally intended for common recitation during the liturgy. The *Credo* is used in a number of variant forms: an elementary version is the so-called "Apostles' Creed" (which by no means goes back to apostolic times); it was expanded as the so-called Nicene Creed (Council of Nicaea, 325), or Constantinopolitan Creed (Council of Constantinople, 381), known as the "Great Confession of Faith." Other creeds, including the Athanasian, Tridentine, etc., are succinct and precise theological statements of faith, but they are not used in the liturgy.

The Latin Mass preferred the singing or recitation of the so-called Constantinopolitan creed, but the current missal for German-speaking regions also permits the use of the Apostles' Creed. There is probably good reason for this because the dogmatic expansions, which are the theological remnant of the early Trinitarian struggles, have—at least in this context— no major kerygmatic significance. Still, it would be a good idea, if the congregation is capable of it, to have them sing the great creed occasionally, and even in Latin. Consequently, the German missal includes it, and certainly not just as window-dressing. At international congresses, pilgrimages, but even at vacation spas, or when foreign workers whose mother tongue is different are present at the community Mass, and in other similar situations, the Latin *Credo* is certainly an impressive testimony to the unity of Catholic faith. In fact, it is still possible for the whole Mass to be celebrated according to the current Latin missal (ed. typ. altera 1975), just as it was before, throughout the whole Church, whenever it is desired or the situation calls for it.

The *Credo* first entered the Latin Mass in Spain. At the third council of Toledo (589) the Visigoths, who had been Arians, converted to the Catholic faith under King Reccared, and because the Nicene creed very explicitly emphasized the unity of nature between Son and Father, it was the most natural thing for it to be incorporated into the liturgy of a Church previously Arian. There, the *Credo* was sung immediately before the Our Father: these two texts, the *Credo (symbolum)* and Lord's Prayer (Our Father) were those that had to be recited as a "short formula of faith" by every catechumen before baptism. Somewhat earlier, under Justinian II (563–578), the creed had also been included in the Mass at Constantinople. In the 7th–8th centuries it then entered the Gallico-Frankish Mass and later was explicitly approved by Leo III, in 810—but without the so-called *filioque*, which teaches the procession of the Holy Spirit from the Father *and* the Son, and remains a painful object of dispute between the eastern and western Church to this day. However, this long-familiar wording remained in use among the Franks. Rome itself first accepted the Franco-German usage at the insistence of St. Henry II at his imperial coronation in Rome in 1014.

While the *Credo* is sung in all Masses in the eastern and mozarabic liturgies, the Latin liturgy had this usage only in special Masses, especially when the mystery celebrated on that day appears in the *Credo:* hence at Christmas, Easter, the Annunciation, the feasts of apostles and certain saints (doctors of the Church, for example), and on all Sundays. The reduction of this usage in the present missal is obvious. The *Credo* is now sung or recited only on Sundays and solemnities, but it can also be included on festive occasions (Rubr.; cf. *GI* 44 and 98)—that is, when there is some reason for special celebration, or when a great many people are present. The rule is somewhat elastic.

By its nature, the *Credo* is one of the parts that belong to the people. It is a response in faith by the whole congregation, even though (in the Latin original) it is couched in the first person singular. When the priest recites it with the people, this simply underscores their community. It is not really indicated that the celebrant should begin the creed, but only that he should introduce it by saying: "Let us recite the Nicene (or Apostles') Creed." Previously, it was the rule that the celebrant would intone the *Credo*.

Genuflection at the affirmation of the Incarnation is now to be done only at Christmas and on the major feast of the Annunciation (March 25), when that event constitutes the mystery celebrated in the feast; otherwise, all should make a deep bow. Unfortunately, this often does not occur. However, we should insist on it, and make a special effort to pay more attention in our preaching to incarnational theology, with all its anthropological and ecclesiological consequences, thus expanding our one-sided paschal theology by incorporating the fullness of the explicit Catholic confession of faith.

(g) The prayer of the faithful

The petitions, also called "general intercessions" and "prayer of the faithful," were reintroduced by the most recent reform as a conclusion to the liturgy of the word, in response to an explicit request of the Council (*SC* 53). We have to do here with an element in the Mass liturgy that had "suffered injury through the accidents of history" (*SC* 50). The petitions were, in fact, among the oldest parts of the Mass and were mentioned twice, and explicitly, by Justin (see above). He speaks of them in connection with the Eucharist after baptisms: When the newly baptized, after receiving the sacrament (and after the community's liturgy of the word) were brought to those assembled, they "make common prayers earnestly for ourselves and for [those who have] been enlightened and for all others everywhere" (First Apology 65). The petitions were also a fixed element in the liturgy of the word on Sundays: "Then [i. e., after the homily] we all stand up together and send up prayers" (ibid., 67). From that point on, the tradition is well attested in east and west: In the east, by the "Apostolic Constitutions" (ca. 380) and to the present time (as a litany before the procession with the gifts); in Rome since Hippolytus, and then in the specific, solemn Roman petitions— which, however, declined after Gelasius (except on Good Friday), and were somehow absorbed in the Kyrie litany at the beginning of the celebration. Today the petitions have been returned to their correct place in the structure. They constitute the conclusion of the *liturgia verbi,* the celebration of the word of God.

These prayers at the end of the liturgy of the word enjoyed a very high status in the liturgy from oldest times. Only those who were baptized and in full communion with the church could participate, because this was considered to be expressly the prayer of the priestly people of God. Hippolytus speaks of a separation of the unbaptized from the baptized before the prayers, because the prayer of the former "is not yet pure." Even Justin says explicitly that only those newly baptized are allowed to participate in the petitions of the assembly.

The liturgy of St. John Chrysostom preserves even today an extensive ritual of prayer for dismissal of catechumens, penitents and the possessed at the end of the liturgy of the word, although it scarcely has any practical significance: only after that is the "prayer of the faithful" recited. Because of this restricted circle of participants, the petitionary prayer retained the name *oratio fidelium,* "prayer of the faithful" in the west for a long time as well. In terms of its content—prayer for the intentions of the whole Church, all people, and the whole world—it was also called the "common prayer," and because of its great esteem in the liturgy it was called *oratio sollemnis,* "solemn prayer." Our missal (Rubr.) calls it "prayer of the faithful" or "general intercessions." "In the general intercessions or prayer of the faithful, the people, exercising their priestly function, intercede for all humanity. It is appropriate that this prayer be included in all Masses celebrated with a congregation" (*GI* 45).

Sacred scripture explicitly teaches the priesthood of the whole people of God, composed of ordained persons and laity: "But you are a chosen race, a royal priesthood, a holy nation. . . ." (1 Pet 2:9). The community is priestly through its union with Christ, whose work as mediator is interpreted particularly by the Letter to the Hebrews as a high-priestly office (on the paradigm of the high priest of the Old Testament and his sacrifice for atonement). Christ, as head of the body of the Church, also works in his members: ". . . as each part . . . working properly promotes the body's growth in building itself up in love" (Eph 4:16). Jesus Christ is "the faithful witness, the firstborn of the dead . . . who loves us and freed us from our sins by his blood, and made us to be a kingdom, priests serving his

God and Father" (Rev 1:5-6). The people of God consciously exercises this universal priesthood on behalf of the whole world when it prays "for the needs of the Church, for public authorities and the salvation of the world, for those oppressed by any need, [and] for the local community" (*GI* 45).

In this way, the "priestly intercessions" of the congregation already constitute a transition to the eucharistic sacrifice, the hinge that binds the liturgy of the word and the celebration of the Eucharist in the narrower sense. This coupling is especially evident in the liturgy of St. John Chrysostom because the prayer of the faithful and the "great entrance" (with the eucharistic gifts) are closely joined, and the petitions are seen as an element in the preparation of the gifts. Nevertheless, in light of the whole liturgical tradition the new order of the Latin missal is more correct: The great intercessions structurally conclude the liturgy of the word; with the preparation of the altar and the gifts for the celebration of the Eucharist, something new begins: the second major part of the Mass liturgy. The Council correctly recognized the necessity of reintroducing the petitions as an integrating element in the Mass, and the Holy Father also places specific emphasis on this element in the apostolic constitution with which he introduced the new missal.

For theological reasons, then, it is "appropriate that this prayer be included in all Masses" (*GI* 45, cf. 33), and not only on those on Sundays. They are optional when Mass is celebrated without a congregation (*GI* 220), but they can be offered even then: "The priest gives the intentions, and the server makes the response" (ibid.).

The content of the intercessions is derived from the intentions of the whole Church, those in public authority, and the needs of the whole world, the intentions of all those in special need, and finally those of the congregation assembled around the altar. At special celebrations such as confirmation, marriage, burial, etc., the sequence can be adapted to reflect the particular occasion (*GI* 46).

On the one hand, the intercessions have a certain integrity of their own as the priestly intervention of the people of God, and thus are significant as an independent part of the Mass. On the other hand, from the point of view of liturgical structure, they constitute the conclusion of the liturgy of the word and hence cannot simply leave unrecognized all the elements of proclamation included in this part of the Mass. Thus the petitions can certainly make reference to what has gone before, especially by suggesting intentions and referring to the mystery of the feast. However, it would be wrong to make the intercessions a moral appendix to the homily, duplicating a parenesis that is quite legitimate in a sermon. The intercessions are prayer, not proclamation, and certainly not instruction for Christian life.

Because of their very nature, the intercessions are a part of the liturgy belonging to the people. They are not a presidential prayer by the presider, as is usually the case with prayers at the end of a liturgical action or some part of it (e.g., the prayer over the gifts after they are prepared, or the concluding prayer after Communion). Still, this does not mean that the priest cannot lead the intercessions in virtue of his office: ultimately, the priest is also part of the people of God, and in the community of intercessory prayer for the intentions of the Church and the world, we find manifested as scarcely anywhere else in the Mass the priesthood of the *whole* community in a most impressive way, and including both the universal priesthood and the special office of ordained priests. Hence the comments in *GI* 47 are to be taken primarily as advice for carrying out the intercessions: "It belongs to the priest celebrant to direct the general intercessions, by means of a brief introduction to invite the congregation to pray, and after the intentions to say the concluding prayer. It is desirable that a deacon, cantor, or other person announce the intentions. The whole assembly gives expression to its supplication either by a response said together after each intention or by silent prayer."

The intercessions recapitulate the old Roman tradition to the extent that they are again placed at the end of the *liturgia verbi;* however, they do not duplicate the most ancient form. The latter can be observed in the so-called *orationes sollemnes* of Good Friday. These begin with a call to prayer and reference to the intention. There follows a period of silent prayer by the people, done kneeling during penitential seasons. Afterward, the presider utters an *oratio* as "summary prayer." In the Mass, a shorter form of litany is used: The intention is announced by the deacon (or cantor or other person), and followed by a single response (which, of course, can vary from occasion to occasion). The opportunity for silent, private prayer between call and response, which really is an expansion of the litany form and augments it in a desirable way, should always be grasped. In that case, the advantages of both forms of prayer—the shorter eastern *ektenia* or litany and the meditative western *orationes sollemnes*—are brought together and combined, as foreseen by the missal. It is to be recommended that the "response said together after each intention" (*GI* 47) be sung and not merely spoken. It is not only more beautiful, because it avoids a none-too-attractive "mumbling" by the congregation, but it is also easier for the congregation to respond in this way.

Chapter Three

The Celebration of the Eucharist

Introduction and Overview

The Eucharist is the heart of the Mass. The other major part, the liturgy of the word, was added in early post-apostolic times in place of the full meal, but there were already comparable verbal elements (in the command and prayer at the Last Supper: cf. Luke 22:19; 1 Cor 11:24) relating to the bread and cup that are to be the Lord's memorial.

As we saw in Part I, this action of Christ was a "thanksgiving" (*eucharistia,* Hebrew *berakah*) to God given over food elements that Christ expressly designated as himself, his body and blood; even before this, he made clear that these were his body *surrendered* and his blood *poured out,* something actually fulfilled afterward in the sacrifice of the cross. These gifts the Lord gave to those at the meal for their consumption. The Church's action in celebrating this *memorial that makes present* is, therefore, the thanksgiving over bread and wine as Christ's body and blood that, in the power of the Spirit, makes the event present, and the subsequent reception of these gifts: in other words, it is a very specific, meaningful meal reduced to essentials. Inasmuch as these gifts present Christ as the one sacrificed—in his body surrendered and his blood poured out—the *sacrifice of Christ* is also present in them, in its saving effects, for the forgiveness of our sins.

Through Christ and with him and in him, the one high priest of the new covenant, the community enters, in the Holy Spirit, into Christ's surrender of his life and presentation of sacrifice to the Father: "Through him, then, let us continually offer a sacrifice of praise to God" (Heb 13:15). Thus the Eucharist is also the Church's sacrifice, not a new sacrifice in addition to Christ's sacrifice on the cross, but participation in it: "I appeal to you therefore, brothers and sisters, by the mercies of God, to present your bodies as a living sacrifice, holy and acceptable to God" (Rom 12:1). This, Christ's cultic sacrifice of praise, into which each concrete congregation enters, is the summit and source of Christian life in faith, hope, and love, the center of all human action; in it, the believer is physically at God's disposal, grasps God's will, and serves the brothers and sisters in love and in works. To this extent, the Eucharist is open to the community and to the world, so that it may always remain clear and evident that liturgy is only one of the Church's self-realizations, and is integrated into its proclamation and caritative service.

Let us summarize: The *nature* of the Eucharist is both that of a meal and of the sacrificial presence of Christ. Its *form* is that of a prayer of thanksgiving over food elements meant for consumption. It is *celebrated* in imitating the action of Christ on the evening before he suffered, when he took bread and wine, said thanks over them, and in them gave himself to his companions at the meal.

Thus the *General Instruction* (§48) says:

> At the last supper Christ instituted the sacrifice and paschal meal that makes the sacrifice of the cross to be continuously present in the Church, when the priest, representing Christ the Lord, carries out what the Lord did and handed over to his disciples to do in his memory.
>
> Christ took bread and the cup and gave thanks; he broke the bread and gave to his disciples, saying: "Take and eat, this is my body." Giving the cup, he said: "Take and drink, this is the cup of my blood. Do this in memory of me." Accordingly, the Church has planned the celebration of the eucharistic liturgy around the parts corresponding to these words and actions of Christ:
>
> 1. In the preparation of the gifts, the bread and the wine with water are brought to the altar, that is, the same elements that Christ used.
>
> 2. In the eucharistic prayer thanks is given to God for the whole work of salvation and the gifts of bread and wine become the body and blood of Christ.
>
> 3. Through the breaking of the one bread the unity of the faithful is expressed and through communion they receive the Lord's body and blood in the same way the apostles received them from Christ's own hands."

A. The Preparation of the Gifts

1. The Meaning of the Preparation of the Gifts

At the institution or origin of the holy Eucharist, Jesus' *taking* the gifts was still something quite simple and unpretentious: the food was ready, having been prepared by the disciples before the meal (Matt 26:19; Mark 14:16; Luke 22:13). Of course, at a paschal meal there were special conditions relating to the memorial: when explaining the symbolism, the head of the household took bread and cup in hand and, during the words of praise and interpretation, lifted them slightly above the surface of the table. This ritual was almost necessitated by the nature of the ceremony, as a way of drawing the attention of the participants to the central objects. The remaining food was simply placed on the table, as usual. "Taking" the gifts by elevating them slightly was a specifically paschal ritual.

In the earliest Christian communities as well, this taking of the gifts by the presider at the celebration would have been very simple. Still, the preparation of bread and wine (and the reception of them afterward) remained the principal way in which the disciples participated, for this meal was not merely a sign of brotherhood and sisterhood with one another; it was also a charitable meal at which the poor members of the community were fed and satisfied. The generous and frequent giving of the things one often in fact needed for one's own sustenance and which were the fruits of one's daily labor, was clearly experienced by the giver as a "sacrifice." Thus in what was brought one gave oneself and one was in a sense identified with what was given. All the sacrifices in human history are based on this primitive religious phenomenon: in giving what is necessary for life, the one sacrificing gives him- or herself. Even when the feeding of the poor and the community meal were separated from the Eucharist, the collecting of these "means of life" for the needy continued, and only a part of the gifts was reserved for the eucharistic celebration itself. Thus it was natural that the preparation of the eucharistic gifts was very quickly interpreted as a spiritual self-donation and shaped in such a way that it became an expressive symbol of the personal surrender of one's life within Christ's unique sacrifice.

In communities that were growing larger, the giving was soon transformed into a bringing forward in a kind of procession, in symmetrical countermovement to the other procession in which the consecrated gifts were received. To the extent that the community reflected theologically on its co-sacrificing action, the preparation of the gifts was also ritually expanded. Even with Hippolytus in the 3rd century we find the idea that only those may bring gifts who can receive the transformed bread again in the Church's communion ("Apostolic Tradition," 20.10; cf. Council of Elvira, canon 28). On the other hand, Cyprian (*De opere et eleemosyna* 15) criticizes those "who come without alms and (in communion) receive part of the sacrifice that a poor person has brought." We could multiply such citations from the era of the Fathers.

A community procession always benefits from the support of a chant or song to minimize noise and distraction, while giving a spiritual interpretation to physical movement. This probably happened very early; psalms were a good accompaniment, or an antiphon could be sung by the congregation in alternation with the chanting of a schola or cantor.

However, such processions with the gifts could easily lead to misunderstanding of the eucharistic sacrifice, at least in the popular mind. The people of antiquity who came to Christian faith were already familiar with "sacrificial processions" to the decorated altars of their gods. The sacrificial animals that were led, and the objects carried in the procession, were already the "sacrifice" itself. Therefore it is and has always been important to give a precise theological and spiritual content to such "sacrificial processions," as the reformed rite for the preparation of the gifts in the missal does in unmistakable fashion. It deliberately avoids the long-familiar word "Offertory" for this first part of the *liturgia eucharistica*, because imprecision can evoke misunderstanding. It is also dangerous to say without qualification, or to sing, as in some of the hymns for the preparation of the gifts, such as "We bring you our sacrifice, the gifts of bread and wine . . ." that the Mass is a "sacrifice of bread and wine." It is, but only in the sense that the visible objects are bread and wine, while in fact and in reality it is the body of Christ that is "given" and his blood "poured out" that are the sacrifice made present in the celebration of the Eucharist.

The Latin verb *offerre* and its associated noun *oblatio* have as a first meaning simply "bring forth," "make available," "present." (The German word *Opfer* comes, in fact, from Latin *operari*, not from *offerre*.)[1] It was certainly a misunderstanding on Luther's part when he feared that multiple Masses were *new* sacrifices alongside the unique sacrifice of Christ and did injury to the latter, as if Christ's sacrifice were not adequate. However, it is true that the preparation of the gifts really and in fact is the beginning of the Eucharist as sacrifice. When the prayers accompanying the preparation of the gifts say: "We bring before you this bread (or: this cup)," the bridge to the strophe in the eucharistic prayer that refers to the bringing of the gifts has already been opened; at both points the Latin text uses the verb *offerimus*. It would thus be inadequate to water down the preparation of the gifts as nothing more than "putting them in place." Theologically and spiritually this is already the real beginning of the Church's eucharistic sacrifice.

2. The Altar and the Eucharistic Gifts

At the beginning of the liturgy of the eucharist the gifts, which will become Christ's body and blood, are brought to the altar.

First the altar, the Lord's table, which is the center of the whole eucharistic liturgy, is prepared: the corporal, purificator, missal, and chalice are placed on it (unless the chalice is prepared at a side table). The gifts are then brought forward." (*GI* 49).

The altar is the "center of the eucharistic liturgy," as is the ambo for the liturgy of the word. Both are located within the sanctuary, correlated to one another spatially as proclamation and sacrament within the Mass. The shift of focus from ambo to altar impressively signals the beginning of something new.

The altar is "the Lord's table." This is a compact way of expressing both its nature and its form. Articles 259–262 of the *General Instruction* provide further details, to which we will simply refer; however, §259 in particular gives some pointers for this particular context: "The altar, where the sacrifice of the cross is made present under sacramental signs, is also the table of the Lord. The people of God is called together to share in this table. Thus the altar is the center of the thanksgiving accomplished in the eucharist." It is the special honor of the people of God that it "shares" in this table. This is a biblical way of speaking, common in the Old Testament and adopted by Paul in 1 Cor 10:18-22: the one who shares in the altar shares in its god—in sacrifices to idols, this is a sharing in the idols; sharing in the "cup of blessing" (v. 16) and the "one bread" (v. 17) is a sharing in the "body of Christ." This is in all probability the starting point for the symbolic equation of the altar with Christ, which we have already discussed in connection with the introductory rites.

While "altar" more strongly indicates the cultic dimension and the connection with the sacrifice of Christ made present, "table of the Lord" expresses primarily the way in which Christ is present—as food to be consumed by the faithful—but also its external form. It would be a mistake to use pagan models in constructing the altar, because Christ's institution contains no sacrificial *ritual;* instead, it is a sharing in "bread" and a "cup of blessing" (1 Cor 10:16). If it is desired to make the theological significance of the Mass as sacrifice symbolically visible, this can be accomplished solely through the cross that stands in the sanctuary and never by giving the Christian altar the form of an altar of sacrifice. The place where Christ really surrendered his life was not a pagan altar; it was the cross. The only legitimate form for the altar is that of a table. Throughout the Church's most ancient period it was, for a long time, still a movable piece of furniture. Later, in order to make its presence felt within the sanctuary, it became heavier and more solidly built to match the spacious basilicas and cathedrals. It was moved closer to the wall under the influence of the law of prayer toward the east, which is no longer felt to be necessary; in the process, the appearance of the altar was relativized by the incorporation of large *retablos,* carved or pictorial backs attached to the altar, and ultimately baroque altar walls. Still, throughout the centuries the term *mensa* ("table") was retained as the common designation for the flat surface of the altar. Recently there has been a return to simpler forms of the altar and its identity as a table. Its essential reality again stands more clearly in the foreground than the decorative "extras," however well meant they may have been in the past. Provisional solutions should soon be overcome, as should inappropriate talk about the "people's altar."

The altar is again freestanding, and it is possible to walk around it. "In every church there should ordinarily be a fixed, dedicated altar, which should be freestanding to allow the ministers to walk around it easily and Mass to be celebrated facing the people. It should be so placed as to be a focal point on which the attention of the whole congregation centers naturally." (*GI* 262).

"At least one cloth should be placed on the altar out of reverence for the celebration of the memorial of the Lord and the banquet that gives us his body and blood. The shape, size, and decoration of the altar cloth should be in keeping with the design of the altar" (*GI* 268). It is no longer required that there be three cloths, especially not the lower *chrismal* previously in use: this was an oil-resistant cloth used especially, since Carolingian times, to keep remaining quantities of oil from the anointing of the altar at its consecration from being absorbed by the other linen. The number three appears first in the Middle Ages, for allegorical reasons. For present sensibilities, a single cloth on the table is appropriate and customary. It is true that linen is not the only material permitted, but there will probably be no desire to change this custom. Linen cloths were regarded for a long time as a reference to Christ's sacrificial death, and especially to his burial (cf. John 19:40). The form of the cloth depends on the altar: It can hang deeper on the sides if the top of the altar rests only on legs; it may be fixed to the corners of the altar if the altar is decorated with an ante-pendium, relief carvings, etc. In any case the decoration of the altar cloth should be well adapted to its reality as something made of cloth: it should never give it the stiffness of a board.

The preparation of the altar (according to *GI* 49) presumes that previ-ously it was empty, and especially that it was not a place to put various books and utensils, which would be a denial of its dignity. The custom of spread-ing the altar cloth at this time is not necessarily to be criticized. It is as old a custom as the removal of the cloth after Mass (cf. Maundy Thursday). Such a preparation of the altar could be recommended for Masses with children, but also occasionally at other times. The corporal, a small (ca. 50x50 cm.), folded linen cloth, should be placed on the altar cloth. It is called "corporal" because within and outside the Mass the body *("corpus")* of the Lord rests on it—consider, for example, the communion of the sick. The purificator, another little cloth, serves primarily for cleaning *(purificare)* the chalice. It is usually placed on the altar next to the corporal.

The missal is also placed on the altar at this time. Previously, the priest had used it at his chair. The chalice is placed on the altar, if the priest himself will mix the wine and water; at concelebrations, for example, and especially at episcopal Masses, this could also be done at the credence table. There is no longer reference to a separate paten for the priest's large host; it is best that the priest's host be laid in the larger dish containing the rest of the bread, which the celebrant takes, lifts slightly while praying, and places on the altar.

The eucharistic bread has been unleavened in the Latin rite since the 8th century—that is, it is prepared simply from flour and water, without the addition of leaven or yeast. At the Last Supper, Jesus probably took bread like this (the so-called *matzoh*), which is interpreted in the paschal memorial as the "bread of tears," the bread of itinerant and homeless herdspeople. However, in the first millennium of the Church's history, both in east and west, the bread normally used for the Eucharist was ordinary "daily bread," that is, leavened bread, and the eastern Church uses it still today; for the most part, they strictly forbid the use of unleavened bread *(azymes)*. The Latin Church, by contrast, has not considered this question very important. At the Council of Unity in Florence (1439), the difference of usage in East and West was simply acknowledged and approved (Denzinger 1303), and some of the uniate Churches of the east still use leavened bread. Wheat bread, on the other hand, is universally used in all rites today. It is the "good" bread of Mediterranean cultures. However, this by no means makes it certain that Christ himself did not use barley bread (cf. John 6:9, 13). It will be best to continue the Latin usage, and not to construct a theological ideology on the basis of the bread question.

In the beginning, the bread was certainly presented in the form of a single loaf. The Lord broke the one bread; the *fractio panis* consequently required a longer period of time in the ancient Church, and in the West since the 7th century the *Agnus Dei* was sung as an interpretative chant during this time. In the Carolingian era, at the earliest, and for practical reasons, small pieces of bread the size of coins came into use. The symbolic power of the one bread (1 Cor 10:16-17) was thus undoubtedly weakened. Today there is a gradual return to the use of one large loaf, or a number of larger hosts. Apparently this is legitimate, for the rubrics at the *Agnus Dei* anticipate that the chant should be "repeated until the breaking of the bread is finished." However, there are also disadvantages to this revived custom, to say nothing of the many crumbs that are showered around. It is true that these are swept into the chalice during the purification, but some of them are rubbed back into the purificator in the process. When Mass is celebrated in a small group, the symbolism of the one bread certainly deserves to be preferred over practicability. For decades I have arranged, for example at a wedding Mass, to give the newly married couple a single broken host. As early as the Didache (9:4) the bread is the symbol of the one Church: "As this bread was scattered over the hills and then was brought together and made one, so let your Church be brought together from the ends of the earth into your kingdom."

The wine must be the unadulterated "fruit of the vine" (Matt 26:29; Mark 14:25; Luke 22:18), which was and is not something that can be taken for granted at all times. The priest must thus be careful about its purity. For the Jews of the Old Testament, the wine was not only a sign of festiveness and joy but also of the undisturbed possession of the land. Of course, for medieval symbolists the wine was also a sign of joy born from sorrow: ultimately the grapes must be crushed before there can be wine.

In antiquity wine was usually mixed with water before drinking. Before or during the meal the two were poured together into the beaker and drunk. Liturgical accounts since Justin are aware of this usage for Mass as well. It is probably to be presumed at Jesus' last supper also. An explanatory symbolism drawn from the mixing was sure to arise; one such has been popular since Cyprian of Carthage (*Ad Caecilianum* 13): "When the wine is mixed with water in the chalice, the people are joined to Christ. If someone offers only wine, the blood of Christ remains without us; if someone offers only water, the people are without Christ." This interpretation was taken over in the same or similar form by almost all liturgies—except for the Monophysites, who emphasize Christ's divinity over his humanity—often with the addition of a reference to the blood and water that flowed from the side of Christ when pierced by the soldier's lance (John 19:34). The Council of Florence says that the Church requires the priest to mix water with the wine in the chalice both because Christ probably did so, and because blood and water came forth together from his side (John 19:34). This mystery is renewed in the mixing. And since in the Revelation of John the nations are called "water" (Rev 17:1, 15), the union of wine and water also represents the union of faithful believers with Christ, the head (cf. Denzinger 1320). These statements of the Council are, of course, not dogmatic teachings of faith, but they indicate the agreement of symbolism in the different churches of East and West, here particularly the Armenian and the Roman. Luther, on the other hand, saw in the unmixed wine of his celebration of the Lord's Supper the image of our redemption by Christ alone, without human aid. He also saw in this praxis a representation of pure teaching without human addition.

The prayer in the missal for the mixing of the wine and water derives, in its content, from ancient liturgical tradition: the union of wine and water is a sign of our participation in the divinity of Christ, who adopted our humanity.

3. The Procession with the Gifts

It is true that the presentation of the gifts by the faithful is by no means the "sacrifice" of the Mass, but it is still a significant expression of their incorporation into the sacrifice of Christ and the Church. The procession with the gifts was shaped by the way in which the character of the Mass as sacrifice was understood. Both Justin Martyr (ca. 150) and Hippolytus of Rome (ca. 225) are acquainted with this procession, but the custom is also attested at an early time in Africa, Milan, Spain, etc. At the beginning of the preparation of the gifts, a procession formed and moved toward the altar. The faithful brought gifts of natural produce: bread and wine, but also oil, wax, flowers, etc. In the Antiochene region the custom seems to have taken a different form: When the people entered the church, they deposited their gifts in a space near the entrance. Deacons then selected the appropriate quantities of bread and wine and brought them to the altar. This was probably the most common usage in the eastern Church and survived in the "Great Entrance" in the Byzantine liturgy, accompanied by the solemn chants of the *cherubikon*.

In Rome also, according to *Ordo Romanus I,* ca. 700, there was sometimes a procession involving only representatives of the people: deacons collected the gifts of the faithful and carried them to the front of the church. However, a procession of all the faithful with their gifts is also well attested for Rome. Theodor Klauser thinks that the transepts of the Roman basilicas from the 4th century onward were, in fact, derived from this practice: The procession moved through the nave to the altar, and the donors laid their gifts on special oblation tables in the transept, which was added to the sides of the sanctuary for that sole purpose; they then returned via the side aisles to their places.

In the west, however, the procession with the gifts declined gradually throughout the early Middle Ages: ordinary bread was leavened, and therefore did not seem appropriate for the Eucharist any longer; besides, the number of communicants became smaller and smaller, so that both processions, the first with the sacrificial gifts and the second for reception of the consecrated elements, vanished little by little. At any rate, it is worth noting that the disappearance of the one procession paralleled the decline of the other: the ritual participation of the faithful at Mass had become very small, or disappeared almost entirely.

Even so, the offertory processions did not entirely die out, although—with a shift from an agricultural to a money economy—the gifts were transformed into donations of coin, especially at funeral Masses (a custom that continues to this day). At ordination Masses, an offering of candles was customary. When a bishop was consecrated, the new bishop brought a container of wine to the one who consecrated him. The practice of receiving money in "collection baskets"—"taking up the collection"—became the general custom.

The practice of bringing forward the gifts has been revived by the present missal. The *General Instruction* says (§49):

> It is desirable for the faithful to present the bread and wine, which are accepted by the priest or deacon at a convenient place. The gifts are placed on the altar to the accompaniment of the prescribed texts. Even though the faithful no longer, as in the past, bring the bread and wine for the liturgy from their homes, the rite of carrying up the gifts retains the same spiritual value and meaning.

The corresponding rubric in the missal anticipates that the faithful, represented by "members of the congregation [bring] up the bread and wine for the celebration of the Eucharist or other gifts for the needs of the Church and the poor." The explanation that follows in the German missal makes good sense: "The monetary collection is another such gift. Therefore, it should be placed in an appropriate spot in the sanctuary. Care should thus be exercised that the taking of the collection be completed before the prayer of offering." There is good foundation for the custom in some places of putting the collection baskets next to the altar: this practice expresses the connection between the Eucharist and care for the poor. The gathering of the collection, by a number of people, should be completed before the Prayer Over the Gifts, on the one hand so that there may be no disturbance during the eucharistic prayer, but primarily because this keeps the contours of the different parts of the Mass fully clear. The Prayer Over the Gifts concludes the preparation of the gifts, and all the associated actions should also be completed by that time.

"The bringing and preparation of the gifts may be accompanied by an appropriate chant or organ music, or it may be done in silence" (German Rubr.). Processional chants, mainly in the form of psalms, are an ancient liturgical custom. Their purpose has already been stated: negatively, the prevention of restlessness, which might otherwise easily arise, and positively, the clarification and internalization of the action.

Article 50 of the *General Instruction* urges that the accompanying chant should be extended until the gifts are placed on the altar. This is sensible: Structurally, the two are closely related, as the chant accompanies the procession. As long as these processions lasted a fairly long time, the chants were extended to match them: usually, a schola or cantor sang the psalm, and the people responded after each verse or two with an antiphon or other easily remembered phrase. With the shrinking of the process of bringing the gifts, the chant became shorter, until in the missal of Pius V (1570) only the antiphon remained; of course, it appeared to have no particular function any longer. Hence *General Instruction* 50 now provides that it should be entirely eliminated if it is not sung. It is also worth noting that, while the missal contains the verses for the entrance and communion (in smaller type), the verse for the preparation of the gifts is no longer given: it is a reasonable accompaniment for movements within the sanctuary, but it is not necessarily a constitutive part of the Mass.

The rubrics for the preparation of the gifts propose as chants the corresponding models in the *Ordo Cantus Missae* or the Roman Gradual or Simple Gradual, as well as vernacular chants or hymns that harmonize either with the spirit of the event (preparation of the gifts) or the character of the day. Organ music and "holy silence" are other possibilities.

4. Prayers Accompanying the Preparation of the Gifts

In the first millennium the preparation of the gifts was done at the altar, presumably in silence. The procession with the gifts was a powerful expression of the mind of the faithful, who, with the donations there represented, desired to enter into the celebration of the sacrifice of Christ and the Church.

When the procession with the gifts disappeared in the Middle Ages, and understanding of the symbol thereby lessened, silent accompanying prayers, at least by the priest, were inserted to interpret the spiritual event. For this purpose, prayers of offering were chosen, quite similar to those in the eucharistic prayer—in fact, almost too similar—so that they were inaccurately called a "little canon:" the *Suscipe, sancte pater . . . hanc immaculatam hostiam* over the bread and *Offerimus tibi, Domine, calicem salutaris* over the chalice, together with the epicletic formula *Veni sanctificator* and, finally, *Suscipe, sancta Trinitas, hanc oblationem. . . .* If one understands *offerre* and *oblatio* in this context to mean "bringing" and "offering" (in the sense of "presentation") of the gifts, the expressions are still absolutely correct from a dogmatic standpoint. Even the appeal to the Holy Spirit is not entirely inappropriate at this point, since it is the Spirit who makes the people of God a holy people. On the other hand, we cannot fail to recognize that almost the same words in the canon mean something fundamentally different: a true sacrifice of the Church.

To avert possible misunderstandings the present missal has deliberately replaced these prayers with others that are more appropriate: Instead of the formula of offering, prayers of praise on the model of Jewish table prayers *(berakoth)* have been chosen; these by no means change the older interpretative sense of these texts, but fully retain it. To assert anything else (as is often done by some traditionalists) is completely unjustified, as a closer look at the two prayers over the bread and wine clearly demonstrates.

These prayers first praise God as the creator of the world and giver of these gifts. They are God's gifts but at the same time the fruit of human labor, the property of the donors, those who bring them as offerings. They bring these gifts (of bread and wine), on behalf of themselves and all participants, into the presence of God (here the earlier *offerre* is deliberately retained!), so that, in the transformative power of the Holy Spirit, they may become the "bread of life" and "our spiritual drink." The consecrated bread and wine are referred to in similar words in the eucharistic prayer, which, as we know, is based on the "Apostolic Tradition" of Hippolytus of Rome. These two terms, "bread of life" and "cup of eternal salvation," are found in the strophe that joins the anamnesis to the offering *(memores offerimus):* "Father, we celebrate the memory of Christ, your Son, . . . we offer to you . . . the bread of life and the cup of eternal salvation." The prayers accompanying the bread and wine at the preparation of the gifts are thus part of the Church's tradition, and are happy reformulations of the ancient teaching.

Whether texts like these should also have been eliminated by the reform, as has often been suggested, is a question that may remain unanswered here. At any rate, the spiritual dimension of the preparation of the gifts for the eucharistic sacrifice is clearly indicated and named. This is beneficial to the offering strophe of the eucharistic prayer, which can thus retain its lapidary brevity and requires no paraphrase or explanatory addition. Thus the preparation of the gifts is interpreted not merely as a physical precondition for the sacrifice, but also as the assent and self-surrender of the faithful who desire to celebrate Christ's sacrifice.

The mixing of wine and water is accompanied by a prayer that suggests their symbolism: the wine is a symbol of divinity, the water of humanity, and their combination is a symbol of God's incarnation in Christ and of human participation in the divinity of the redeemer. This formula is merely a remnant of the previous prayer, which we find even in the oldest sacramentary, the Leonine, as a Christmas *oratio:* Christ's birth is the precondition for the miraculous "exchange of life."

Bread and wine, priest and people, may be (silently) incensed. The incense that is consumed in the fire is a vivid allegory for our surrender to God.

Two brief prayers for purity emphasize the preparatory character of this phase. After the preparation of the bread and wine, the priest bows and prays quietly, "Lord God, we ask you to receive us and be pleased with the sacrifice we offer you with humble and contrite hearts." During the hand-washing at the side of the altar, the priest also says inaudibly: "Lord, wash away my iniquity; cleanse me from my sin" (Ps 51:4).

All these prayers for the preparation of the gifts are, by their nature, not official prayers of the priest, but private prayers that are therefore to be spoken quietly. This is the provision of the rubrics. However, if there is neither singing nor organ music during the preparation of the gifts, the priest is permitted to speak the texts over the bread and wine in an audible voice; in that case, the congregation adopts the prayer as its own by means of an acclamation.

5. Prayer over the Gifts

The prayer over the gifts *(oratio super oblata)* concludes the preparation of the gifts. It summarizes the content and meaning of the action—the preparation of the gifts and the congregation—and leads onward to the eucharistic prayer, forming a transition without a noticeable break. This is theologically correct.

The old name for this *oratio,* long in use, was "secret prayer" because, although it was an official prayer of the priest, spoken in the *orans* posture, it was uttered quietly, in a low voice. This interpretation, however, is apparently recent. The name "secret" is found even in the old sacramentaries from the first millennium, although often in the form *oratio super (oblata) secreta:* prayer over the gifts set aside, that is, over the portions of bread and wine that have been selected to be used for the Eucharist from among the gifts carried in the procession. Today, the prayer over the gifts is again spoken in an audible voice, as an official prayer.

The earlier editions of the German missal (before 1962) preceded the prayer over the gifts with a request by the celebrant to the clergy present, later directed to the whole congregation *(Orate, fratres)* that they pray for him in order that the sacrifice to follow might be pleasing to God. This invitation to prayer represents the most ancient incorporation of Roman material on Frankish soil; it is first attested by Amalar of Metz (d. 850). In its intention, this exchange is most closely allied to the prayers over the gifts. Before the rise of the liturgical movement in the 20th century, the *Orate, fratres* was answered quietly by the altar servers or, at solemn Masses, by the clergy with the *Suscipe,* but it was eagerly adopted as one of the few acclamatory prayers that enjoyed great popularity. This opportunity is still offered as Form C of the invitation to pray over the gifts in the new rubrics of the German missal.[2] But since the responsorial prayer and prayer over the gifts are very similar in their content, they may easily appear to be an unnecessary duplication. Consequently, Form A has transformed the *Orate, fratres* into an expanded call to prayer, like that in the intercessions for Good Friday. Its wording is: "Let us pray to God, the almighty Father, to accept the gifts of the Church to his glory and for the salvation of the whole world." But even the simple and unexpanded "Let us pray," or other variations on the invitation to prayer are possible. If they are well formulated and do not seem garrulous, they can be helpful to the congregation.

As one of the priest's three *orationes,* the prayer over the gifts has the same structure as the collect and closing prayer: appeal to God, predication, and supplications, with a concluding formula. However, the style is less strict overall. The content is often a variation on the same intention that informs the whole preparation of the gifts: they represent the willing submission of the whole community, but that attitude is to be reawakened in order that the celebration of the Eucharist may also be the Church's sacrifice in spirit and truth.

The concluding formula of the prayer over the gifts is more succinct than that of the collect; it omits the appositions of Christ (your Son, our

Lord and God) that are customary at the collect, as well as the "eternity" formula ("forever and ever").

B. The Eucharistic Prayer

> Now the center and summit of the entire celebration begins: the eucharistic prayer, a prayer of thanksgiving and sanctification. The priest invites the people to lift up their hearts to the Lord in prayer and thanks; he unites them with himself in the prayer he addresses in their name to the Father through Jesus Christ. The meaning of the prayer is that the entire congregation joins itself to Christ in acknowledging the great things God has done and in offering the sacrifice. (*GI* 54).

From a form-critical point of view this part, as we have said, may be traced to Jewish table blessings, which appear in an expanded form at Passover. This form of *berakah* is found frequently in the Old Testament and is characteristic of the piety of the covenant people as a whole: In a listing of the proofs of God's power, or of God's gifts—as in the psalms— God is praised as Lord of creation and divine protector of the people. God is implored to maintain fidelity for all times. Thus thanksgiving and confident petition are closely intertwined. The gospel songs are also rooted in this same spirit: the *Magnificat* of the mother of God (Luke 1:46-55), the *Benedictus* of Zechariah (Luke 1:67-79), the *Nunc dimittis* of the ancient Simeon (Luke 2:29-32). So Christ also prayed, when instituting the Eucharist: He spoke the blessing—the praise of God—over the gifts given to human beings by God, and in this praise and thanksgiving he gave them their new meaning and reality. Such a "thanksgiving" (Hebrew *barak*, Greek *eucharistein* or *eulogein*, Latin *benedicere* or *gratias agere*—all these words are fully congruent) is thus not just any form of giving thanks, but this very specific form of "Eucharist," as Jesus and the apostolic community knew and practiced it. The carrying out of such a eucharistic thanksgiving, the "prayer of thanksgiving and sanctification" with which the Mass reaches "its center and high point" (*GI* 54), is called in Latin *prex eucharistica*, and in English simply "the eucharistic prayer."

1. Name and Content

The eucharistic prayer begins with the preface, which follows the prayer over the gifts and is introduced by a dialogue between priest and congregation:

> "The Lord be with you."
> "And also with you" [German missal: "And with your spirit"].

"Lift up your hearts."

"We lift them up to the Lord."

"Let us give thanks *(gratias agamus)* to the Lord our God."

"It is right to give him thanks and praise" [German missal: "It is right and just"].

The eucharistic prayer ends with solemn praise, the great doxology: "Through him, with him, in him . . . ." The continuing flow of praises is impressively illustrated in the eucharistic prayer of Hippolytus, cited above, and stemming from the earliest days of the Church. It gave this central element of our Mass liturgy, the eucharistic prayer, its name.

In the Latin Church this part of the Mass was long called the "canon," often not including the Preface, which was separated from the rest by the Sanctus. However, that is completely wrong, as the history of the form very clearly shows. "Canon," in fact, means "level" (in the sense of a carpenter's tool). It was an aid used by builders in ancient times to test the "rightness" of a wall, by comparing the horizontal beam with the vertical support. "Canon" is the abbreviation of the original term: *Canon actionis gratiarum,* "order of the thanksgiving," the Eucharist. This term is related to the call to prayer: *Gratias agamus Domino Deo nostro,* and designates the traditional and quickly solidified structure of this official priestly prayer accompanying, marking, and determining the sacred actions. The previous missal still had the old direction, *Infra actionem,* above; here also the word *gratiarum* had been lopped off. The Greeks prefer to call the eucharistic prayer *anaphora*. With that name they in all probability refer to the other call to prayer, "Sursum corda" *(anó tas kardías)*. Within Christ's threefold act of institution (taking, giving thanks, distributing), the essential center and high point was the giving of thanks.

2. The Roman Canon

(a) Origins

The Roman canon, now called "Eucharistic Prayer I," possesses an honorable seniority: it is more than 1,500 years old. We can guess that it existed, at least in its fundamental features, as early as the second half of the 4th century; it may have received its basic form under Pope Damasus I (366–384), a Spaniard by birth, who was of the highest importance for the Latin shaping of the Roman liturgy. The official Latin translation of the Bible, Jerome's "Vulgate" (ca. 380) was prepared at his direction. With

Damasus the Greek liturgy of the early period, for which Hippolytus is the most important witness, came to an end in Rome.

Unfortunately, we have no Roman witnesses to the earliest Latin canon, but Ambrose of Milan (339–397), in his *De sacramentis* (IV.5,21–6,27) cites the essential passages. The power of this eucharistic prayer as a model thus passed swiftly beyond Rome into other Latin provinces. In Ambrose's version we do not yet find the various intercessions (with the list of saints), but they are mentioned in advisory letters from Popes Innocent I (401–417), Boniface I (418–422), and Celestine I (422–432). The Roman canon may well have assumed its form very soon after 400.

The Latin liturgy was given its fundamental shaping in the era of Damasus. This did not involve a word-for-word translation of the previous Greek liturgy of the city of Rome; instead, the liturgy was reshaped in the Roman style and spirit. This is especially evident in the *orationes*, the priestly presidial or official prayers—brief, highly succinct and significant prayer-speeches that have no Greek models in this form. The same is true also of the canon.

Compared with Hippolytus's eucharistic prayer, the Roman canon has two special characteristics: One is the interruption of the originally free flow of the prayer by a variety of insertions (see section b, below); the other, and more significant, is the symmetrical and concentric stylization around the unvarying block of prayer in the middle of this canon, the words of Christ (words of institution) and anamnesis (see section c, below).

(b) Formal history

As regards the history of the form, this new Roman canon has its origins also in that of Hippolytus. But whereas in Hippolytus's work the praise continually refers, in a series of relative clauses, to God, whose name is pronounced at the beginning and who is the recipient of the thanksgiving, with the whole series culminating in the final doxology, the new Latin canon is a series of more or less independent or interlocking pieces which are then composed into a whole through the principle of mirroring. The result is a highly artistic new creation, even though encumbered by some artificiality. This *canon actionis gratiarum* was scarcely varied thereafter. To retain its clear structuredness it had to be used as it was, without alteration. Time polished and honed it, but only to bring it more fully into conformity with its structural principle. The Roman canon is as solid as a Roman, keystone-anchored arch, imposing, but also very rational and perhaps somewhat too coldly elegant.

The oldest of the insertions is the *Sanctus,* and in its ultimate consequences it is also the most influential, not from its origins, but because of its gradually expanding form. At the beginning, the *Sanctus* was only part of the words of praise offered to God's creative deeds and ultimately a descendant of the first part of the Jewish prayer after meals (see above). At the mention of the creation of the world, human beings and angels simultaneously put it into action, in biblical terms, singing the threefold "Holy!" of Isa 6:3. This quotation did not necessarily have to lead to the later fracturing of the eucharistic prayer into "preface" and "canon," as we can see, for example, from the so-called "Ambrosian" hymn of praise, the *Te Deum,* where the threefold *Sanctus* is fully integrated into the strophe. In the Old Gelasian (*Cod. reg.* 316) and *Missale Gothicum* also, the preface and canon flow without interruption. But the *Sanctus* quickly acquired an acclamatory character; the audience knew the text and joined in it, possibly in a spontaneous fashion at first. Choral speaking is always awkward, and song is more beautiful. However, it is not only more beautiful, it is also longer, especially when it is meditatively provided with melismata; this, in turn, could easily lead a somewhat impatient celebrant to continue with the prayer, and then to go on praying in more audible tones once the song has ended.

Thus *Ordo Romanus I* (ca. 700) reads: *surgit pontifex solus in canone,* "the bishop begins the canon alone." The *Ordo Romanus XV,* then (already a Frankish composition) provides: "he continues in a low voice, audible only to those standing at the altar." Thus, the more the *Sanctus* expanded, the more parts of the canon were spoken quietly. In its origins, this low-voiced recitation certainly had nothing to do with "the silence of mystery" or the arcane discipline. The old mystery religions were already long forgotten.

In Merovingian France the "silence during the canon" created no problems: No one among the invading Germans understood Latin anyway. But in the end this silence was strictly prescribed, with the canon coming to be regarded as a "great mystery" and the words of institution as the most sacred words of all; because of their power they were employed superstitiously for magical purposes: *hocus pocus* is a parody of *Hoc est Corpus.* Pseudo-Germanus of Paris reports that boys heard the words of institution in the church and repeated them in wanton ways, whereupon bears appeared and tore them to pieces!

In the earliest editions of Anselm Schott's missal (1883ff.), the canon is printed, but not the words of Christ. In the hymnal of my youth, the *Sursum corda* of Paderborn, in use until 1948, I find on p. 27, with reference to the canon: "Because these mysterious words have their power and significance only on the lips of a legally ordained priest, they are omitted here out of reverence. O Christian, cast yourself down in the dust and adore with faith, repentance, humility and love your Savior present on the altar!" As late as 1921 the Congregation of Rites, completely ignoring structural laws and historical development, ordered that the *Benedictus,* the second part of the *Sanctus,* should only be sung after the consecration, with the result that the eucharistic prayer was completely covered up by the choral singing, something that had already occurred in the orchestrated polyphonic Masses.

A second group of insertions was made up of prayers of offering and petitions for blessing and for the consecration[3] of the gifts. They are much more extensive than the *Sanctus,* and were introduced from the beginning into the body of the symmetrically composed canon. For that reason, unlike the expanding *Sanctus,* they always retained their fixed location. As a whole, they are an expression of theological reflection on the Mass as the Church's sacrifice.

The canon begins, immediately after the *Sanctus,* with a prayer for acceptance *(Te igitur):* "We come to you, Father . . . we ask you to accept and bless these gifts we offer you in sacrifice." This insertion mirrors the final statement before the doxology: "Through Christ our Lord you give us all these good gifts. You fill them with life and goodness, you bless them and make them holy."

Near the center of the canon, surrounding the words of Christ and the anamnesis, there are two double-strophed petitions for acceptance and consecration: the *Hanc igitur* and *Quam oblationem* before, and the *Supra quae* and *Supplices* afterward. Together, they constitute almost half of Eucharistic Prayer I.

The intercessions that are inserted in the canon constitute two major blocks, one for the living (for the Church, pope, and local bishop) before the first double-strophed petition, and a corresponding one for the dead and for those present after the second group of petitions. To each of these groups is appended a list of apostles and martyrs especially venerated at Rome. Finally, all these petitions express the idea that the Eucharist is celebrated in communion with the whole Church. It joins heaven and earth.

In the course of time the canon (with still further emphasis on its mirror-image quality) was ritually adorned with a number of signs of the cross: three at the first petition for acceptance *(haec + dona, haec + munera, haec + sancta sacrificia)* and three at the last *(sancti+ficas, vivi+ficas, bene+dicis);* five at the first petition for consecration *(. . . bene+dictam, adscrip+tam, ra+tam, ut nobis Cor+pus et San+guis fiat . . .),* and five more at the anamnesis *(hostiam + puram, hostiam + sanctam, hostiam + immac-*

ulatam, Panem + sanctum vitae aeternae et Calicem + salutis perpetuae).
Five signs of the cross were also made with the host over the chalice before
the elevation at the final doxology. To begin with, these signs of the cross
were probably mere gestures with the right hand toward the gifts lying on
the altar. Under the influence of the analysis of the sacramental signs into
word and action, "form and matter," they were transformed into gestures of
blessing. That was a misunderstanding arising from the Latin *benedicere,*
which was understood to mean "blessing." The two signs of the cross over
the bread and wine, each connected with the word *benedixit* before the
words of Christ, reveal the error. The equation of *"benedicere"* with "blessing," and that in turn with "make the sign of the cross" is inaccurate. Here
benedicere really means "praise and thank," and is no different from Greek
eucharistein and Hebrew *barak.*

The accumulation of signs of the cross has been reduced by the missal
now in force, especially in Eucharistic Prayer I, to a single cross over bread
and wine together, at the first petition of the *Te igitur.* With the corrected
translation of the twofold *benedixit,* so that it now reads: "gave you thanks
and praise," the two signs at the heart of the eucharistic prayer also disappeared. Obviously, at the Last Supper Christ did not make these much later
signs of blessing. Since the high Middle Ages there were also parallel genuflections and elevations of bread and wine, after each separate consecration.

The artistic rules of late antiquity for formal, and especially juridical,
language are evident in the many synonymous doublets (*rogamus ac
petimus; de tuis donis ac datis,* etc.), in sets of three terms in sequence (*haec
dona, haec munera, haec sancta sacrificia; hostiam puram, hostiam sanctam,
hostiam immaculatam,* etc.), or even of five (*benedictam, adscriptam,
ratam, rationabilem, acceptabilemque; creas, sanctificas, vivificas, benedicis
et praestas,* etc.). This kind of cumulative rhetoric is found also in
Germanic and English legal language: bed and board, wife and child, home
and family, etc. It is not common otherwise, and the effect is one of over-
loading. However, the Roman canon bestowed a sacrosanct significance
and special dignity even on the laws of language.

(c) Structure of the canon

We have already referred to the symmetry or mirror-image quality of the
structure of the canon. It may not have been so strict at the outset, because
it presumes the sharp separation of the preface from the canon, which
occurred somewhat later. Only the canon, and not the more independent
and variable preface, has been subjected to this structural rule. Since about

600, the time of Gregory the Great, the text, as we find it in the various groups of sacramentaries, has changed very little.

For what follows it will be absolutely necessary to open the text of the canon and to refer to the schematic structure in Appendix II below in order more easily to grasp the connections. Otherwise, the structure will be difficult to understand.

The center of the eucharistic prayer, the axis of the symmetrical structure, is the anamnetic block constructed around the *memores offerimus*. In the performative memory of the Lord's action in the supper room, its content and significance deriving from the sacrifice of the cross and the resurrection, the "prophecy of death drenched in the hope of resurrection" (Heinz Schürmann), the Church enters into the sacrifice of the Lord present under the forms of bread and wine as his "body given" and "blood poured out," available to us in the signs of a real symbol, under the form of food and drink. Thus this part also retains the memory of that performative action, the "commemorative repetition," on the one hand, and on the other, in the *offerimus*, the entry of the Church into this one, present sacrifice of Christ. The two elements are combined as intimately as possible.

Around this center are grouped interpretive strophes or prayers, as a distinctive frame is placed around a valuable painting. The frame exists to serve what is central and essential, but its splendor gives it an additional accent.

The parts of the frame that border most closely on the center are the prayers of offering that interpret the sacrifice. First the community, in the priest's prayer, brings gifts to God (*Hanc igitur . . .* = Father, accept . . .), and asks for God's gracious acceptance in the gifts that, during their preparation, have been made a self-representation of the people of God. The community knows that it is unworthy, but prays for eschatological peace, freedom from sin, and ultimate perfection. This part is somewhat paraphrased and expanded at Easter and Pentecost. In the next part of the prayer (*Quam oblationem . . .* = Bless and approve our offering . . .), closely connected with the first, the Church prays God, in a kind of consecratory epiclesis, to be active in this sacrifice: God alone can incorporate the community represented by the gifts into the sacrifice of Christ. *Epiclesis* means "calling down," especially calling down the Spirit of God. Although the Holy Spirit is not expressly named here, as in the liturgy of the Byzantine Church, it is always the Spirit "who comes forth from the Father" who sanctifies humanity.

In the same way, the Church again prays after the memorial of Christ's action for the acceptance of this sacrifice (*Supra quae . . .* = Look with favor . . .): God is asked to accept those assembled in their gifts. This is done, entirely in the tradition of prayer in the old covenant, with reference to God's faithful actions on behalf of the ancestors, and their sacrifices pleasing to God, which are the expression of complete surrender of one's life: Abel, Abraham, Melchizedek. But there is more happening here than in the old covenant: This sacrifice is that of Christ, which is certain of being received, "[whose] blood . . . speaks a better word than the blood of Abel" (Heb 12:24). This plea for acceptance is, like the first one before the consecration, closely united with a prayer for God's action, which—in light of the parallels in Eucharistic Prayers II–IV (but also in that of Hippolytus)—we may call a "Communion epiclesis." Only through God's acceptance of the sacrifice does it become fruitful for those who receive the body and blood of Christ: They are "filled with every grace and blessing." In and of itself an epiclesis, a "calling down," presumes a movement from above to below, from God to the sacrifice on earth; here the idea is reversed: the angel creates a union between heavenly and earthly liturgies, and thus at the same time ratifies the sacrifice as something pleasing to God. We may perhaps assume that this "angel" is the *Christos angelos,* the Father's "messenger" in proclamation and sacrament. To this extent, then, the epicleses at the consecration *(Quam oblationem)* and communion *(Supplices)* in the Roman canon represent the twofold dialogical movement of our redemption: from the Father through Christ to human beings, and from the faithful through Christ to the Father. Here again it is striking that the Spirit is not named, as is the case in the Greek liturgies. We can therefore speak here of *logos epicleses* in contrast to Spirit epicleses. Ultimately, however, their meaning is the same.

Around the first layer of framing, a second is laid: In these prayers there is a remembrance of those for whom the sacrifice is made as atonement. Both times, the mention of these different groups is followed by a list of saints especially venerated in Rome, who are implored as intercessors to plead before the throne of God. The unity of the Church on pilgrimage with the Church perfected is well expressed here. While in the first cycle of prayers in the innermost frame the sacrifice of Christ in the anamnesis was more strongly interpreted as a sacrifice of praise to the Father, here in the multiple petitions of an ecclesial nature it is more sharply emphasized as a sacrifice of atonement for Church and community.

First the Church is named in terms of the pope and bishop. This petition is very closely united with the plea for acceptance through its beginning *(Te igitur . . .* = We come to you, Father . . .), and with a relative clause *(in primis, quae tibi offerrimus;* in the vernacular sensibly reshaped as a new independent sentence: "We offer them for . . ."). Thus those whom the Church especially wishes to commend are named first: either because of their rank (earlier there was often reference to other patriarchs, the emperor, etc.) or their special services to the Church or the present sacrificial celebration. Their names were formerly written on folding tablets, so-called diptychs, and were mentioned during the canon (N.N. = *nomina nominanda*, the names to be mentioned). The naming and commendation of these groups of persons is followed by the naming of the saints often called upon (*Communicantes*. . . = "In union with. . ."), whom the Church knows as members of the whole people of God, and whose memorial (*memoria*) it celebrates.

In addition, on major feasts (Christmas, Epiphany, Easter, Ascension and Pentecost) after the word *memoria* the mystery of the feast is given particular expression, because, even more than the naming of the saints, it emphasizes the unity of the Church, which is documented in the unified celebration of the great feasts. In the list of saints, after the mother of God, the apostles are named first (St. Joseph was introduced only by Pope John XXIII), then the early bishops of the city of Rome (Linus, Cletus, Clement, Sixtus II, Cornelius), and other martyrs: Cyprian, bishop of Carthage (d. 258), who was revered early at Rome, Lawrence the deacon (d. 251), and five laymen: Chrysogonus of Aquileia (d. 304); John and Paul (d. 362), officials at the court of Emperor Julian; and the Persian physicians Cosmas and Damian, who died at Rome, the *anargyroi*, (meaning that they heal "for nothing," without payment), to whom the people of Rome appealed in various emergencies of body and soul.

Juxtaposed with this block of petitions is another, corresponding block after the communion epiclesis. In the text, it is attached to the material that precedes it, where there is a plea for the grace and blessing of heaven. Here, the dead are named first (*Memento etiam*. . . = "Remember, Lord, those who have died . . ."), along with those who (because of their services to the community or a special request by the family) are to receive special mention, as well as all others who have died in Christ. This naming of the dead is followed by the commendation of the whole community present, who know themselves to be a Church of sinners, but also a Church of the promise. Just as in the first petition, the host of heavenly intercessors is again mentioned, all of them martyrs this time, beginning with John the Baptist, then seven men and seven women: Stephen, the deacon of Jerusalem (Acts 7:58); the last-chosen apostle Matthias (Acts 1:26); Barnabas, the companion of Paul (Acts 4:36; 9:27; 11:22, and frequently; 1 Cor 9:6; Gal 2:1, 9, 13); Ignatius, bishop of Antioch, martyred at Rome in

107; Pope Alexander (d. 119), who is venerated at Santa Sabina on the Aventine; the Roman presbyter Marcellinus (d. 304), and the exorcist Peter, who is usually mentioned with him ("Marcellinus and Peter"); then follow the women martyrs Felicitas and Perpetua (d. 202 in Carthage); Agatha (d. 215?) and Lucy (d. 304?) from Sicily; and finally the Romans Agnes (d. 304), Cecilia (d. 177 or 203), and Anastasia.

Two relatively short transitional formulae join the body of the eucharistic prayer to the two great units of praise at the beginning and end, the first as a prayer for acceptance (*Te igitur . . .* = "We come to you, Father . . .") after the preface, the second a blessing of the non-eucharistic gifts before the final doxology. It was often customary to bless the first fruits of the land (beans, grapes, etc.) or special devotional gifts (such as wine for mixing the "St. John's wine" on 27 December, small loaves of special bread, etc.) at this point; they were then taken home as *eulogia*.

The Roman canon, which has no special elements of praise in its central portion, is enclosed in two powerfully expressive prayers of praise, the preface at the beginning and the great trinitarian doxology at the end, the latter already appearing in a similar form in Hippolytus's canon at the beginning of the third century.

The congregation's "Amen" is an essential element of the canon, as the people's acceptance, which is made explicitly their own through the "Amen." There are two references to it in the first account of the Mass, in Justin's First Apology, first in chapter 65: "When [the presider] has finished the prayers and the thanksgiving, all the people give their assent by saying 'Amen.' 'Amen' is the Hebrew for 'So be it;'" and then in chapter 67: ". . . the president . . . sends up prayers and thanksgivings . . . and the people assent, saying the Amen."

(d) The preface

Of all the parts of the Roman canon, the preface has preserved the character of the *eucharistia* most perfectly. In it, something of the model of Hippolytus lives on and ultimately something also of the *berakah* of the apostolic community and the way in which Christ prayed. The dialogical formula of invitation to prayer is followed by praise to God for God's saving deeds in history and in the present. This praise culminates in the threefold "Holy!" of the angels. Thus the preface has three clear parts: dialogue, praise, and *Sanctus*.

The dialogue rests on Jewish models: a formula to gain attention and an invitation to prayer, less in its present wording than in its structure. Such words for gaining attention and invitations are called for especially at the prayer after meals, to prepare for the transition. The initial blessing and response are modeled on Jewish peace-formulae, translated into Christian terms. "Lift up your hearts" is already an Old Testament expression: "Let us lift up our hearts as well as our hands to God in heaven" (Lam 3:41). Paul enjoins: "Seek the things that are above, . . . Set your minds on things that are above, . . ." (Col 3:1-2). Hippolytus of Rome knew this acclamation in the early third century in the same words, and so did the African Cyprian, who a few years later reports: "Therefore the priest precedes the eucharistic prayer with a few words of introduction and prepares the hearts of the sisters and brothers by saying: 'Lift up your hearts,' that the congregation, which answers this with: 'We have them with the Lord' may be reminded that they are to think of nothing except the Lord" ("On the Lord's Prayer," 31). *Gratias agamus,* "Let us give thanks to the Lord our God," is probably borrowed from Judaism and at the same time makes clear that the somewhat generalized vernacular expression does not call for thanksgiving in general, but for the specific praise of the *berakah/eucharistia,* still more easily detected in the Byzantine liturgy of St. John Chrysostom's *eucharistäsomen.* The response, "It is right to give him thanks and praise," by contrast, has Hellenistic origins: In the assembly of the *polis,* the acclamation of agreement was *"axios"* (= worthy, right). The purpose of the dialogue portion of the preface is to make everyone conscious of the community of the people of God with their official presider and speaker. To that extent, the *Dignum et justum* of the introduction and the "Amen" at the end of the canon stand in close correspondence to each other and document the community of those assembled as brothers and sisters and their ecclesial unity.

The second part, the praise itself, is closely connected with the dialogue and takes up the people's formula of agreement. It is really true: God is always and everywhere worthy to be praised. God is the "Lord," the "Father" of the people, by nature the "all-powerful and ever-living God." This beginning is always the same in every preface. It is followed by the naming of the special reasons for praise, derived from the mystery of the feast or more generally from God's saving deeds. The diction is for the most part terse and succinct, lapidary Roman style without wordiness. The prefaces, like the *orationes,* belong to the most impressive prayer material of the Roman Church. The listing of God's saving deeds is followed then by the third part, the conclusion, which emphasizes the unity of earthly and heavenly liturgy and culminates in the song of the seraphim (Isa 6:2-3), the threefold *Sanctus.* This hymnic element within the otherwise clear wording of the preface is very old, but perhaps not original: for example,

Hippolytus does not have it, but the first letter of Bishop Clement of Rome to the Corinthians (before 100) already knows it. The *Sanctus* is a fixed element in the "Apostolic Constitutions" (VIII, 12, 27) at the end of the 4th century, but also in most of the eastern liturgies, including Jerusalem (Liturgy of James), Constantinople (Liturgy of St. Basil), and Armenia.

The wording of this hymn begins (in this it is comparable to the Gloria) with a biblical praise of God: here it is taken from Isa 6:3. However, it then combines various liturgical acclamations and composes them into a single hymn. The very mention of the joining of "heaven" in the song of praise, and not the earth alone, represents an addition to the biblical text, even though it is an easy conclusion from the context, because it is the angels who here call out these words. The expansion was already current in Judaism and the common material for all liturgies. The praise of God's "glory" (already in Isa 6:3) refers to God's existence above all worlds: This "glory" (Hebrew *kabod,* Greek *doxa*) is a specific predicate of God throughout the Old Testament; it belongs to God alone.

Hosanna is the Hebrew word *hosian-na* adapted to Greek. Its original meaning was: Save us, come to our aid (cf. Ps 118:25: "Save us, we beseech you, O Lord! O Lord, we beseech you, give us success!") Even in the synagogue liturgy this petition had been transformed into praise of the one who helps, as we may gather from Matt 21:9, the cries of the people on Jesus' entry into Jerusalem: "*Hosanna* to the Son of David!" This passage from Matthew was quite evidently incorporated here, especially the expression about "coming in the name of the Lord." This "coming," in the context of the eucharistic prayer, has the character of a reference. It points to the expected presence of the Lord in the eucharistic gifts. The second part of the *Sanctus,* beginning with the word *Benedictus,* has the character of an acclamation and even with the word *benedictus* (= Hebrew *baruch*) reveals its relationship to Jewish prayer practices: the praise offered by the presider is always followed by the people's acknowledgment (cf. the prayers accompanying the bringing of bread and wine). We may refer also to Rom 9:5, where the mention of the name of God immediately moves Paul, the Jew, to add, according to synagogal usage: "God blessed forever. Amen."

(e) Weaknesses of the Roman canon and its reform

The Roman canon is undoubtedly a most venerable witness to the Church's eucharistic celebration, not because of its age alone, but also because of the way in which it testifies to the doctrine of the Eucharist. However, the artificiality of its structure made a full comprehension of this eucharistic prayer difficult from the outset. To illustrate with an example: it is difficult even for a professional archeologist, when excavating a large, symmetrical complex of baths, to understand every trend in the walls immediately, unless he or she has previously "learned" the plan thoroughly and has it constantly at hand, either on paper or in his or her head. This is multiplied the more historical layers lie one on top of the other, thus making the ancient structure, difficult to begin with, still less clear. The ingenuity of the architect is certainly worth admiring, but the unpracticed observer is easily confused and understands the connections only with difficulty, no matter how clever the plan may be.

Such an observer would be more comfortable in an easily comprehended building, planned like a house, for example; he or she would know at every moment where he or she stood and what functions the individual parts had. The same is true of the Roman canon in its final version before the present reform: It had stood too long and was over-objectified; it was considered to be as unalterable as the inspired word of God itself, but internally it had suffered displacements due to insertions, and it had been rendered unclear by allegorical additions. For the simple faithful who, in the wake of the liturgical movement, again desired to take an active part in the liturgy, it presented too many obstacles; they could not recognize it as an expression of their praise of God, something that they expected and desired to underscore with their "Amen" at the end.

The weaknesses of this canon were many. Especially striking was its poverty with respect to praise, which was its proper content from the beginning. It is true that there were such elements of praise in the preface, but during more than half the year the common preface was prayed, and it consisted of a framework of praise made up of a stereotypical beginning and end without any real content, an "empty formula" in the truest sense. Only on feast days could one hear the "proper." In the canon itself, such a special unit was inserted only on a few feast days, but its effect was more didactic than inspirational. On most Sundays, by far, the preface of the Trinity was used, an adapted piece of dogmatic teaching with the christological vocabulary of a time long past.

The intercessions in the eucharistic prayer occupied far too much space, especially because, for that very reason, they were seen as highly essential to the whole of the Mass, since, after all, it was for their sake that one had offered a Mass stipend in the first place. The vernacular recitation of prayers during the canon, especially petitions, contributed to the same effect. The lists of saints was completely colorless: who called on Linus, Cletus, Clement, Sixtus, Cornelius, or Cyprian for help in their daily needs?

Local saints, or those venerated especially in one place, whose images were better known from history, art, and legend, had no place in the canon.

The epicletic elements were never enunciated clearly, at least not as clearly as the *Veni sanctificator* at the preparation of the gifts, where the epiclesis had lodged in a most inappropriate place. Almost nothing was said in the canon about the Holy Spirit, the soul of God's people and Church. A well-known representative of the eastern Church described this as a "remarkable allergy of the Latin Church toward the Holy Spirit," something he regarded as very sad. He was certainly not entirely wrong. Moreover, the eschatological dimension of the assembly of the community here and now, awaiting the Lord "until he comes again" was completely lacking, even though in Paul's account of the Lord's supper (1 Cor 11:26) this plays such an essential role.

Stylistically, the canon was so fragmented by the many insertions and repeated "amens," which practically hacked apart the individual strophes or pieces of the canon, that the grammatical connections and references often remained up in the air: for example, the *Communicantes,* and even the consecration, which begins with an unreferenced relative pronoun: *qui pridie . . .* , the very easily misunderstood *pro Ecclesia tua . . . quam . . . regere digneris toto orbe terrarum, una cum famulo tuo Papa nostro N. et antistite nostro N.*, as if God made arrangements for the government of the Church with the pope and each individual local bishop, for example the leader of the tiny Italian diocese of Borgo. The relationships simply did not work any longer! If the canon of early days could be praised for its resemblance to a skillful Roman arch of well-shaped keystones, those stones had now been displaced as if by an earthquake. They no longer fit together. Absolutely unbearable were the many signs of the cross, one after another, especially when the celebrant made them obediently, following the rubrics, but in a completely inappropriate fashion and much too fast, which often gave him the appearance of sawing or chopping something with his hand.

These complaints are idle and superfluous, because there was a distinct turn for the better in the wake of the reform. Thus the elements of praise have been happily expanded by the addition of a great many prefaces, attuned to the feasts and seasons of the liturgical year; the empty "common preface" no longer exists. The numerous recent expansions of the canon text to apply to specific situations are an aid to the faithful, providing impulses for thought and suggestions for participation in the celebration. The intercessions have recovered a defensible degree of proportionality to the whole; the lists of saints have been shortened, and according to need and spiritual benefit to the participants they may be varied somewhat. The two epicleses, the consecration and the Communion prayer to the Holy Spirit have had their meaning clarified, more in the translations than in the Latin model.

It is easier to retouch the text when translating it into the vernacular than to change the original, the wording of which, understandably enough— for the sake of reverence for history—one is somewhat reluctant to change in any drastic way. The awaiting of the Lord's return has been clearly accented by its placement at the center of the anamnetic block, and thus at the heart of the sacrificial event, in the new acclamation of the people. This acclamation has its advantages. The *mysterium fidei* has been eliminated from the words of consecration and has become the "spark" for a special activity of the people, which, with its acclamation, also expresses an essential aspect of the Eucharist. Scarcely anyone will weep for the loss of the old ritual trimmings, such as the 21 signs of the cross in place of a single, truly meaningful one, kissings of the altar, etc. Anyone who does is pretty much a hopeless case, liturgically speaking! Nowhere has the reform resulted in any genuine loss or abbreviation in doctrine, or in the liturgical execution that is possible today, or in the spiritual dimension of the community celebration. On the contrary, it is only because of the reform that the ancient and venerable canon has a chance of survival.

3. Other Texts for the Eucharistic Prayer

Some months before the publication of the constitution *Sacrosanctum Concilium* in April 1964, a liturgical commission was constituted at Rome for the carrying out of the conciliar decisions; they in turn appointed a study commission for the eucharistic prayer. The task of this study commission was one of the most ticklish in the whole liturgical reform, because many bishops and liturgists were of the opinion that a liturgical monument like the Roman canon should be regarded as fully complete in its development and that it should be entirely excepted from any reform, apart, perhaps, from a few light retouchings here and there. But a majority of the bishops wanted new eucharistic prayers that would be on an equal footing with the Roman canon. Even so, the commission members were instructed that new eucharistic prayers must "correspond to the genius of the Roman liturgy." It would be necessary "to preserve the coherence between new eucharistic prayers and the traditional liturgy of the Mass."

Formally, what was understood by "the genius of the Roman liturgy" was its ancient style: succinct and not wordy, neither a hymnic poem nor a dogmatic tract. Structurally, the primary object was to preserve the special character of the prefaces, although these were to be greatly increased in number. For while the *anaphoras* in the eastern church incline to summarize all the events of salvation in a single eucharistic prayer, it seems to have been the custom in the West, from the very beginning, to relate the words of praise as nearly as possible to the particular feast within the liturgical year and in doing so, to shift the focus to the preface; the remaining parts of the eucharistic prayer (prayers concerning the presentation of the Church's sacrifice, the epicletic moments, and the intercessions) placed more concentrated emphasis on the sacrificial action. In addition, the single epiclesis of the eastern Church *after* the words of Christ had been divided in the west, from the earliest period, into its two essential elements: a prayer for the transformation of the gifts before the consecration and a Communion epiclesis after the consecration, which in turn formed a transition to the subsequent reception of the Eucharist. These instructions of the liturgical commission did, in fact, harmonize with the Latin tradition and were therefore well-founded.

The study commission went to work right away, and was able to present its results to the meeting of the full liturgical commission in April 1967. It first suggested that the old, slightly corrected canon be known in future as Eucharistic Prayer I *(prex eucharistica I),* but that four additional eucharistic prayers be added. The first would be a short prayer based on materials from the canon of Hippolytus, but reconstructed in such a way that, as was the Latin custom, the interchangeable prefaces would recite God's saving deeds and conclude with the *Sanctus,* while the eucharistic prayer itself would correspond more closely to the material content of the Roman canon.

A second, new composition was proposed, constructed primarily of materials from the old canon, but with a view to a more comprehensible structure and logical succession; a third would be drawn from prayer materials in the Antiochene tradition (especially "Apostolic Constitutions" VIII), somewhat less Roman in character, because the praise material would echo beyond the preface and Sanctus: by its nature, then, this prayer would not allow for interchangeable prefaces. As a fourth eucharistic prayer, the commission suggested an adaptation of the Alexandrian liturgy of St. Basil. In all four eucharistic prayers the words of Christ in the last supper account (but not the framing additions) would be exactly the same and in accordance with the old canon, so that there would always be an identical recitation in every eucharistic prayer, and the celebrant would not be required to look in the missal for a special form each time. This gave an opportunity to insert the relative clause, "which will be given up for you," from Luke 22:19, in the words over the bread; astonishingly enough, it had been omitted from the Roman canon in spite of its emphatic sacrificial theology.

After long deliberations, and some considerable opposition by a few individuals, the revised Roman canon (as described above) and three other eucharistic prayers, together with (for the time being) eight prefaces, were officially published on Ascension Day 1968. The fifth suggested eucharistic prayer (modeled on the liturgy of St. Basil) had not received approval. The four eucharistic prayers were incorporated soon afterward into our present missal.

Despite all differences, the three new eucharistic prayers have a unified structure, the elements of which are accurately described in *GI* 55:

The chief elements making up the eucharistic prayer are these:

a. Thanksgiving (expressed especially in the preface): in the name of the entire people of God, the priest praises the Father and gives thanks to him for the whole work of salvation or for some special aspect of it that corresponds to the day, feast, or season.

b. Acclamation: joining with the angels, the congregation sings or recites the *Sanctus*. This acclamation is an intrinsic part of the eucharistic prayer and all the people join with the priest in singing or reciting it.

c. Epiclesis: in special invocations the Church calls on God's power and asks that the gifts offered by human hands be consecrated, that is, become Christ's body and blood, and that the victim to be received in communion be the source of salvation for those who will partake.

d. Institution narrative and consecration: in the words and actions of Christ, that sacrifice is celebrated which he himself instituted at the Last Supper, when, under the appearances of bread and wine, he offered his body and blood, gave them to his apostles to eat and drink, then commanded that they carry on this mystery.

e. Anamnesis: in fulfillment of the command received from Christ through the apostles, the Church keeps his memorial by recalling especially his passion, resurrection, and ascension.

f. Offering: in this memorial, the Church—and in particular the Church here and now assembled—offers the spotless victim to the Father in the Holy Spirit. The Church's intention is that the faithful not only offer this victim but also learn to offer themselves and so to surrender themselves, through Christ the Mediator, to an even more complete union with the Father and with each other, so that at last God may be all in all.

g. Intercessions: the intercessions make it clear that the eucharist is celebrated in communion with the entire Church of heaven and earth and that the offering is made for the Church and all its members, living and dead, who are called to share in the salvation and redemption purchased by Christ's body and blood.

h. Final doxology: the praise of God is expressed in the doxology, to which the people's acclamation is an assent and conclusion.

The eucharistic prayer calls for all to listen in silent reverence, but also to take part through the acclamations for which the rite makes provision.

(a) The second eucharistic prayer

A great many of the building blocks for this eucharistic prayer, as we have already said, stem from the canon of Hippolytus. But these verses have been rearranged or conformed more strongly to the "spirit of the Roman liturgy." Hippolytus's listing of God's saving deeds in creation and (sharply abbreviated) in the christological history of salvation up to Christ's death and resurrection now constitutes the preface; the *Sanctus* is added; and, after a transition, the first part of Hippolytus's epiclesis is brought forward as a consecration epiclesis; then follows the consecration, with the people's acclamation and the anamnesis, which, as in the Roman canon, is followed by a petition for a sharing in Christ's body and blood in the Communion epiclesis. The intercessions, clearly arranged and adaptable, then follow and lead to the great concluding praise with the community's "Amen." It will be helpful if the reader places the Hippolytus text (see above) alongside Eucharistic Prayer II (see Appendix III) for comparison.

We may say that this composition both makes use of Hippolytus's model and reshapes it. For example, while in the model it is always the Father who appears as the one acting in Christ, the new preface retains this theology but drops it after the *Sanctus*. The offering-strophe corresponds both to Hippolytus' and the Roman canon, but afterward the structures of the Roman eucharistic prayer control almost exclusively, which is entirely sensible and logical, especially because in this way the whole Church, extending beyond the group of those now celebrating, is clearly brought into view in the intercessions. The Mass is not simply the communion of individuals with Christ, but also with the whole Church, both earthly and heavenly.

The preface for this eucharistic prayer is invariable. To this extent it appears somewhat un-Roman, since the mystery of no single feast is singled out; instead the history of salvation from creation onward is mentioned, although very briefly, and a number of decorative passages in the model have been dropped. Apparently there was a desire not to exceed the measure of a normal Roman preface. God's action in the old covenant, which is commemorated at special length in Eucharistic Prayer I and particularly in Eucharistic Prayer IV, is absent here, as it is in the model.

(b) The third eucharistic prayer

This eucharistic prayer is most clearly in harmony with the traditional Roman canon: it has no preface of its own. Many of its formulations have been drawn from the Roman model. To oversimplify somewhat, one could say that here the old canon has been reshaped according to the new structural principles, and enriched with many formulations stemming from other liturgical sources.

The connection of the variable preface to the rest of the text with "*Vere sanctus . . .*" ("Father, you are holy indeed . . .") is very fortunate. But in addition, God's saving deeds, already mentioned in the preface, are resumed and briefly summarized. Thus here the Church appears as the high point of God's saving will and as the one who brings the "perfect offering . . . from east to west," as prophesied by Malachi (1:11). The insertions planned for Sundays and feast days, like those already familiar from the Roman canon, constitute a further structural backward reference to the praises in the preface. They emphasize the firm closure and unity of the whole eucharistic prayer.

The epiclesis is also well situated in its context. It connects immediately to Malachi's prophecy about the perfect offering, asks that the Spirit be sent upon these particular gifts, the memorial whose celebration has been mandated for the Church by the Lord himself. It then moves seamlessly into the Last Supper narrative and anamnesis. This also refers to the eschatological aspect of the Lord's return. The Communion epiclesis is at the same time a well-formulated testimony to prayerful theology: "the Victim whose death has reconciled us to yourself" is "your Church's offering," which it offers to the Father "in thanksgiving." The fruit of this sacrifice of Christ is the gift of the Spirit and the unity in Christ that finds its tangible expression in the communion of the table. At the same time, the community itself is to enter into this sacrifice. First the Spirit makes of it a gift pleasing to the Father.

Here the connection to the petitions of the community, which follow, is very successful: the request to enter into the promised inheritance expands the view vertically toward the perfected saints in heaven, and horizontally to the whole number of the redeemed, including "all your children wherever they may be." Then those who have died in the grace of God are included in the prayer, and finally the horizon is again widened—really exploded—with a glance at the heavenly liturgy of the end-time at the coming of Christ, when all will "enjoy forever the vision of your glory." [The German text speaks of "sitting at table in your kingdom."] The old petition of the canon for the blessing of the gifts of nature also reappears here, but eucharistically reshaped and forming a preparation for the conclusion to the eucharistic prayer, which remains the same for all four.

Anyone who often meditates and prays through the whole of this third eucharistic prayer will clearly sense that here the rich tradition of the Roman Church's treasury of prayer has been very well researched, expanded, and consistently reshaped in such a way that it combines the dynamism and fluidity of Greek anaphoras with the spare tectonics and closer relationship of individual parts to one another that marks the Roman tradition.

(c) The fourth eucharistic prayer

While the second eucharistic prayer adopted elements from the canon of Hippolytus, and the third drew primarily on the Roman canon, the fourth relies on parts of the Antiochene "Apostolic Constitutions." One might call this eucharistic prayer the most ecumenical, because it has a structure strongly reminiscent of those in the eastern Church, especially since the Sanctus does not separate the preface from the eucharistic prayer, but instead—as in the beginning—is an embedded section of the praise that continues after the *Sanctus*. Ultimately, the structure of this eucharistic prayer is derived also from Jewish prayer after meals and presumes the work of Hippolytus: praise of God, then of God's creation of the visible world and the universe, the praise of the angels who sing the *Sanctus* and of human beings, created in the image of God, who, although they lost God's friendship through their disobedience and became subject to the power of death, were never abandoned by God, but received the offer of God's covenant and were taught by the prophets to expect salvation in Christ. Then follows praise for God's saving work in the New Testament, culminating in Christ's death and resurrection, continuing and perfected in the sending of the Spirit, and in the Church, the ever-living Christ.

The reference to the sending of the Spirit leads to the consecration epiclesis and the central section, familiar from the other eucharistic prayers, but here somewhat expanded, consisting of the framing text with the words of the Lord (consecration), the acclamation, and the anamnesis of Christ's death, descent to the ancestors, resurrection and ascension, and the anticipation of his return. This real memorial is both the presence of the sacrificed Lord and the entry of the community into that sacrifice, in which it has a share through the one bread and the one cup, in order to become one body in the Holy Spirit and one living sacrificial gift in Christ. It is the Spirit who effects this communion. The community is then specifically named: pope and bishops, priests and deacons, the donors of the gifts and the whole congregation, the entire people and all humankind who seek God with sincere hearts, those who have departed in Christ and all the dead whose faith is known to God alone. An appeal then to Mary, the apostles, and all the saints leads to the expectation of the future revelation of the reign of God and the final doxology with the congregation's "Amen."

This redaction reveals many significant advantages. From a purely external point of view it is, at first glance, not very unlike the Latin liturgy, since it clearly contains a preface and *Sanctus*. But the fact that the preface is not interchangeable and is an integrative part of the entire eucharistic prayer gives a Greek impression. Another Greek feature is found in the fact that the eucharistic prayer has less to do with a single feast than with the whole event of salvation, in which the Father appears as the one acting and disposing of events: from the creation of the visible and invisible world, through the leading of the ancestors in faith, the redemption through Christ and its continuation in the Church until the final consummation of the world in the coming of Christ. The central proclamation at the heart of the eucharistic prayer (the words of the Lord and the anamnesis) are thus integrated as intimately as possible within the depiction of the whole event of salvation, something we find in the tradition of the ancient Church's liturgy. Thus this fourth eucharistic prayer succeeds in accomplishing a genuine ecumenical breakthrough, as in it the traditions of east and west are joined together.

C. The Communion

In the commemorative repetition of the action of Christ in the supper room, the communion corresponds to the last act of the three (taking, giving thanks, distributing). "Through the breaking of the one bread the unity of the faithful is expressed and through communion they receive the Lord's body and blood in the same way the apostles received them from Christ's own hands" (*GI* 48, 3). Article 56 of the *General Instruction* says of the procedure for carrying out this action within the Mass: "Since the eucharistic celebration is the paschal meal, it is right that the faithful who are properly disposed receive the Lord's body and blood as spiritual food as he commanded. This is the purpose of the breaking of the bread and the other preparatory rites that lead directly to the communion of the people."

In the very earliest period, the distribution of the consecrated bread probably took place without any particular ceremony, as Justin Martyr reports. However, it is also probable that the celebrant's prayer of thanksgiving very soon incorporated elements of petition for the fruitful reception of the gifts in the power of the Holy Spirit. Some of these elements have survived in the communion epiclesis described by Hippolytus. The breaking of the bread into pieces according to the number of participants at the meal was already part of the action of Christ and at first was a purely functional necessity. However, we find a spiritual interpretation even in Paul's account: "The bread that we break, is it not a sharing in the body of Christ? Because there is one bread, we who are many are one body, for we all partake of the one bread" (1 Cor 10:16-17). The manifold unity and mutual love of the community, expressed in the sharing of the one bread made up of many grains, was formulated even in the earliest eucharistic prayers, as in Didache 9:4: "As this bread was scattered over the hills and then was brought together and made one, so let your Church be brought together from the ends of the earth into your kingdom. For yours is the glory and the power through Jesus Christ forever."

A second concern, besides that of unity, appears to be worthiness: "Examine yourselves, and only then eat of the bread and drink of the cup" (1 Cor 11:28). The Didache (following Matt 7:6) warns: "Do not give what is holy to dogs" (Didache 9:5). This petition for a proper disposition appears again and again in the Mass, from the communion epiclesis in the eucharistic prayer through the final petitions of the Lord's Prayer (Our Father), with the insertion that follows, the singing of the *Agnus Dei* and the silent prayer of preparation, and the "Lord, I am not worthy."

The gestures of breaking and distributing the bread, very simple to begin with, acquired a series of expressive actions and preparatory prayers in the course of time:

1. The "Lord's Prayer" as table prayer,
2. Prayers for peace and accompanying gestures,
3. Expanded texts for the breaking of the bread,
4. The chant for the Communion procession, with interpretive formulae for the distribution,
5. The closing prayer.

1. The Lord's Prayer

In the Latin rite, the Lord's Prayer (Matt 6:9-13; cf. Luke 11:2-4) begins the third part of the eucharistic liturgy. It is regarded as the table prayer for the communicants, especially because of the fourth petition: "Give us this day our daily bread." Even Cyprian and Ambrose interpreted this desire in eucharistic terms. The fifth petition: "And forgive us our trespasses, as we forgive those who trespass against us" suggests the ideas of unity and peace, and easily introduces the concern for the worthiness of reception, expressly named in the sixth and seventh petitions (for freedom from temptation and from evil). An insertion (embolism) paraphrases these petitions, expands them eschatologically, and concludes in a doxological acclamation that turns the thought back to the beginning of the Lord's Prayer, the expectation of the inbreaking of the fullness of the reign of God. With its petition for bread and for the unity and worthiness of the re-cipients, the prayer summarizes all the major concerns of the Communion celebration.

The Lord's Prayer has certainly been a part of the Mass since the late 4th century and is attested in the West by Jerome (*Adv. Pelag.* 3, 15), Ambrose (*De sacr.* 6, 14), Augustine (*Ep.* 149), and others, and in the East by Cyril of Jerusalem (*Cat. mystag.* 5, 11-18). The Easterners usually pray the Lord's Prayer after the breaking of the bread, immediately before Communion, while the Latins—certainly since Gregory the Great—have it before the breaking of the bread. Gregory even considers it part of the eucharistic prayer.

The Lord's Prayer is the common prayer of priest and people. From Carolingian times onward it was for a long time the priest's prayer, except for the final petition, although the older introductory formula in the plural (*"we* have the courage to say") could only refer to the whole community. The acclamatory "Amen" of the congregation that, for a long time, followed the priest's prayer, disappeared when the congregation again assumed the part belonging to it.

The Lord's Prayer in the Mass has an introduction, an insertion after its recitation, and a final acclamation. Earlier, there was only a single form of invitation to pray (cf. Cyprian, *Lord's Prayer* 2). Today a number of vari-ations are possible, and still others can be added according to the feast or season (Rubr.); these give a thematic expansion to the usual "Let us pray." However, the invitation to pray is distinguished from these by not being a call for a period of silent prayer; instead, it is meant to insure that all will begin the prayer simultaneously: all should speak the opening words, the address to God, which belongs to the whole congregation. The intonation of a part of the prayer or of a hymn by the celebrant, which suggests itself from other analogies ("Glory to God in the highest," "I believe in God"), with the congregation joining in afterward, is always awkward in light of the distribution of roles in the liturgy. At the *Credo,* this practice has now been overcome through a corresponding invitation to prayer uttered by the priest, but it remains in many ways unsatisfying at the *Gloria.*

The Our Father is again, as in the early period, the prayer of the people, and no longer an official prayer of the priest, although now as before the priest assumes the *orans* posture, with arms raised—which is really inconsistent. More lovely and more meaningful than a common recitation of the Lord's Prayer, of course, is a festive chant.

The insertion (embolism, *Libera nos*) derives from more recent times. Until the present missal it was prayed in silence by the priest, but it is now spoken aloud. The embolism is not the people's part. It is more succinct than before, and heterogeneous petitions that had crept in at different times have been omitted. In its content it continues the final petition of the Our Father and takes up the idea of peace as well. It is a pity that, through the opening paraphrase, asking that we be delivered "from all evil," the ecumenical agreement about the final petition has practically been erased ("Deliver us from the Evil One/Thing" rather than the earlier "Deliver us from evil"), which— in harmony with the original Greek text—apostrophizes both *that which* is evil and *the* personal Evil One, God's opponent.[4] The text ends with the expectation of the eschatological coming of the Redeemer (according to Titus 2:13). This leads easily to the people's acclamation: "For the kingdom, the power and the glory are yours, now and forever." This acclamation derives from the very oldest liturgy and from there it even entered many biblical manuscripts as a gloss (after Matt 6:13). It was handed down in the Didache (9:4) and in many eastern liturgies from earliest times. In particular, the addition of "For thine is the kingdom . . ." in the Churches of the Reformation has become a characteristic of the "Protestant Our Father." Catholics in German-speaking countries do not use it as a rule except in the Mass. Certain groups who are blind to history regard its appearance as an acclamation in the Communion of the Mass as "proof" that the Catholic liturgy has been protestantized. These people are referred to what I have said above, as well as to the liturgies of St. James and St. Mark.

2. The Exchange of Peace

In the Roman missal the complex action of breaking the bread and extending the greeting of peace became confused over a period of time. The reform of the missal has restored good order especially in this part of the Mass.

Justin tells us that the peace was exchanged at the very beginning of the Mass of the Faithful: when the intercessions were ended, "we greet one another with a kiss," and then the gifts for the Eucharist were brought in.

The situation is similar for Hippolytus ("Apostolic Tradition" 22, 6), in the *Apostolic Constitutions* (VIII, 1, 9), and in most of the eastern rites. Even in Rome and Milan it appears that it was this way in the beginning, as Justin and Hippolytus suggest. The practice was different, however, in North Africa, and it was from there that the custom of giving the peace just before communion reached Rome in the 4th century. There is good reason for this greeting at both of those points in the Mass.

Regular Communion at every Mass declined in late antiquity. Even then, it seemed inappropriate to remain present if one was not to participate in the Communion. But to prevent people from simply straggling out of the church, those departing were given a parting blessing; this, in turn, soon began to be regarded as a kind of substitute for Communion. Even Augustine (*Ep.* 149) knows of this blessing; Caesarius of Arles (*Prd.* 73, 2) requires in the early 6th century that all should remain in the church until "the Lord's Prayer is spoken and the people are blessed." Gregory of Tours (d. 594) reports explicitly (*Miracles of St. Martin* 2, 47) that the Communion of the people begins after the dismissal of those who are not communicating. Even in Rome we find the notice of the next station Mass given before Communion, (as in *Ordo Romanus I* and the Gelasian Sacramentary, ed. Mohlberg, 186), which certainly indicates that a great number of the faithful were already leaving at that point.

In the course of time, this custom of dismissal and the disruption of the course of the Mass caused this part of the liturgy to become very disorganized. Thus in the missal of Pius V the breaking of the bread took place during the embolism *(Libera nos);* part of the host was dropped into the chalice, accompanied by three signs of the cross (which originally were probably part of the blessing at the dismissal of those leaving), during the exchange of peace; only then came the *Agnus Dei,* which was properly a chant accompanying the breaking of the bread (which, however, was now already past). The exchange of peace (among the clergy alone, and then only at solemn Masses) took place after the first silent prayer of preparation and the petition for peace. Since the reform, the gesture and wish for peace have been combined with the breaking of the bread and the chanting of the *Agnus Dei,* which properly belongs there.

The rite for the exchange of peace now has three parts:

— the priest's prayer for peace,
— the priest's expression of the wish that the congregation may have peace, together with their response, and
— a gesture of peace given to one another by those assembled.

The introductory prayer for peace in the Latin missal (edition of 1970; 2nd ed. 1975) is the first of what previously were three silent prayers of preparation, but now phrased in the plural. This prayer was drawn from collections of private prayers, and was introduced into the Mass in the early Middle Ages. It continues the third appeal of the *Agnus Dei (dona nobis pacem)* and motivates the exchange of the kiss of peace among the clergy in the sanctuary, which previously followed it. As a private prayer, it was phrased in the singular. Now it has really become a presidential or official prayer, which scarcely fits its style. The rubrics of the Latin missal dictate that the priest should speak the prayer for peace with hands extended. In the German version we find a reshaping of this: The first half of the prayer for peace has been transformed into an invitation to pray, motivating the congregation's own petition for peace and variable according to the season of the liturgical year; the real prayer for peace then follows. The *orans* posture was not accepted. The prayer is addressed to Christ, as are other elements before the communion ("Lamb of God," "This is the Lamb of God," "Lord, I am not worthy"). On the whole, the German form is more satisfactory than the Latin.

The wish that the congregation may have peace, with their answer, is an ancient liturgical formula. It corresponds to the bishop's greeting at the beginning of the Mass. The more precise designation of that peace as "the peace of the Lord" reveals the Christian and ecclesial dimension: this is more than mere worldly peace (John 14:27). The origin of the formula, however, was secular, and it is common especially in Semitic usage (Hebrew *shalom,* Arabic *salaam aleicum*). Most of the Pauline letters begin and end with such greetings. That peace is itself a component of eschatological salvation, the fruit of communion. The usage of spreading the hands during the greeting, because of its origins, signifies a collective embrace; it is thus different from similar gestures of invitation to prayer ("Let us pray") or the *orans* posture during the official prayer.

The peace gesture was not introduced in Germany as intended, although the missal for the German-speaking dioceses contains the following rubric: "The deacon or the priest may invite the people to declare to one another their willingness for peace and reconciliation in a way that corresponds to the customs of the locality, such as: 'Let us offer each other a sign of peace and reconciliation.'" In that case, the priest himself offers the kiss of peace to the deacon or an acolyte. It is a matter for the bishops' conference to provide for such a sign (or several possibilities). An embrace (the *accolade* of Romance lands) or a kiss on the cheek are rather uncommon in our latitude; in many places a handshake has become customary at this point, and for us (when more than merely a polite greeting) it can be a sign of real human affection. Some thought really should be given to this, because gestures are more powerfully expressive than mere words. It is true, however, that it is difficult to find an appropriate posture or gesture for this purpose.

3. The Breaking of the Bread

"[The priest] takes the host and breaks it over the paten. He places a small piece in the chalice, . . ." (Rubr.)

(a) The rite

The breaking of the bread was necessary as long as a single loaf of bread was consecrated, requiring that it be broken into as many pieces as necessary for distribution to those communicating. The appearance of small hosts the size of a coin really made this ritual superfluous. According to the previous missal, only the priest's host was broken: first into two pieces, with a small piece of one half being broken off and placed in the chalice for "commingling." However, this ritual had a different origin and meaning (see section 3b, below).

The functionally necessary breaking of the *one* bread acquired a symbolic significance, already clearly echoed in the New Testament accounts of the Last Supper: The one bread is Christ, who in the broken bread gives a share in his own life. "Breaking of bread: this gesture of Christ at the Last Supper gave the entire eucharistic action its name in apostolic times. In addition to its practical aspect, it signifies that in Communion we who are many are made one body in the one bread of life which is Christ (see 1 Cor 10:17)" (*GI* 56c).

It is not quite certain that the "breaking of bread" in apostolic times (Acts 2:42), mentioned in this article, really means the eucharistic celebration, as the text of the *General Instruction* suggests. The passage in Acts could refer to table fellowship in general, since Jews spoke of "breaking" bread with reference merely to the blessing over the bread before the meal. This is essentially different from Christ's distribution of the one bread (Matt 26:26; Mark 14:22; Luke 22:19; 1 Corinthians), for Christ's action reaches beyond the momentary event perceptible to the sense and probably points back to a paschal ritual that has been reinterpreted in the New Testament: whoever ate only a piece of the paschal lamb as big as an olive had a share in the whole blessing of Passover. So the bread that we break is a sharing in the body of Christ (1 Cor 10:16), who is himself our slaughtered paschal lamb (1 Cor 5:7).

The rite of breaking the bread conveys a great deal of meaning; therefore its execution deserves full respect and care, today as well as in the past.

The practical difficulties we have already mentioned (shower of crumbs, awkwardness in reception, etc.) should not lead us to minimalize it. For this reason, *GI* 195 provides that, as a rule, large hosts should be broken, although small hosts should not be completely eliminated. Attention should therefore be paid to *GI* 283:

> The nature of the sign demands that the material for the eucharistic celebration truly have the appearance of food. Accordingly, even though unleavened and baked in the traditional shape, the eucharistic bread should be made in such a way that in a Mass with a congregation the priest is able actually to break the host into parts and distribute them to at least some of the faithful. (When, however, the number of communicants is large or other pastoral needs require it, small hosts are in no way ruled out.) The action of the breaking of the bread, the simple term for the eucharist in apostolic times, will more clearly bring out the force and meaning of the unity of all in the one bread and of their charity, since the one bread is being distributed among the members of one family.

Especially at wedding Masses, eucharistic celebrations in small groups, concelebrations, etc., it is advisable to make it possible for those present to participate in the symbolism of this breaking of the bread. Moreover, it is no longer prescribed that the priest alone must consume the large host. It can easily be treated in such a way that it is shared with the lectors and other ministers. In any case, it is important and helpful that, even if it is not a single loaf that is shared, the hosts for those communicating be taken from a single dish. Article 293 of the *General Instruction* is specific about this: "For the consecration of hosts one rather large paten may properly be used; on it is placed the bread for the priest as well as for the ministers and the faithful." The small paten for the priest's host that was formerly customary can now be dispensed with. The breaking of the host is no longer done over the chalice, but in the dish or paten (Rubr.).

"It is most desirable that the faithful receive the Lord's body from hosts consecrated at the same Mass . . . ." (*GI* 56h). The distribution of hosts preserved in the tabernacle should remain an exception. Unfortunately, the practice nowadays is often still the reverse. Certainly thoughtlessness plays a role here, but sometimes practical considerations dominate. Nevertheless, one should not withhold from the community the sign of the *one* bread taken from the *one* altar—a reiterated wish of the Church according to Pius XII's 1947 liturgical encyclical *Mediator Dei*. When, in addition, the bread is distributed by members of the congregation, it makes sense that *the same* bread, as the gift just consecrated, should be distributed. After all, we generally know approximately how many communicants to expect. To ask before Mass who wants to receive communion can be disturbing and seem tactless. In many congregations the practice is for the communicants, using tongs, to place a host in the dish. Obviously, it will often prove necessary, in any case, to place the remaining hosts in the tabernacle and distribute them at another Mass.

(b) The commingling

"Commingling: the celebrant drops a part of the host into the chalice" (*GI* 56d; Rubr.). This ritual has a complicated and multi-layered tradition. Probably it was retained chiefly for ecumenical reasons, although it can be made accessible to believers today only by explanation. However, the *General Instruction,* surprisingly enough, offers no clarification at all.

The origin of this custom probably lies in the household communion of the early period: the faithful took the sacred species home with them, unless, in emergencies, they were brought by the deacons (Justin, "First Apology" 65 and 67). While leavened bread may be kept a long time under certain conditions, it quickly becomes stale and hard. Therefore, before being eaten it was dipped or soaked in wine or water to soften it. (In some rural districts and mountain valleys, one still encounters the practice of softening dry, stale bread in a cup or dish and eating it with a spoon.) The idea that the wine itself was "consecrated" by contact with the body of Christ was widespread. At the "Mass of the Presanctified," celebrated in the eastern Church on weekdays in Lent since the 6th century, but customary for us only on Good Friday, this practice of softening by mixing was useful. The customary way of distributing Communion in the eastern Church, by immersing the body of Christ in the chalice and placing it in the mouths of the faithful by means of a small spoon, probably goes back to the same preconditions and customs.

Especially in Syria, but elsewhere as well, this practice of commingling acquired a symbolic significance: while the separate consecration of bread and wine demonstratively represented—in the "mortal" division of flesh and blood—the death of Christ, the commingling and joining of the separated elements represented his return to life, his resurrection. Thus the Mass was understood and experienced in a vivid manner as "the memorial of his death and resurrection." This idea was particularly effective in giving the "commingling" an unexpected ritual significance.

Two especially Roman customs significantly influenced this practice. In order to illustrate the historical-vertical unity of the one sacrifice of

Christ, a part of the host from a previous Mass—the so-called *sancta*—was placed in the chalice before Communion. This was done especially in papal Masses, as the *Ordo Romanus I* (often cited above) reports. Added to this was another custom that was meant to express the local-horizontal unity of the one sacrifice in many Masses: the pope sent a small piece of the eucharistic bread—the so-called *fermentum*—to his Roman titular priests, which they added to the sacred blood during their community Masses. Thus this custom became a lovely sign of the unity of the Roman presbytery, and the individual congregations experienced their ecclesial community beyond the boundaries of the local assembly.

All these customs have different origins and different histories, even though their ultimate source is the softening of stale bread, which was given a variety of symbolic meanings. Still, these historical backgrounds can, under certain circumstances, be instructive, in order that the rite of commingling may not simply lie there in the middle of the Communion of the Mass like an erratic block deposited by a long-ago glacier. The Latin missal has retained the previous designation *Commixtio* in the formula of commingling; the vernacular translation simply speaks of the "mingling of the body and blood of Christ."

Apparently it is not desired to give too much attention to the rite of commingling any longer. This can certainly be justified, especially since not every rite that has been adopted in the course of history needs to be preserved if it no longer has any meaning. After all, the community does not consist simply of historians. This rite would have meaning only if or when one wished to adopt the Byzantine custom (permitted for us also) of distributing the eucharistic bread, saturated with the sacred blood, from the chalice, using a spoon and placing it in the mouth of the recipient. This could be recommended in border regions or areas where there is a mixture of western and eastern Churches, but it will scarcely ever be the case in our country. That means that the custom will remain relatively meaningless, a mere relic of what was once a rather significant historical development and symbolism that has now disappeared and lost its point of reference.

(c) The Agnus Dei *as accompanying anthem*

The *Agnus Dei* is the chant that accompanies the breaking of the bread. Its text stems from the words of John the Baptist, referring to Jesus (John 1:29, 36), combined with Rev 5:6 and 13:8: The "lamb that was slain" is the one, enduring sacrifice of reconciliation for humanity. From this fact of salvation arises the appeal for mercy and eschatological peace. In the previous missal the acclamation "grant them [eternal] rest" was used, but this is no longer the case.

In the Middle Ages it was frequently the custom to chant the *Agnus Dei* even before the breaking of the bread (in Lyons, among Carthusians and Dominicans, etc.)—perhaps because there was a desire to emphasize the saving significance of the Lamb, to be sure, but on the other hand not to create a contradiction to John 19:33, where it is expressly noted that the soldiers did not break Jesus' legs when they perceived that he was already dead; this the evangelist apparently saw as a fulfillment of Exod 12:46 and Ps 34:21.

The *Agnus Dei* is Greco-Syrian in origin and was placed in the Latin Mass by Pope Sergius I (687–701), a Syrian born in Palermo. Many acclamatory and hymnic elements (*Gloria, Kyrie,* etc.) are the heritage of the eastern Church, which—despite language barriers—always enjoyed a significant participation of the people in the Mass. Since the 12th century it has been customary to repeat the chant three times, and the third time to vary the appeal for mercy (similar to that in the *Kyrie*) with a petition for peace. This is also offered as a possibility in the present missal, but it is not prescribed. One may—as in the Greek liturgy of St. James, from Syria—repeat the chant until all the bread is broken (Rubr.). "During the breaking of the bread and the commingling the *Agnus Dei* is as a rule sung by the choir or cantor with the congregation responding; otherwise it is recited aloud. This invocation may be repeated as often as necessary to accompany the breaking of the bread. The final reprise concludes with the words, grant us peace" (*GI* 56e). This chant is the people's part. The priest should therefore not intone the chant or recitation, and should not sing or speak it with the people.

An *Agnus Dei* hymn may also be sung (Rubr.) One may further note that the Latin text is printed in the German missals: Our congregations should be able to sing the *Agnus Dei* to a simple choral melody.

It was the custom for a long time to strike the breast at the petitions of the *Agnus Dei.* The *General Instruction* and the rubrics no longer provide for this, but one should not necessarily forbid it, because symbolic gestures that are rooted among the people have great significance. Originally, this striking of the breast was probably more an emphatic underscoring of "us" than a specific penitential gesture.

4. The Reception of the Eucharistic Gifts

(a) Preparation

"The priest prepares himself by the prayer, said softly, that he may receive Christ's body and blood to good effect. The faithful do the same by silent prayer" (*GI* 56f). Of the three preparatory prayers previously used only the second and third have been retained, and they are alternative choices. The prayer that was previously the first preparatory prayer now introduces the priest's greeting at the rite of peace, and the reorganization and clarification of the preparatory rite before Communion has therefore omitted it at this point. The remaining prayers, stylistically speaking, are private: there is no invitation to pray, they are addressed to Christ, there is no "Amen" acclamation, and they are spoken with hands folded, rather than in the *orans* posture proper to official prayers. We can find them in this order since the 11th century; they arose out of the concern of the Church that the mystery be celebrated with recollection and conscious attention. However, their character as private prayers does not detract from their quality and reflectiveness. The first of the two prayers now offered for selection was present in the Carolingian sacramentary of Amiens (9th c.). The Carthusians and Dominicans used only this single preparatory prayer instead of the three.

The corresponding rubric provides that the priest's prayer should be spoken inaudibly. The congregation should also pray quietly, in the same or similar manner; the presider at the liturgy may indicate this by a brief direction. Obviously, the prayer should not be recited in unison. Reflective silence, which is not an "empty space" in worship, but "part of the celebration" (*GI* 23), will certainly be experienced by all participants as beneficial, especially if it has been preceded by a special gesture of peace and the singing of the Agnus Dei.

(b) Invitation

"The priest then shows the eucharistic bread for communion to the faithful and with them recites the prayer of humility in words from the Gospels" (*GI* 56g). To begin with, the ritual of showing is interpreted by repeating the cry of the precursor of Jesus (John 1:29). The priest and congregation recite together the humble and confident words of the centurion of Capernaum, "Lord, I am not worthy . . ." (Matt 8:8). Wisely, the somewhat antiquated phrase "under my roof," which does not correspond to the German unified translation [but is in the NRSV], has been retained in the German prayer because it has been so familiar for such a long time; the change from "my servant" to "my soul" changes the scriptural text to correspond to the situation, but the German continues to use "my soul" instead of the ordinary "I" (which is now used in some other vernacular translations, [including the ICEL]). We may entirely welcome the fact that the formula we have known from ancient times has not been altered. The single acclamation, rather than the previous threefold repetition, answers to modern sensibilities; nowadays a repeated, stereotypical recitation of the same thing is not experienced as emphasis or intensification. The fact that priest and people pray together manifests the community of those celebrating the one meal. Previously, priest and people (if they were to receive Communion) each recited the prayer three times (for a total of six); between the two sets, the *Confiteor* and absolution formula were recited. This corresponded to the form for Communion of the sick and shows how much the reception of the body of the Lord had sometimes been extrapolated outside the Mass and was regarded as an extra ritual within the Mass itself.

The priest can (at least according to the German missal) add an interpretative verse to this prayer. [In the American missal, this verse is incorporated in the words of invitation before the recitation of the "Lamb of God . . . ."] A number of models are suggested, and they really should be used as a means of avoiding monotony. The first suggestion is: "Happy are those who are invited to the marriage feast of the Lamb," taken from Rev 19:9. It points to the eschatological dimension of the Eucharist and the liturgy of heaven, but is somewhat more difficult to understand than the others, and presupposes a more biblically literate group of faithful, which cannot always be the case. Hence it would certainly not be wise to use only this verse, simply because it is the first suggestion. Unfortunately, that is what often happens! The second suggested verse is from Ps 34:9: "Taste and see how good the Lord is." At an earlier time Psalm 34 was often *the* Communion psalm, a beautiful song of trust in God and confident reliance on divine protection; verse 9 was the antiphon that was repeated throughout by the people. It deserves special consideration.

The third variant, "Whoever eats this bread will live forever," corresponds to John 6:58 and is meant to nourish the faith of communicants. It is the culminating point of the Johannine eucharistic theology as found in the so-called discourse of assurance in the synagogue at Capernaum. The suggestion of the rubrics that "another communion verse from the missal" may be chosen, "especially from the Mass of the day" illuminates the purpose of this priestly speech: like the Communion chant, it is intended to promote the right eucharistic mood in the congregation. One difficulty for the celebrant seems to lie in making a gesture (showing the eucharistic bread) while at the same time reciting a fairly long passage from the missal. However, this can be overcome.

(c) Distribution of Communion

After the breaking of the bread and the invitation to the table of the Lord, the eucharistic meal is ready for the congregation. Christ himself is "present . . . in the person of his minister" (SC 7). He "gives the bread" and "extends the cup" (Matt 26:26-27; Mark 14:22-23; Luke 22:19; 1 Cor 11:24) through the presider at the liturgy, who—especially when there are large gatherings and whenever it is sensible to do so—is assisted by a deacon, acolytes, or ministers of Communion. But if the congregation is not too large, it is certainly better from the point of view of symbolism and the "distribution of roles" that only the celebrant should distribute the body and blood of Christ to those present.

In all rites, the sequence is such that the priest communicates first, and then the congregation. Because Christ is the true giver of the Eucharist, the presider is the first to share in the Lord's supper. This position belongs not so much to the person as to the office. On the other hand, modern sensibilities might also tempt us to suggest that the person in office should first serve the community, and only then partake of the Eucharist, especially because it would then be possible to consume any hosts that may remain and the residue of the sacred blood without "communicating twice." Such an accommodation to modern feelings is not left to the discretion of the individual priest, but it should be carefully considered. In smaller groups, for example in home Masses, the order of concelebrants (GI 197–9) could be used: then the priest distributes the body of the Lord to each individual, but all communicate simultaneously.

The priest receives the Lord with the optative formula (spoken in a low voice) that has been retained in its essential form from the previous missal: "Lord, may I receive these gifts in purity of heart. May they bring me healing and strength, now and for ever." In the Latin and vernacular texts the Hebraizing "my soul" has been changed to the personal pronoun "me," with good reason, because this sentence, unlike the "Lord, I am not worthy," has nothing to do with the congregation's habitual expectations.

Afterward the priest distributes the body of the Lord to the congregation, showing each one the host by lifting it slightly above the dish and saying: "The body of Christ." The communicant answers: "Amen," and receives the consecrated bread. The deacons, acolytes, or ministers of communion do the same. The formula for distributing Communion to the faithful is the ancient one, known already to Ambrose (De sacr. IV, 5, 25) in the 4th century. In the previous missal, the formula expressed the priest's wish for the communicant: "May the body of Christ keep your soul to everlasting life." The new form is much better: the communicants are no longer purely passive, allowing the priest or minister to wish them a fruitful reception; they are active, responsible persons who confess their faith in the body of the Lord.

The question whether the sacred body should be received in the hand or on the tongue has unfortunately become the subject of controversy, which makes little sense. It is certain that, when Christ instituted the sacrament, Jewish meal customs were followed: the bread over which the blessing was spoken lay on the table or on a cloth (or mat), and at the blessing it was taken in the hands and broken. That is what Christ did: he took the bread, broke it, and distributed it—placing it in the hands of his companions at the meal, obviously. If he had acted differently, it would have been something unusual, and would certainly have been described by the evangelists. Later depictions of the Lord's supper, such as those in the Rabulas codex from Syria (586) or in medieval pictures, of course prove nothing. The reception of the bread with hands covered by a cloth is, in each case, only the depiction of the rite at the particular time. It corresponds to a ceremonial of courtly devotion, impossible to practice now: things received from the emperor were accepted *manu velata,* with covered hands (just as, in turn, everything given to the emperor was first kissed).

Distribution of Holy Communion on the tongue arose in the early Middle Ages out of fear that tiny crumbs or bits could fall off and thus be desecrated (possibly at first in connection with the Communion of the sick). Communion on the tongue is thus merely one kind of ritual emerging out of carefulness and reverence, but it is not ultimately derived from the action of feeding (except in the case of small children). Moreover, surely no one will want to say that the tongue is always a more appropriate part of the body to receive Communion than the hand: Paul, in fact, says (1 Cor 12:12-27) that the members of the body all have their function for the sake of the whole, and none can claim priority over another. James even warns about the tongue (Jas 3:5-10) that, although "a small member," it is "a fire . . . a world of iniquity" that "no one can tame, . . . a restless evil, full of deadly poison." But he also knows (3:9) that "with it we bless the Lord and Father." The same is true of the hand: it can do evil and strike, it can work, caress, and bless.

The suggestion that the priest's hand is different because it has been anointed at ordination only applies to the last thousand years since the Carolingian era; previously it was no more so than that of ordinary believers. Thus the issue can only be one of assuring reverence for the sacred body of the Lord. However, fixed rites of veneration in themselves by no means guarantee such reverence once they become habitual. Gestures of reverence retain their vitality only through conviction, for which they are an expression. By their nature, then, they can be extraordinarily variable; the only condition is that they must remain deliberate and spontaneous. Therefore to receive the eucharistic bread in the left hand, supported by the right, and then place it in the mouth with the right hand can be just as much—or just as little—an expression of reverence as receiving it on the tongue with a Communion paten (as suggested by *GI* 80c) held underneath, out of concern for falling bits of the host. This style of reception could be suggested, for example, to people with severe handicaps, the very old, bedridden persons, etc. But otherwise, the freedom of individuals and their personal responsibility must be respected. To make this a matter for dispute among communicants directly contradicts the spirit of the Eucharist. Each person should feel responsible for his or her own reverent state and behavior.

"Holy communion has a more complete form as a sign when it is received under both kinds. For in this manner of reception a fuller light shines on the sign of the eucharistic banquet" (*GI* 240). Communion of the faithful in the cup declined in the Latin Church only in the high Middle Ages. It was retained solely for the ministers at papal Masses and for members of the Latin rite participating in eastern liturgical celebrations (*CIC* 1917, canon 866). All the eastern Churches have Communion under both forms, as do the Churches of the Reformation, but for different theological reasons. The Constitution on the Liturgy (article 55b) at first suggested reception of Communion under both species only for special occasions, but in the meantime this has been extended (cf. *GI* 242). Apart from the danger of spillage there are a number of practical considerations, particularly on the part of the faithful, and these do not relate simply to hygiene. Still, one should not be too easily frightened away, especially since *GI* 240 speaks expressly of the "more complete" quality of the sign. The character of the Eucharist as a meal is more explicitly rendered, and the new covenant, which is specifically in the *blood* of Christ (Exod 24:8; Mark 14:24; Matt 26:28; Luke 22:20; 1 Cor 11:25; Heb 9:20, and frequently) is clearly evident. The Lord himself placed special emphasis on the connection between the cup and the eschatological meal (Matt 26:29; Mark 14:25; Luke 22:18).

Article 240 could also—and primarily—have referred to Christ's explicit will that we should drink the cup (John 6:54-56). However, as *GI* 241 emphasizes, the promotion of Communion in the cup should not detract from Catholic doctrine that "Christ, whole and entire, as well as the true sacrament are received even under one kind only; that, therefore, as far as the effects are concerned, those who receive in this manner are not deprived of any grace necessary for salvation." We may rejoice that the same article continues: "At the same time the faithful should be guided toward a desire to take part more intensely in a sacred rite in which the sign of the eucharistic meal stands out more explicitly."

A purely mechanical introduction of Communion in the cup or a casuistic determination that it is possible and permitted, or even the appearance of a privilege granted to certain persons on particular occasions (cf. *GI* 242) without a deeper understanding of its significance as a real symbol would certainly not be profitable for fruitful participation by the faithful. The use of a large number of chalices, even one for every communicant, would again detract greatly from the symbolic power of Communion in the cup: if possible, there should be only one "cup of blessing" (1 Cor 10:16) that is given to all. It corresponds to the *one* bread that is broken.

"The blood of the Lord may be taken by drinking from the chalice directly, through a tube, with a spoon, or even by intinction" (*GI* 200). This direction is presented at greater length and in more detail in articles 244–51 of the *General Instruction*. Christ originally gave his blood to be drunk directly from the cup, and that is how the apostolic communities knew the practice. Therefore, in spite of some difficulties, it deserves preference over all other forms, not only because it is mentioned first here; it is simply the natural way of drinking. It has been retained in this form, unchanged, by the eastern Syrians and Ethiopians through the centuries. Communion through a tube was customary for a long time at papal Masses. Its reintroduction in our country would be difficult because whenever possible we drink directly from a cup or glass and, at least for the present, the association of a straw with the drinking of bottled soft drinks would be highly embarrassing. Distribution by use of a small spoon, placing the contents on the tongue of the communicant, is usual in the Byzantine liturgy. It originated in connection with the softening of stale leavened bread (discussed above at 3b, with regard to the commingling), and probably most often in the eastern Church's reception of the "presanctified gifts." The last form named in *GI* 200, which, however, makes Communion in the hand impossible, is the immersion and soaking of the host in the sacred blood, but what is envisioned is only the dipping of the lower margin. Care should be taken, in this case, that the parts of the host are not too small. Probably when this form of distribution is used, a separate Communion paten will be necessary.

Communion in the hand best matches drinking from the cup; both forms have the best *Sitz im Leben* in the world today. Probably drinking through a *fistula* will never become customary here. The other two forms are best suited when it is preferred that Communion on the tongue should be retained.

(d) Communion song

> During the priest's and the faithful's reception of the sacrament the communion song is sung. Its function is to express outwardly the communicants' union in spirit by means of the unity of their voices, to give evidence of joy of heart, to make the procession to receive Christ's body more fully an act of community. The song begins when the priest takes communion and continues for as long as seems appropriate while the faithful receive Christ's body. But the communion song should be ended in good time whenever there is to be a hymn after communion (*GI* 56i).

This song was originally a processional chant, accompanying the progress of the communicants to the altar and back to their places. The people's joining together in song internalizes the physical action and creates a spiritual unity; it is also an expression of festivity. Its form is closely related to that of the entrance song: "For the Communion song, the same rules naturally apply as for the entrance song" (German Rubr.) As far as its content is concerned, it can be a whole psalm with a repeated verse, simply a Communion verse, or even a popular hymn; in terms of participation, it may be sung by everyone or by a schola or cantor and the congregation alternating, or even by the schola alone. Here one may adapt the usage to the opportunities as well as to the sense of the community for what is appropriate. It need not be the business of every individual to sing loudly all the way to and from the altar; some will prefer to keep a meditative silence. In any case, the content of the new communion verse, which is to be chosen with care, should always be integrated into the celebration, perhaps in the invitation to Communion (see section 4b, above), or as a suggestion for silent meditation and thanksgiving after Communion (see the following section).

(e) Purification of the vessels

It should be a fundamental principle that a period of silence follows the conclusion of the Communion procession and song. There can be no doubt that this is at least as necessary here as it is, for example, at the penitential rite or after the readings and homily. Without a deliberate cultivation of communion devotion all promotion of active participation in Mass is meaningless. Hence one should avoid any unnecessary movement and walking around in the sanctuary and every kind of fussing with the altar; this only disturbs and distracts.

After distributing the eucharistic food, the priest returns to the altar, consumes any remaining hosts, if there are only a few, and, if necessary, the rest of the sacred blood. If there are very many hosts he, or the deacon, deposits them in the tabernacle, whether located in the sanctuary or the chapel of adoration (cf. *GI* 276). The priest carefully collects in the chalice any particles of the host remaining on the corporal or in the dish. This requires reverence, which, however, has nothing to do with anxiety or scrupulosity. Especially after the controversy surrounding Berengar's sacramental theology in the early Middle Ages it became the custom to handle the sacred species with special care. This was a sign of deep faith and great reverence.

Christ is present even in the particles of bread and drops of wine. But they must still appear to the natural senses as bread and wine, not as molecular fragments. Even the strictest understanding of the doctrine of transubstantiation since the high Middle Ages and the Council of Trent says that Christ is present in the *substance* of the bread, while the accidents of bread remain. Thus, for example, the regulation that the priest must hold thumb and index finger together from the consecration to the purification no longer applies. Of course, it is another matter to discard reverence along with "particle panic"! The applicable rule in the *General Instruction* is:

> Whenever a particle of the eucharistic bread adheres to his fingers, especially after the breaking of the bread or the communion of the people, the priest cleanses his fingers over the paten or, if necessary, washes them. He also gathers any particles that may fall outside the paten (*GI* 237).

> The vessels are purified by the priest or else by the deacon or acolyte after the communion or after Mass, if possible at a side table. Wine and water or water alone are used for the purification of the chalice, then drunk by the one who purifies it. The paten is usually wiped with the purificator" (*GI* 238).

The transfer of the purification to the credence table at the side makes very good sense. After all, it is the usual practice to wash the dishes and cutlery somewhere other than at the dinner table.

In addition, article 120 of the *General Instruction* suggests: "It is also permitted, especially if there are several vessels to be purified, to leave them, properly covered and on a corporal, either at the altar or at a side table and to purify them after Mass when the people have left." This would certainly benefit the period of silence, as well as the recollection of the priest, who otherwise would be incessantly occupied, to its detriment. The accompanying prayer, to be spoken softly, asks that what has been received with the lips may be accepted with a pure heart and that temporal nourishment may be medicine for immortality: its purpose is the same. Thus one should make as little ritual to-do about the purification of the vessels as possible, while preserving an appropriate reverence.

(f) Silent meditation or song of thanksgiving

Previously it was customary for the (often very few) communicants to remain in the church for some time for private thanksgiving, while the body of the congregation, paying little attention to the playing of the organ, proceeded, more or less hastily, to the exits. Today, the church generally empties completely after the dismissal, which is taken quite literally: The people are told to depart, and they do. It would be a great loss if, while the number of communicants is happily growing larger, the good old practice of private prayer should completely die out. It is always beneficial for liturgical action to be closely united to contemplation, each saturating the other as much as possible and thus drawing benefit from the other. Hence it really represents progress when the rubrics of the missal for our language area provide that "[after the distribution of Communion] the priest may return to the chair. A period of silence may now be observed, or a psalm or song of praise may be sung."

It should be the concern of all those responsible to make a good habit out of this permissive instruction. All experience speaks unconditionally in its favor. The length of the silence must be varied according to the group of persons present and the situation. However, it should be long enough that the faithful can enter into prayer. Polls have shown that this is also the desire of everyone. One of the principal reproaches raised against the renewed liturgy is that there is so much activity and instruction that one never has a chance to pray. There is "always something going on." After communion would undoubtedly be the best time to activate prayer and adoration within the Mass. Again, the period of time should not be made so long that restlessness (manifested by nervous coughing and throat-clearing) will appear among those who really do have important things to attend to, such as mothers with small children. The sense of an arbitrary "lengthening of the Mass" will only achieve the opposite of what is desired. Undoubtedly, a suggestion from the celebrant for prayer or meditation could be helpful, perhaps in association with the Communion verse of the day if it has not already been sung. However, the atmosphere must be easy and relaxed; there should not be an additional "pressure to accomplish something." Private adoration at another time, outside Mass, can only profit from this period of contemplation.

Article 56j of the *General Instruction* contains the suggestion that a psalm of thanksgiving or hymn of praise be sung. That can be an addition or an alternative to the silence, but it requires careful consideration with respect to individual cases and special situations. Silence is certainly more essential than singing, especially if there has already been a lot of the latter. It would be good at this point to choose hymns that, because of their subjective character, are otherwise not well suited to replace liturgical hymns or other parts of the ordinary of the Mass. For this very situation, the hymnal offers a good selection. German hymnody contains a rich treasure of traditional devotion.

5. The Prayer after Communion

"Then, standing at the altar or at the chair and facing the people, the priest says, with hands outstretched: 'Let us pray.' There may be a brief period of silence, unless this has been already observed immediately after communion. He recites the prayer after communion, at the end of which the people make the response: Amen" (*GI* 122). As the place for this final prayer, the altar is generally, and reasonably, to be preferred over the priest's chair. *Orationes* always conclude a liturgical action or an essential part of the worship service. The place for the eucharistic celebration is the altar; the Communion is also immediately connected with it. Thus the action is best concluded where it took place. On the other hand, the *oratio* is also the conclusion to the period of silent prayer, carried out by all participants at their places. Therefore it is defensible for the priest to speak the *oratio* after Communion at his chair, especially if silent adoration or thanksgiving has replaced the pause after "Let us pray."

The closing prayer is an official prayer of the priest and is therefore subject to the stylistic laws of presidial prayers: call to prayer, *orans* posture, and acclamation of the congregation with "Amen." The conclusion of the prayer, like that of the prayer over the gifts, is the briefer form (compared with that of the collect): "through Christ, our Lord."

The meaning of the concluding prayer is enunciated by article 56k of the *General Instruction*: "In the prayer after communion, the priest petitions for the effects of the mystery just celebrated and by their acclamation,

Amen, the people make the prayer their own." The selection of motifs for the prayer is relatively small. For the most part this *oratio* combines thanksgiving with a petition that the reception of the sacred body (and blood) of Christ may prove fruitful in daily works of love and, as a deposit for eternity, may bring us to perfection.

Notes

[1]Translator's note: the English word from *offerre* is "offer," which does not in itself have sacrificial significance. The English "sacrifice," the equivalent of German *Opfer*, is obviously derived from a quite different word, Latin *sacrificium*.

[2]Translator's note: this prayer is a standard part of the Mass in English; no options are given.

[3]Translator's note: The usual English usage for this action is "consecration," but the customary German is *Wandlung*, which in itself means "change" or "transformation" and points toward the technical term "transubstantiation." It thus bears more dogmatic freight than English speakers are accustomed to. In this translation I will regularly render *Wandlung* in the eucharistic context with "consecration."

[4]Translator's note: German has two words *(das Böse, das Übel)* for the Greek word that translates in English as "evil." The author's point is that *das Böse* can either be personified ("the Evil One") or simply a substantive ("evil"), so that the last petition can mean either "Deliver us from the Evil One" or "Deliver us from evil" without changing the wording in German. *Das Übel*, on the other hand, cannot be personified and so is univocal. English lacks an equivalent for the equivocal or ambiguous German word. See the NRSV text of Matt 6:13: "but rescue us from the evil one," and footnote: "Or 'from evil.'"

Chapter Four

The Conclusion of the Mass

The concluding rite of the Mass has always been amazingly brief and succinct, even in antiquity. The reason for this may be that it was never properly developed, because frequent Communion declined relatively early and many of the faithful left the church even before or during the priest's communion.

1. Announcements

The time between the *oratio* after Communion and the blessing and dismissal is the best moment, psychologically, for brief announcements, declarations, news bulletins, and calendar notes. This is certainly better than making them in connection with the sermon, where they tend to be distracting.

The announcements can usually be short, and they should be of interest to everyone. If they are extensive, it is better to publish them in the church bulletin or the parish newsletter, or to post them in the church vestibule (such would include the Mass intentions for the week, marriage banns, the calendar of events for parish organizations, etc.). In any event, it is hard to remember such matters merely from hearing them. It might be more appropriate to announce baptisms and deaths, so that these events may be integrated into the community's life.

2. Final Blessing

The blessing is introduced by a greeting corresponding to that at the beginning of Mass. This is a matter of course: we speak to each other when arriving and leaving, and in this way we show our community with one another. While a number of variations are provided for the greeting at the beginning of Mass, here ordinarily the only one used is "The Lord be with you," "And with your spirit." It is unnecessary to further paraphrase this greeting or to expand it with personal wishes (for the week, etc.). Instead, one might combine special wishes for the community, perhaps for the elderly and the homebound sick, with the previous announcements. In combination with the venerable and brief liturgical greeting, they easily have a banal effect.

The priest's blessing as part of the Mass is relatively recent and was added only in the late Middle Ages. Previously, the priest blessed individuals who asked for it on the way to the sacristy, often with the chalice, paten, and especially the corporal, which was laid on particularly sick and painful limbs (the eyes, the cheeks if there was toothache, etc.). This custom of blessing during the departure is now used only by bishops, although it is often very ritually stylized ("once to the left, once to the right"). From this late addition of the blessing arises the curious fact that, before 1967, the dismissal preceded the blessing. If the faithful had promptly done what they were asked to do (luckily in Latin), the priest could only have blessed their backs as they rushed for the door! The rearrangement, or correction, was thus long overdue.

The formula of blessing is deprecative: "May almighty God bless you, the Father, and the Son, and the Holy Spirit." While naming the most Holy Trinity, the priest makes a large cross with the right hand. The people cross themselves at the same time and answer with the acclamation: "Amen." "On certain days and occasions another, more solemn form of blessing or the prayer over the people precedes this form of blessing as the rubrics direct" (*GI* 124). Such forms of blessing correspond to ancient tradition, especially the dismissal of the non-communicants before the exchange of peace. On ferial days in Lent it is added to the *oratio* after communion as an *oratio super populum*.

The present missal contains a great many three-part formulae for the solemn blessing. These are intended for feasts and festal seasons, but for the rest of the Church year as well. They can be used not only at the end of Mass, but also at liturgies of the word, at one of the hours of the daily office, or to conclude the administration of a sacrament. The deacon (or the priest himself) first urges: "Let us kneel for a blessing." Instead, the ancient *Humiliate capita vestra Deo,* "Bow your heads before God," could also be revived. The priest then extends his arms over the people and says (or sings) the three-strophe blessing, incorporating a form of "May almighty God bless you" as a continuation: "And may . . . ." The people can answer

"Amen" after each strophe of the blessing, or simply at the end of the whole. These expansions are undoubtedly a great acquisition, because they add appropriate aspects to the general formula of blessing and interpret them as well.

In addition to these three-part formulae of blessing, the prayers of blessing over the people have also been revived; they had always been used on ferial days in Lent and are now available for every day in the year. They represent a rich treasure of prayer. They may be chosen for each particular situation, and one should really do this, not simply settling for the first that comes to hand. Ordinarily they will be spoken rather than sung; to that extent they seem less festive than the final blessing, which is printed with musical notes in the missal. During this prayer of blessing, also, the priest extends hands over the people, not lifting them, as previously during Lent, in the *orans* gesture, although in style they are official prayers and are followed by the people's "Amen." These prayers over the people flow into the blessing at the end: "And may the blessing of almighty God, the Father, and the Son, and the Holy Spirit, come upon you and remain with you for ever." The congregation answers: "Amen."

The "blessing for good weather" can be combined with the final blessing. This has been very popular for a long time, especially in rural areas. Two formulae are provided in the missal, one patterned on the solemn, three-part final blessing, the other designed as the first prayer of blessing over the people. Both are easily comprehended by people today; demonological and apotropaic remnants have been removed. The texts for the blessing for good weather are excellent examples of the way in which blessings of natural things can be translated into terms that are credible today: God's presence is invoked on these things, and God's protection for them is implored.

3. Dismissal

"Immediately after the blessing, with his hands joined, the priest adds: "Go in the peace of Christ," or: "Go in peace to love and serve the Lord," or: "The Mass is ended, go in peace," and the people answer: "Thanks be to God" (*GI* 124). These formulae of dismissal may be used at all Masses. The earlier *Benedicamus Domino* in Masses without a Gloria and *Requiescant in pace* in Masses for the dead have been eliminated, as has the prayer *Placeat*, originally a private prayer of the priest on the way from the altar to the sacristy. Only because the priest, in the course of time, attached the blessing to the end of the Mass itself—although only after the *Ite missa est*—the *Placeat* forced its way into the ordo of the Mass. In addition, the beginning of the Fourth Gospel is no longer recited. It was never a genuine proclamation, but was regarded as an element in the blessing: by virtue of the power of the word of God, with the *initium* of the gospel standing for the whole (as was earlier the case in the stations of the Corpus Christi procession).

The formula of dismissal in the Latin missal is the familiar *Ite, missa est,* with the response *Deo gratias.* The word *missa,* which gave its name to the whole Mass, is the late Latin form of *missio,* dismissal (similar, for example, to *collecta* from *collectio, secreta* from *secretio,* etc.). In the German and English translations there was no way to retain the association, because German *Entlassung* [= dismissal] awakens no echo of *missa,* while the English word "dismissal," which does contain "*missa,*" is not used in any formula of dismissal. Therefore the alternatives adopted (the German is *Gehet hin in Frieden* = "Go in peace," the same phrase contained in all three of the English options) are sensible; "go in peace," for example, echoes a biblical way of speaking (e. g., Mark 5:34, and frequently), and corresponds to the dismissal formula of the Byzantine liturgy, "Let us go in peace."

"When the dismissal is sung, the twofold alleluia can be added throughout the Easter season" (German Rubr.). If another liturgical action (such as a procession) follows immediately after the Mass, the concluding rites, with blessing and dismissal, are of course omitted.

4. Kissing the Altar and Departure

"The priest kisses the altar as at the beginning" (Rubr.). The beginning and end of the Mass are mirror images of each other: at the beginning, the priest silently greets Christ by kissing the altar, then greets the community with a blessing and opens the service; at the end he greets the people with a blessing, dismisses them, and finally kisses the altar representative of Christ. Such an arrangement of beginning and end is a natural reflection of the way any gathering, or even a conversation, proceeds. A letter is usually constructed in the same way, with greetings at beginning and end; in antiquity this was even more strictly regulated than today. In his community letters Paul explicitly incorporates these parts in the form of blessing-formulas, which solemnly frame the whole letter.

The kiss given to the altar at the end of the celebration is ancient liturgical tradition; it is used in most rites. In the Latin Mass, its meaning was unclear until very recent times, because, since the late Middle Ages, the various blessings by the priest during departure—as a common final blessing for all—were simply tacked onto the old conclusion of the Mass (consisting of *Dominus vobiscum,* post-Communion prayer, and altar kiss). From the moment when the blessing was combined with another *Dominus vobiscum,* the altar kiss was interpreted not as a parting kiss given to the altar, but as part of the greeting, for it was the custom for a long time for the priest to kiss the altar before this exchange of greetings, so that his wishes would also emanate from the altar (= Christ).

The many kissings of the altar at this point have been rightly eliminated because all experience shows that an accumulation of the same thing tends rather to dampen than strengthen its expressive power. When, in 1967, in a quest for a logical sequence to the rites, the blessing was placed before the dismissal, the kiss remained combined with the exchange of greetings. The present missal has restored good order: final greeting, blessing and dismissal of the people, priest's (and deacon's) kiss of the altar, and departure of the celebrant and his ministers.

The altar is kissed in silence, because the gesture is expressive enough in itself. The east Syrian liturgy has a prayer that well reflects the spirit of this kiss: "Rest in peace, holy altar of God. I know not if it will be given to me to approach you again. May the Lord permit me to see you again in the church of heaven."

The priest "kisses the altar, makes the proper reverence with the ministers, and leaves" (*GI* 125). This sign of reverence is ordinarily a deep bow, or a genuflection if the tabernacle is on the altar. The exit is simpler than the entrance, when cross and book were carried in procession. However, on festive occasions there is no reason why the exit may not follow the same pattern as the entrance. In many places it has become customary for the congregation (or part of it) to remain together for a while, in the parish house or somewhere else. In this way the Mass appears more clearly as the center of community life.

Recollection of a Westphalian in Vienna

A reminiscence of Professor Johannes H. Emminghaus (1916–1989)

The two years after the name "Emminghaus" above are like the pillars of a bridge between which stretches the curve of a life on earth. It was not quite spring when he was born and not quite fall when he died. Nevertheless, the years 1916 and 1989 mark the beginning and end of a full life, the high point of which was attained in Vienna.

The flickering light in the Gothic death lamps on the Stiftsplatz in Klosterneuburg burns for many deceased priests. Since 9 September 1989, it shines also for a priest from the archdiocese of Paderborn. The *Tucz* column, as it is called, points to the nearby chapel of St. Sebastian, which shelters in its crypt the tomb of the Augustinian canons of Klosterneuburg. There Johannes H. Emminghaus, departed in his 74th year of life, also found his grave. On the stone that closes his burial niche one may read: *Praelatus et Can. hon. DDr. Johannes H. Emminghaus. Univ.-Professor. Geb. 1. 3. 1916. Gest. 2. 9. 1989.* Here are very few dates to mark the life of a man who, as priest and scholar, lived and worked in the liberating hope that cannot be walled up in the narrow chamber of death, but explodes all the boundaries of the life given to us on earth and transcends all temporality in Christ. The whole ambience of the broad, handsomely built plaza before the foundation of Klosterneuburg near Vienna proclaims life in many ways. Only those who are fairly familiar with the place are aware that its chapel of St. Sebastian also shelters a chamber for the dead.

Johannes H. Emminghaus was *ordinarius* professor for liturgiology and sacramental theology at the University of Vienna beginning in 1967.

He always considered it his "good fortune" and a high honor to be allowed to be part of the rich tradition of the Vienna faculty of theology as a tenured professor. When he retired in 1984, he decisively declared: "I will remain where I am." Of course, by this he meant not only Vienna, but also the town of Klosterneuburg, close to the Austrian metropolis, the parish of St. Martin, and not least the convent of the Augustinian canons. Professor Emminghaus liked to say that Klosterneuburg was his "chosen homeland," lying "beautifully situated between the Danube and the Vienna Woods." In 1984 the canons named the professor from Westphalia, who had given them so much valuable inspiration, and who had cooperated for many years with the successors of Pius Parsch, as *canonicus honorarius,* honorary canon. Therefore on 9 September 1989, as I have mentioned, the body of the deceased was laid in the crypt with the canons.

It is not simply the wine from Klosterneuburg and its custom of "barrel-sliding" on St. Leopold's day that are known far and wide. The imposing foundation on the Danube acquired an importance in the 1920s and –30s, through its canon, Dr. Pius Parsch (1884–1954), and the "Popular Liturgical Movement," that puts everything else in the shade. In the whole German-speaking world and in many other lands, the name "Klosterneuburg" is known for it, and at that time it became something almost like a program for action: Bible and liturgy as the sources of Christian life and true Catholic devotion; living with the Church; praying with the Church; internal and external, living and active participation; conscious celebration of the sacred liturgy as a community. Even the modest little Romanesque church of St. Gertrude, built by St. Leopold near the pilgrim hospital belonging to the convent, became very well known because Pius Parsch used to speak of it everywhere as the "cradle of the popular liturgical movement." In front of the steps leading to the choir of St. Gertrude one may find the grave of this tireless pioneer of biblical-liturgical renewal.

We may comfortably regard it as proven that the popular liturgical impulses from Klosterneuburg inspired an especially lively echo in the parishes of the Ruhr. Thus Klosterneuburg very early became something special to Johannes H. Emminghaus, too. In the foreword to his most important book, *Die Messe. Wesen - Gestalt - Vollzug* (the fifth edition of which is represented by this English translation), this Viennese scholar, now deceased, born and reared in Bochum in the Ruhr, recalled: "For nearly fifty years, I have felt a great gratitude to Pius Parsch. When I was a boy, wise pastors in the parish of St. Meinolf in Bochum not only taught me how to be an altar boy, but at the same time instructed me in the liturgy. Even before I received my first 'Schott' as a Christmas present from my parents in 1928, I was collecting the 'Sunday leaflets' by Pius Parsch (entitled 'Live with the Church') that were used in the congregation. Later came his 'explanation of the Mass' and 'liturgical calendar,' which were combined in three handy volumes under the title *The Church's Year of Grace*, and furnished the spiritual accompaniment to my theological studies." Professor Emminghaus respectfully dedicated his book on the renewed liturgy of the holy Mass, first published in 1976, "to the memory of Pius Parsch," as evidence of his gratitude.

Before the founding of the Ruhr bishopric of Essen in 1958, Bochum, where Johannes H. Emminghaus first saw the light of day on 1 March 1916 (son of the sculptor Heinrich Emminghaus and his wife Maria, born Hoffmann), was part of the archdiocese of Paderborn. After his *Abitur* (secondary school diploma), Emminghaus began the study of theology in 1936 in Paderborn and in that Westphalian city he was ordained priest on 22 March 1947. When Archbishop Lorenz Jaeger (1892–1975), who became a cardinal in 1965, laid hands on him, the *Felix Paderae Civitas* lay deeply wounded, a heap of ashes and ruins. It reflected the crisis of a generation that suffered severely from the consequences of the Nazi regime, war, imprisonment, and exile. In the summer of 1938 Emminghaus, then a seminarian, was torn from his studies to enter "work service for the Reich." He lost the years 1940 to 1946 to war service and imprisonment in England. When he became a priest in 1947, he was 31 years old.

While an assistant pastor in Dortmund-Hörde (1947–1950), Johannes Emminghaus studied theology and art history in the Westphalian Wilhelms-University in Münster. On 12 December 1949 he received his Ph.D., with a dissertation on Westphalian "hunger cloths" from the post-medieval era and their liturgical origins. His doctorate in theology followed on 28 July 1954, also in Münster. His dissertation, directed by Professor Bernhard Kötting, was on early Christian baptismal locations in Syria and Palestine. This work was supported by a fellowship from the Federal Republic of Germany, still very new at that time, and was aided especially by two years of study in Rome, combined with extended research trips in the winter of 1951–1952. From 1960 until he was called to the professorate of liturgiology and sacramental theology in Vienna in the spring of 1967, Dr. Emminghaus was rector of the Catholic Academy of the diocese of Essen, "Wolfsburg" in Mülheim on the Ruhr. During this period he obtained his *Habilitation* in Münster (1965).

For Professor Emminghaus's 65th birthday, one of his Vienna students, Heribert Lehenhofer, edited the bibliography that appeared in the periodical *Bibel und Liturgie* (1981), and that needs to be updated as soon as possible, because to the end of his days Professor Emminghaus continued to work with dedication. His publications are concentrated first of all in the fields of liturgy, archeology and art history, and the combination of liturgiology and art history (with reference also to the results of archeological research) led him to pay special attention to liturgical spaces and their decoration, always in combination with the topic of church architecture as a whole. In addition, my colleague Professor Emminghaus's scholarly works are devoted to the nature of liturgical celebration, themes of liturgical reform, and questions of liturgical performance. This is the rule and in every well-founded sense the way in which historical, theological, pastoral, and spiritual aspects are com- bined into a unified whole.

Professor Emminghaus was anything but an "iconoclast." He was deeply anchored in the traditions of all that is Christian; he knew them well and loved them. Certainly he was not a man who was tempted by euphoric en- thusiasm for reform to squander what is valuable or lightly to throw treasures out the window. No, he understood himself to be a guardian of the tradition, the Church's heritage, but as theologian and as pastor he was entirely atten- tive to the present and sought to do justice to its unavoidable demands. That in pastoral questions primacy belongs to life, and especially the life of faith: this was a position in which Emminghaus the prelate was thoroughly at one with many representatives of practical theology, including his colleague and friend of many years, Ferdinand Klostermann, the *ordinarius* professor of pastoral theology in Vienna.

Johannes H. Emminghaus was sober enough to see clearly that even the most beautiful or best liturgy was not able to solve all the conflicts of modern people and present-day Christians with secularism. Faith and re- pentance must sustain the people of God and enable them to stand up as witnesses in the modern world. Pastoral care in all its forms of presentation, for Emminghaus, was part and parcel of care for the liturgy of the Church, as a precondition for its genuine, truthful, and believable execution.

Nothing was more disgusting to the deceased than cheap hot air and mere words spoken out of foolish arrogance. His love for the Church in its concrete form—with all its strengths and weaknesses—was greater, and his search for the truth was characterized by deep humility. "I never had the courage," my "fellow countryman" once wrote—characteristically for him— "to feel myself more strongly led by the Holy Spirit than the Pope and the Council and the absolute whole of the people of God." Nevertheless, this Westphalian, whose thinking was characterized as much by love of life as by sobriety, had deep understanding for those "arts of ecclesiastical behavior" that might from time to time make someone see red, but are especially affected by the character or temperament of human beings. As far as I can see, and from all I know, well-founded knowledge and insight, as well as a considerable share of professional sobriety, always preserved Johannes H. Emminghaus himself from hasty thought or action. He was a man of superior spiritual and human qualities. I was very sad when I learned that this colleague had died.

"No one dies of a malady, but only when, according to God's will, an earthly life reaches its end" (Joseph Cardinal Höffner). For Professor Emminghaus the *hora mortis* struck on 2 September 1989, when, after suffering a heart attack, he seemed to be on the road to recovery. His memorial card is quite unusual: it shows a sumptuous baptismal font with a quotation from Col 2:12a: "With Christ you were buried in baptism, [and] you were also raised with him."

In Klosterneuburg, one must ask for a key to visit the grave of Johannes H. Emminghaus. But perhaps it is enough to know that the light in the *Tucz* column on the plaza burns also for the author of this book, the priest and professor from Westphalia, who in the best years of his earthly existence worked at the University of Vienna and lived in Klosterneuburg. That light in the darkness well shows what is meant by the confident words of the prayer to the Lord of all life: *Lux aeterna luceat ei.*

Theodor Maas-Ewerd

Bibliography

Basic sources are the Constitution on the Sacred Liturgy of Vatican Council II and the *General Instruction of the Roman Missal*. The German editions of the missal and lectionary employed by the author and editor are:

Die Feier der heiligen Messe. Meßbuch für die Bistümer des deutschen Sprachgebietes. Authentische Ausgabe für den liturgischen Gebrauch. Herausgegeben im Auftrag der Bischofskonferenzen Deutschlands, Österreichs und der Schweiz sowie der Bischöfe von Luxemburg, Bozen-Brixen und Lüttich. Einsiedeln u. a. 1975.

Die Feier der heiligen Messe. Meßlektionar für die Bistümer des deutschen Sprachgebietes. Authentische Ausgabe für den liturgischen Gebrauch. Herausgegeben im Auftrag der Bischofskonferenzen Deutschlands, Österreichs und der Schweiz sowie der Bischöfe von Luxemburg, Bozen-Brixen und Lüttich. 8 vols. Einsiedeln u. a. 1982–1986.

Other resources:

Adam, Adolf, and Berger, Rupert. *Pastoralliturgisches Handlexikon.* Freiburg, Basel, and Vienna: Herder, 1980; 5th ed. 1991.

Adam, Adolf. *Die Eucharistiefeier - Quelle und Gipfel des Glaubens.* Freiburg, Basel, and Vienna: Herder, 1991. ET: *The Eucharistic Celebration : The Source and Summit of Faith.* Translated by Robert C. Schultz. Collegeville: The Liturgical Press, 1994.

Baumstark, Anton. *Vom geschichtlichen Werden der Liturgie.* Ecclesia Orans 10. Freiburg, 1923; new printing 1971.

Bugnini, Annibale. *Die Liturgiereform, 1948–1975. Zeugnis und Testament.* Freiburg, Basel, and Vienna: Herder, 1988. ET: *The Reform of the Liturgy, 1948–1975.* Translated by Matthew J. O'Connell. Collegeville: The Liturgical Press, 1990.

Eisenhofer, Ludwig. *Handbuch der katholischen Liturgik*. Herders Theologische Bibliothek. 2 vols. Freiburg: Herder, 1932/1933; 2nd ed. 1941.

Emminghaus, Johannes H. "Der gottesdienstliche Raum und seine Ausstattung," 347–416 in R. Berger, et al, *Gestalt des Gottesdienstes. Sprachliche und nicht-sprachliche Ausdrucksformen*. Gottesdienst der Kirche. Handbuch der Liturgiewissenschaft 3. Regensburg, 1987.

Franz, Adolph. *Die Messe im deutschen Mittelalter. Beiträge zur Geschichte der Liturgie und des religiösen Volkslebens*. Freiburg im Breisgau and St. Louis, Mo.: Herder, 1902; new printing Darmstadt: Wissenschaftliche Buchgesellschaft, 1963.

Hänggi, Anton, and Pahl, Irmgard., eds. *Prex Eucharistica. Textus e variis antiquioribus selecti*. Spicilegium Friburgense 12. Fribourg: Editions universitaires, 1968.

Häußling, Angelus A. *Das Missale deutsch. Materialien zur Rezeptionsgeschichte der lateinischen Meßliturgie im deutschen Sprachgebiet bis zum Zweiten Vatikanischen Konzil. 1. Bibliographie der Übersetzungen in Handschriften und Drucken*. Liturgische Quellen und Forschungen 66. Münster, 1984.

Heinz, Andreas. *Die sonn- und feiertägliche Pfarrmesse im Landkapitel Bitburg-Kyllburg in der alten Erzdiözese Trier von der Mitte des 18. bis zur Mitte des 19. Jahrhunderts*. Trierer Theologische Studien 34. Trier: Paulinus-Verlag, 1978.

Hermans, J. *Die Feier der Eucharistie. Erklärung und spirituelle Erschließung*. Regensburg: F. Pustet, 1984.

Jungmann, Josef A. *Der Gottesdienst der Kirche, auf dem Hintergrund seiner Geschichte kurz erläutert*. Innsbruck, Vienna, and Munich, 1955. ET: *Public worship: A survey*. Translated by Clifford Howell. Collegeville: The Liturgical Press, [1958]

_____. *Missarum Sollemnia. Eine genetische Erklärung der römischen Messe*. 2 vols. Vienna, 1948; 5th ed. 1962. ET: *The Mass of the Roman Rite: Its Origins and Development*. Translated by Francis A. Brunner. Rev. by Charles K. Riepe. New York : Benziger Bros., [1959]

_____. *Liturgie der christlichen Frühzeit bis auf Gregor den Großen*. Fribourg: Universitätsverlag, 1967.

_____. *Messe im Gottesvolk. Ein nachkonziliarer Durchblick durch Missarum Sollemnia*. Freiburg, Basel, Vienna: Herder, 1970.

Klauser, Theodor. *Kleine Abendländische Liturgiegeschichte*. Bonn, 5th ed. 1965. ET: *A Short History of the Western Liturgy. An Account and Some Reflections*. Translated by John Halliburton. London: Oxford Univ. Press, 1969.

Kleinheyer, Bruno. *Erneuerung des Hochgebetes*. Regensburg: F. Pustet, 1969.

Lechner, J. *Liturgik des römischen Ritus* (originally by Ludwig Eisenhofer). Freiburg, 6th ed. 1953.

Lengeling, Emil J. *Die neue Ordnung der Eucharistiefeier. Allgemeine Einführung in das Römische Meßbuch (lateinisch und deutsch). Einleitung und Kommentar*. Lebendiger Gottesdienst 17–18. Münster, 1970; 2nd ed. 1971.

Luykx, Boniface. "Der Ursprung der gleichbleibenden Teile der heiligen Messe," 2–119 in *Priestertum und Mönchtum. Liturgie und Mönchtum* 29 (1961).

Maas-Ewerd, Theodor. *Liturgie und Pfarrei. Einfluß der Liturgischen Erneuerung auf Leben und Verständnis der Pfarrei im deutschen Sprachgebiet.* Paderborn: Verlag Bonifacius-Druckerei, 1969.

Maas-Ewerd, Theodor, and Richter, Klemens. *Gemeinde im Herrenmahl. Zur Praxis der Meßfeier.* (Festschrift for E. J. Lengeling). Einsiedeln-Zürich and Freiburg-Vienna, 2nd ed. 1976.

Maas-Ewerd, Theodor. *Vom Pronaus zur Homilie. Ein Stück "Liturgie" in jüngster Geschichte und pastoraler Gegenwart.* Exemporalia. Fragen der Theologie und Seelsorge 8. Eichstätt-Vienna, 1990.

Martimort, Aimé Georges, ed. *The Church at Prayer : An Introduction to the Liturgy.* 4 vols. ET of *L'église en prière* by Matthew O'Connell. Collegeville: The Liturgical Press, 1986–1988.

Mayer, Anton L. *Die Liturgie in der europäischen Geistesgeschichte. Gesammelte Aufsätze.* Darmstadt: Wissenschaftliche Buchgesellschaft, 1971.

Meyer, Hans Bernhard. *Luther und die Messe. Eine liturgiewissenschaftliche Untersuchung über das Verhältnis Luthers zum Messwesen des späten Mittelalters.* Konfessionskundliche und kontroverstheologische Studien 11. Paderborn: Verlag Bonifacius-Druckerei, 1965.

_____. "Die Feier der Eucharistie auf dem Weg zu katholischer Vielfalt," 84–106 in Theodor Maas-Ewerd, ed., *Lebt unser Gottesdienst? Die bleibende Aufgabe der Liturgiereform* (Festschrift for B. Kleinheyer). Freiburg, Basel, Vienna, 1988.

_____. *Eucharistie, Geschichte, Theologie, Pastoral: zum Gedenken an den 100. Geburtstag von Josef Andreas Jungmann am 16. Nov. 1989.* Gottesdienst der Kirche. Handbuch der Liturgiewissenschaft 4. Regensburg: F. Pustet, 1989.

Rennings, H., and Klöckener, M., eds. *Dokumente zur Erneuerung der Liturgie. I: Dokumente des Apostolischen Stuhls 1963–1973.* Kevelaer, 1983.

Schermann, J., and Meyer, H. B., eds. *Der Gottesdienst im deutschen Sprachgebiet. Liturgische Dokumente, Bücher und Behelfe.* Studien zur Pastoraltheologie 5. Regensburg, 1982.

Schürmann, Heinz. *Der Abendmahlsbericht Lukas 22,7–38 als Gottesdienstordnung, Gemeindeordnung, Lebensordnung.* Die Botschaft Gottes. Eine biblische Schriftenreihe II, 1. Leipzig, 1955.

Appendix I

Structure of the Mass
and the Significance of Its Parts

Elements of the Mass	Meaning of the Action
The Lord is present among those gathered in his name (Matt 18:20)	
Entrance and Entrance Song	Creation of community and preparation for celebration
Opening Rites Kissing the altar	In kissing the altar, the priest kisses Christ as the true Lord and priest of this assembly, and with the greeting, strengthens the spirit of love and peace within the community.
Sign of the cross, liturgical greeting, introduction	
Penitential action, *Kyrie*	The community acknowledges that it is a community of sinners, and asks God for pardon; it also knows itself to be a community of the redeemed, and praises the triune God.
(Gloria)	
Collect of the day	The community reflects on the saving mystery of the day or the feast.

The Lord is present to his Church in the word

Liturgy of the Word	First reading and responsorial psalm	The Lord comes and is present in the word;
	(Second reading and) verse/alleluia	the community receives him willingly and in
	Gospel	faith and reflects on what has been proclaimed.
	Homily	The preacher actuates the word that has been proclaimed for the concrete here and now.
	(Credo)	The community responds (in its confession of faith and) in priestly
	General Intercessions	prayer for the well-being of the world.

The Lord is sacramentally present to his Church in bread and wine

Preparation of the gifts

Eucharist (sacrificial real memorial)	Procession with the gifts	The gifts presented symbolize the willing surrender of the community,
	Presentation of the gifts	for the gifts are gifts of God and also the fruits of human labor.
	Private prayer of the priest/ washing of hands	Self-surrender can only occur in a spirit of humility and purity, in order that the gifts may become the body and blood of Christ.

Eucharistic Prayer

Dialogue, with preface and *Sanctus*	God is to be praised in the divine Son as creator of the world and as Lord of salvation history.
Consecration epiclesis Institution narrative	In the power of the Holy Spirit, Christ's surrendered body and blood poured out are present as sacrifice in the bread and wine;
Anamnesis	Christ incorporates the sacrificial surrender of the Church in his unique sacrifice and
Communion epiclesis	wills to give himself to the Church, in the power of the Holy Spirit, in the sacred meal.
Intercessions	The Church prays, in this atoning sacrifice, for the salvation of all humankind and acknowledges its communion with the dead and those in heaven,
Doxology	culminating its thanksgiving in praise of the triune God.

Communion

Our Father	In its table prayer, the community prays for the eucharistic bread and for freedom from sin,
Prayer for peace	renewing in itself the spirit of love and peace,

	Breaking of the bread	breaking the one bread (1 Cor 10:17) as a participation in the body of Christ;
	Administration of Communion	it is fed by Christ's flesh and blood
	Concluding prayer	and prays to receive the fruits of this Holy Communion in daily life and for eternity.

	Announcements	Concrete expression of community life.
Concluding		
Rites	Final blessing	The seal of fruitful participation in this celebration and
	Dismissal	sending of the community anew to its service to the world in daily life.

Appendix II

Structure of the Roman Canon (Eucharistic Prayer I)

Texts

Preface (with *Sanctus*)

Te igitur / We come to you, Father

In primis / We offer them
Memento Domino famulorum / Remember, Lord, your people
Communicantes / In union with the whole Church

Hanc igitur / Father, accept this offering
Quam oblationem / Bless and approve our offering

Qui pridie / The day before he suffered
Simili modo / When supper was ended
(*Mysterium fidei* / Let us proclaim the mystery of faith)
Unde et memores / Father, we celebrate the memory

Supra quae / Look with favor on
Supplices te rogamus / Almighty God, we pray

Memento etiam / Remember, Lord, those who have died
Nobis quoque peccatoribus / For ourselves, too, we ask
et societatem donare digneris / Though we are sinners,

Per quem haec omnia / Through Christ our Lord

Per ipsum et cum ipso / Through him, with him

Appendix III

Structure of Eucharistic Prayers II–IV

	II	III	IV
Dialogue	the same in all the eucharistic prayers: "The Lord be with you . . ."		
Preface	related, but changeable	changes by season	a fixed part of the prayer, unchangeable
Sanctus	the same in all the eucharistic prayers: "Holy, holy . . ."		
Transition (post-*Sanctus*)	Lord, you are holy indeed . . .	Father, you are holy indeed . . .	Continues the praise for salvation history
Consecration epiclesis	Let your Spirit come upon these gifts . . .	And so, Father, we bring you these gifts . . .	Father, may this Holy Spirit sanctify these offerings . . .
Framing text	The day before he suffered . . .	On the night he was betrayed . . .	Having always loved those who were his own in the world . . .
Words of Christ	the same in all the eucharistic prayers: "Take this, all of you, and eat [drink] . . ."		
Acclamation	the same in all the eucharistic prayers (several options)		

Anamnesis	In memory of his death and resurrection . . .	Father, calling to mind the death your Son endured . . .	Father, we now celebrate this memorial of our redemption . . .
Communion epiclesis	Look with favor on these offerings . . .	Look with favor on your Church's offering . . .	Lord, look upon this sacrifice . . .
Intercessions	for the Church, with pope and bishops, the dead, the community	for the community, the Church with pope and bishops, the whole world, the dead	for the Church, with pope and bishops, the whole world, the dead, the community
Transition to doxology	Through Christ our Lord . . .	through your Son, Jesus Christ . . .	through whom you give us everything . . .
Doxology	the same in all the eucharistic prayers: "Through him and with him and in him . . ."		
Acclamation	the same in all: "Amen."		

Index